OPEC's Dilemma and the Future of Oil

The UN's Net Zero goal is to limit the rise in mean global temperatures to 1.5°C by 2050. They suggested that it could be achieved by reducing global emissions by 45 percent by 2030 and then to zero by 2050. This book is a new stress test in applied econometric analysis of oil-producing countries. It includes a positive economic analysis using a sample of 11 OPEC (Organization of Petroleum Exporting Countries) nations from 1970 to 2019; and presents an empirical analysis of OPEC's operating model – the state-owned oil monopoly, hence its dilemma. The book estimates a production function for every OPEC nation and then uses counterfactual scenarios to show that OPEC's strategy to peg the price of oil by cutting oil production by more than 45 percent by 2030, results in a reduction of permanent income, which has negative macroeconomic consequences, such as on social welfare losses. The book begins by defining the dilemma, describing the stylized facts of OPEC economies and oil production organizations, their political environments, the dominant features of these economies such as oil rent, productivity, oil dependence, and the long-run and cyclical correlation between oil and output. It provides a microeconomic foundation for the macro analysis by testing the monopoly vs. competition price mechanism. Finally, there is a discussion of the policy options available to OPEC to deal with the UN's Race to Zero. Students, scholars, and researchers will benefit from the innovative ideas presented in the book and it will be a useful guide for policymakers and global governance experts.

Weshah Razzak is Honorary Research Fellow at the School of Economics and Finance, Massey University, Palmerston North, New Zealand.

Routledge Studies in the Economics of Business and Industry

The Professional Standards of Executive Remuneration Consultants
Calvin Jackson

International Trade and the Music Industry
Live Music Services from the Caribbean
Lisa Gordon

Sustainability Management in the Oil and Gas Industry
Emerging and Developing Country Perspectives
Edited by Joshua Yindenaba Abor and Amin Karimu

Economic Policy, COVID-19 and Corporations
Perspectives from Central and Eastern Europe
Edited by Katarzyna Mroczek-Dąbrowska, Aleksandra Kania and Anna Matysek-Jędrych

Artists and Markets in Music
The Political Economy of Music During the Covid Era and Beyond
Cameron M. Weber, Ying Zhen and J. J. Arias

Intangible Assets, Productivity and Economic Growth
Micro, Meso and Macro Perspectives
Carter Bloch, Aimilia Protogerou and Nicholas S. Vonortas

OPEC's Dilemma and the Future of Oil
Navigating the Path to Net Zero
Weshah Razzak

For more information about this series, please visit *www.routledge.com/Routledge-Studies-in-the-Economics-of-Business-and-Industry/book-series/RSEBI*

OPEC's Dilemma and the Future of Oil

Navigating the Path to Net Zero

Weshah Razzak

Routledge
Taylor & Francis Group
LONDON AND NEW YORK

First published 2025
by Routledge
4 Park Square, Milton Park, Abingdon, Oxon OX14 4RN

and by Routledge
605 Third Avenue, New York, NY 10158

Routledge is an imprint of the Taylor & Francis Group, an informa business

British Library Cataloguing-in-Publication Data
A catalogue record for this book is available from the British Library

ISBN: 978-1-032-78485-4 (hbk)
ISBN: 978-1-032-78488-5 (pbk)
ISBN: 978-1-003-48812-5 (ebk)

DOI: 10.4324/9781003488125

Typeset in Galliard
by Apex CoVantage, LLC

Contents

Figures

Tables

Preface and an Executive Summary

- The Net Zero Paris Agreement (2015) called for emissions to be reduced by 45 percent by 2030 and reach net zero by 2050 to keep global warming to no more than 1.5°C. It is arguable whether, or not, such targets are achievable.
- Such targets could not be achieved without some *permanent* decline in the demand for oil and global oil consumption among other fossil fuels.
- We are unsure what policies are used to achieve Net Zero in every country; there could be taxes on carbon production and consumption, subsidies of alternative energy production and consumption, specific regulations, or all of the above. Also, carbon credit and offset markets may reduce emission.
- It should be plainly obvious that Net Zero and major oil producers have conflicting objectives. Nonetheless, the Organization of Petroleum Exporting Countries (OPEC) expresses a peculiar agreement with Net Zero objectives. OPEC makes up 70 percent of the world oil reserve. OPEC signed off on the Net Zero agreement and publicly announced its commitment to adhering to it.
- The OPEC economies (1) have a high share of oil in real gross domestic product (GDP); (2) are rentier economies; (3) have low productivity, and (4) have high sensitivity to changes in oil price. Put simply, real GDP and the real price of oil share a long-run common trend and also a common cycle.
- OPEC is an oligopoly. The oil industries in every OPEC country, however, are state-owned. Oil production decisions are, largely, made by governments. Global oil consumption and global emission share a long-run common trend. Global oil consumption and oil production in each OPEC economy also share a long-run common trend.
- Furthermore, (every) OPEC country's oil production is highly responsive to global oil consumption. A 1 percent fall (rise) in the latter reduces (increases) the former by more than one percent. Thus, exactly like the monopolist, in order to keep the price of oil at a *certain breakeven level*, OPEC governments respond to the fall in global oil consumption by cutting oil production, and these cuts exceed the reduction in oil production required by Net Zero.

- OPEC has been cutting oil production by more than the reduction stipulated by the Net Zero. The objective of such an excessive oil production cut is to increase the price of oil, which it did (apparent in the data). However, it must have reduced real GDP too because oil production has a significant share in aggregate output.
- It seems that OPEC cares more about the price of oil, but not real GDP. A reduction in real GDP in low-productivity growth economies has far more adverse effects than the benefits of the increase in the current price of oil.
- From a public finance standpoint, higher oil prices increase government revenues and spending, but it is not so promising from a macroeconomic view. OPEC's dilemma is that *expected income* 2020–2050 (i.e., *permanent income*) will fall below baseline estimates; current consumption would decline too, thus a welfare loss.
- A competitive oil industry, on the other hand, would be a price taker; hence it would not cut oil production by more than the decline in global oil consumption. We do not predict a decline in permanent income under such a scenario.
- The predicted decline in *permanent income* under the current state-owned oil monopoly model suggests a need for changing the oil policies and the political and economic institutions.
- OPEC could resolve this dilemma by cutting production by less than they currently do and less than what they did in 2022 and 2023 in response to the fall in global oil consumption, or they could target a lower breakeven oil price to prevent the decline in permanent income.
- Optimally, however, it should create a competitive oil industry. To do so, the governments should transfer oil wealth to the citizens directly, creating and establishing private ownership of oil and gas resources to foster economic development. This may sound grand, but many countries have transformed their economies into market economies, e.g., the UK, Poland, Russia, the Czech Republic, and so on in the past and they all succeeded in doing so. Even China has realized that the government should not intervene in production and pricing decisions. It requires a political commitment. We are conscious that this proposal would be most certainly met with resistance by people with entrenched interests in the *status quo*.
- Finally, the record shows that the majority of OPEC governments fully understood decades ago that they must diversify their incomes away from oil. However, very little has been done to do so for obvious reasons. The main reasons in my opinion are that the governments have had no intention to relinquish power and control over oil and that the job is beyond the ability of the governments and its bureaucracy. This job must be left to the people to do. The people must own their wealth, oil, gas, and land. Once they do, they will naturally know how to allocate resources efficiently and grow their economy and wealth. They would have the incentive to do so. There has been no pressure on the governments in the past, and high oil prices

worked as a tranquilizer. The governments panic when the price of oil falls and revenues dwindle. Time is running fast now. There is a UN target, Net Zero by 2050. The new generations of young people who will be in charge in the future governments *seem* committed more than ever to achieving this target. Skeptics may say that will not happen or it would take much longer than 2050 to reach the target. This might be, however, everyone knows that fossil fuel production and consumption are in the crosshairs.

1 The Dilemma, the Stylized Facts, and the Objectives

Abstract

We provide some stylized facts about the OPEC countries. The facts are that The OPEC countries are dominantly not, or relatively, less democratic; more autocratic; and the government makes the decisions about oil production. OPEC countries are oil-rich; relatively unproductive rentier economies, heavily dependent on oil, and only thrive when the price of oil is high at a certain, often high, breakeven level. We provide empirical evidence of significant oil-dependence.

1.1 OPEC's Dilemma

According to the UN Webpage, the Net Zero (UNFCCC, the Paris Agreement 2015) objective is to keep global warming to no more than 1.5°C. It, loosely, suggests that emissions need to be reduced by 45 percent by 2030 and reach net zero by 2050.[1] Put simply, it means cutting greenhouse gas emissions to as close to zero as possible, with any remaining emissions re-absorbed from the atmosphere, by oceans and forests for instance. It should be plainly obvious that Net Zero and major oil producers have conflicting objectives. However, the Organization of Petroleum Exporting Countries (OPEC) expresses a peculiar agreement with Net Zero. Claes and Garavini (2020, 10) say that the OPEC secretary general has declared that the biggest challenge OPEC has to face today is environmental activism that is present even within the families of OPEC officials when their children are asking us about their future because they see their peers on the streets campaigning against this industry.[2]

We have no information about how every signatory country to the Paris Agreement on Climate Change will achieve this goal including OPEC. Countries could impose a carbon tax to reduce consumption (demand), regulate the industry and household fossil fuel consumption, subsidize alternative clean energy uses, or all of the above. Also, carbon credit and offset markets could reduce

1 I say loosely because it is not at all clear how the 45 percent target by 2030 was obtained, but we will assume that it is the goal.

2 OPEC Statement delivered at the UN Climate Change Conference (2017) and said it adheres to the UN goals of 45 percent and zero by 2050, hence Net Zero.

DOI: 10.4324/9781003488125-1

emission.[3] We will provide evidence that global carbon emission and global oil consumption are cointegrated, i.e., they share a common long-run trend. Furthermore, we estimated that the elasticity of oil production with respect to global oil consumption is >1. Most importantly, the share of oil in real GDP is relatively large in most OPEC countries, especially the rich ones in the Gulf Cooperation Council countries (GCC) (Razzak, 2023). Therefore, a reduction in oil production is not only associated with a higher price of oil but also associated with a reduction in real GDP. OPEC is best described as an oligopoly, whereby it is made of a number of oil sellers whose share in the global oil market is substantial. In addition, the oil industries in the OPEC countries are state-owned; they enjoy government monopoly powers in that particular market even though some countries have production-sharing agreements with foreign oil companies.[4] It is very important to understand that there is one decision maker who decides how much oil to produce and sell. The typical sizable and strong oil monopoly structure in OPEC oil industries stems from, and is protected by, entrenched interest groups. Big governments can create big monopolies (Hayek 2012).

In price theory, the monopolist cuts output significantly when it faces adverse demand shocks because the monopolist charges a relatively higher price for its product and wants to prevent this price from falling below its breakeven price (the price of oil needed to finance fiscal expenditures). Therefore, cutting oil production not only raises the spot price of oil (and perhaps *current* oil revenues and maybe *current* income) to balance the budget; it reduces the *expected* real GDP (permanent income) because the share of oil in income is relatively large. As *permanent income* declines, *current* consumption also falls sharply and hence welfare loss. We will show that in order to keep the price of oil at a certain *breakeven level,* OPEC cuts oil production by much more than the reduction in global oil consumption.

A competitive oil producer, however, would be a price taker. It would cut oil production to meet the declining demand and it would not cut oil production in excess of the UN-required 45 percent by 2030. Most importantly, the competitive industry's oil cut should not reduce *permanent income* and welfare. OPEC's state monopoly model, which cuts oil production *in excess of* the UN-stipulated reduction in oil production in order to peg the price of oil, is the dilemma that faces OPEC under the Net zero state of the world. It is the state-owned oil producer's dilemma.

3 See https://carboncredits.com/the-ultimate-guide-to-understanding-carbon-credits/#1 – The Ultimate Guide to Understanding Carbon Credits, which is a very useful document.

4 The definition of the "state" is fuzzy. The literature is scattered across many fields. Max Weber (1919), for example, defined it as polity, which has a monopoly on violence, among other things. James Buchannan in a number of publications (1975, 1977, 1986, 1988, and 1991), on the other hand, attempted to provide a normative theory of the state. In all these different literatures, the state and the government were two different things. However, they are used interchangeably in this book because they do share common features in our context, most importantly that the decision regarding the production of the quantity of oil is centralized, in the hands of the politicians, i.e., non-market determined. In a few cases, there are private oil producers in OPEC countries, e.g., Nigeria, Iraq, and Gabon, but the government is the ultimate decider on oil production via the laws and regulations it makes.

1.2 Organization of Petroleum Exporting Countries

OPEC is an oil cartel founded in Baghdad (Iraq) in 1960. Initially, it included five countries, Iraq, the Islamic Republic of Iran (before the establishment of the Islamic Republic in 1979), Kuwait, Saudi Arabia, and Venezuela. OPEC then includes Indonesia, the United Arab Emirates (UAE), Algeria, Nigeria, Gabon, Angola, Equatorial Guinea, Libya, and the Congo, DR. Qatar and Ecuador joined OPEC but withdrew later. OPEC members share common features.

1.3 Stylized Facts

1.3.1 Political Instability

OPEC countries are developing countries, which have colonial pasts (except Saudi Arabia perhaps) and a history of political instability. S*ome* have held elections; have some quasi democratic institutions, and court systems. We do not speculate on the causes of political instability because it is beyond the scope of this book. Generally, countries that are oil-rich, mostly tribal culture, and surrounded by powerful industrial countries experience political instability. The majority of OPEC has been suffering from political, economic, and social instability throughout the periods of their independence from colonial powers. Nonetheless, there are exceptions. Saudi Arabia and the UAE are exceptionally politically stable absolute monarchies. Kuwait is an absolute stable monarchy; however, it experienced a military invasion by Iraq in 1990 and was the subject of total destruction. Its oil fields were torched and burned for months. Since its inception, the Islamic Republic of Iran engaged in a brutal eight-year war with its neighbor Iraq. And, it has had a very complex relationship with the Western countries, which has been dominated by economic and financial sanctions that hindered economic development. Iran has been subject to the US–UN sanctions since 2005. Iraq, Iran's next-door neighbor, could easily be described as a politically unstable country since its establishment in 1921. It experienced many military coups, internal armed insurgencies, wars with its neighbors, long and grueling UN sanctions, and foreign invasions. In 1990, it invaded neighboring Kuwait and was evicted violently by the US in 1991 (the First Gulf War). Immediately after, it was placed on a UN sanction until 2003; it was not allowed to sell oil or export and import anything without the direct involvement of the UN; see Gordon (1999) for example. In 2003, the US invaded Iraq (Second Gulf War) and toppled the government. Since 2003, the US government has considered Iraq a democracy. Iraq, however, is clearly still politically unstable. Recent elections did not result in peaceful transfers of power. The court is politicized. Democratic institutions are fragile; see, for example, Knights (2023).

The African countries in OPEC have very capricious political histories, which began after independence from colonial powers, and included military coups, civil wars, foreign military interventions, and UN sanctions. The Democratic Republic of Congo is a populated African resource-rich country. It has the world's largest reserves for metals and rare earth metals (Cobalt, Zinc, and

Copper) that are used in the production of car and cell phone batteries and other electronics. Congo has been in turmoil since independence from Belgium in 1960. The country changed its name more than once. A long period of Western-backed dictatorship began in 1965 and lasted until 1997. The first Congo war was 1996–1997 and related to the Rwandan Genocide. In 1998, a second Congo War broke out. It came to an end in 2002 with about 3 million people dead. The DRC joined OPEC in 2018 only. Angola also has a very complicated history. Its oil production has been rising significantly. Immediately upon independence from Portugal, Angola had a civil war in 1975. It lasted 27 bloody years. Nearly one million people died. The war and foreign entanglements devastated the infrastructure and the economy. Angola held the first round of its presidential election on 29–30 September 1992. Gabon is slightly different from the other African countries. It is a previous French colony, which has been relatively politically stable. However, the political system was a one-party system from 1960 to 1993. A multiparty political system was adopted in 1993, which led to elections and coalition-based government. Nonetheless, there is one dominant party in the government, the Democratic Gabonese Party. Nigeria is a very large African country in terms of area and population. Its recent history is also a colonial one. Britain was involved in the country since 1851. It gained full independence in 1960 and became a republic in 1963 but yielded to military rule after a bloody coup d'état in 1966. A separatist movement later formed the Republic of Biafra in 1967, leading to the three-year Nigerian Civil War. Nigeria became a republic again after a new constitution was written in 1979. The military took over the government in 1983. A number of military coups took place in Nigeria. A two-party system was introduced in 1992/1993, but that did not end the military control. This political volatility in Nigeria remained a feature of the political system for nearly 40 years. It was not until 1999 that Nigeria was able to establish some civil order. The West did not approve the 2007 presidential election. Another election in 2011 followed with a slightly more favorable Western opinion. Ahead of the general election of 2015, a campaigner in 2015 who was a popular anti-corruption fighter won the election by over two million votes. The election was generally praised as being fair. The election marked the first time an incumbent president had lost re-election in Nigeria. In the 2019 presidential election, the president was re-elected for a second term in office. For the first time since the elections of the Second Republic, four candidates ran for the presidency in the 2003 election, and for the first *time* since the return of democracy, no former military ruler ran for president. As far as oil is concerned, production and revenue rose and the Nigerian government became increasingly more dependent on oil revenues. The Economic Intelligence Report describes the political system in Equatorial Guinea as a dictatorship with a repressive internal security apparatus.[5] Political stability is and will nonetheless remain fragile, owing to power struggles within the ruling family over the presidential succession.

We have two North African countries in OPEC, Algeria and Libya. There is more volatility in Algeria. The most recent history of Algeria, which has a very old history, begins with the French colonial rule in 1830. It became

5 https://country.eiu.com/Equatorial%20Guinea

independent in 1962. Algeria was ruled by a single party from independence in 1962 until the approval of a new constitution in 1989, which introduced multi-party politics and ended the monopoly of the Front of National Liberation (FLN from the French name). The FLN and the military run the country. The second president of the country who was associated with the FLN and the military had in fact come to power through a military coup in 1965. In 1978, another president took over after the death of the previous one and had promised to steer Algeria away from the control of the military to a more civilian system. The formation of political parties began, and by 1991, 33 political parties were registered. The political reforms led to a local election victory of the Islamists (Islamic Salvation Front). When it became clear that they would win the parliamentary election, the military intervened and canceled the second round of voting. The president resigned in protest and was replaced by a series of civilian presidents, but the military reserved eventual control on the government. The Islamic Salvation Front was disbanded and a very violent civil war started, and Algeria was completely paralyzed from 1992 to 1999. Libya's story is just as bad. It was under a strong centralized dictatorship from 1969 to 2011. It remains a fractured country with two separate governments and no obvious economic and political objectives.

We have one South American oil producer in OPEC, Venezuela. The population is about 32 million, and the land area is 916,000 sq km; it has the largest oil reserve in the world. Venezuela has been ruled by the military for many periods post-independence. The country has 24 constitutions over the period from its independence from Spain in 1811–1956 (Lott 1956). The first democratic period was from 1945 to 1948, followed by periods of dictatorships from 1948 to 1958, and democratically elected presidents from 1960 to 1990. From 1990 onward, the government has been dominated by one political party. The country has been under sanctions for quite some time. The US, the EU, Canada, Mexico, Panama, and Switzerland have applied individual sanctions against people associated with the government since 2018. Beginning in January 2019, during the Venezuelan Presidential Crisis, the US applied additional economic sanctions in the petroleum, gold, mining, food, and banking industries. A report published by the UN High Commissioner for Human Rights stated that the new sanctions have had a severe impact on the economy. In April 2019, Human Rights Watch and Johns Hopkins Bloomberg School of Public Health published a joint report show that most early sanctions did not target the Venezuelan economy in any way, adding that sanctions imposed in 2019 could worsen the situation (OHCHR 2019).[6]

And finally, Indonesia is a large country, which joined OPEC in 1962. Immediately after the surrender of Japan in August 1945, the Proclamation of Indonesian Independence was announced. Indonesia became authoritarian with an increase in the power of the Communist Party of Indonesia (PKI). Tensions

6 Oral update on the situation of human rights in the Bolivarian Republic of Venezuela, OHCHR, the UN Human Rights Office, 20 March 2019, retrieved 23 March 2019. www.ohchr.org/en/statements/2019/03/oral-update-situation-human-rights-bolivarian-republic-venezuela?LangID=E&NewsID=24374

between the military and the PKI culminated in an attempted coup d'état in 1965. A new dictatorship was established in March 1968. A 'new order' administration was supported by the US. In 1999, East Timor seceded from Indonesia. Since 1998, democratic processes have been strengthened by enhancing regional autonomy and instituting the country's first direct presidential election in 2004.

Almost all OPEC countries experienced Political instability. Furthermore, OPEC countries have high levels of corruption. The Corruption Perception Index published by Transparency International in 2022, for example, ranked the UAE 27 in the world, which is the least corrupt OPEC member. This must be taken with a very large grain of salt. Saudi Arabia ranked 54 and Kuwait 77, which is also murky. The rest of OPEC members are among the most corrupt countries in the world. Indonesia ranked 110; Algeria and Angola ranked 116; Gabon 136; Iran 147; Nigeria 150; Iraq 157; Congo, DR 167; Equatorial Guinea and Libya 171; and Venezuela 177.[7]

The political and economic histories of the OPEC countries have affected economic development and the quality of the economic time series data. For example, when Iraq invaded Kuwait in 1990, Kuwait's data were missing for two years. For Iraq, the data from 1980 to 2002 are questionable. From 2012 onward, the Venezuelan's data are unusable. Volatility is reflected in uneven economic development, which is evident in the data. Breaks in time series make empirical analysis and statistical tests very challenging. Generally, OPEC data are unreliable quality; there are breaks in some cases, missing values, and in other cases, the data are missing totally (e.g., Libya has no data). In some cases, the data look very inconsistent with basic economic logic, e.g., Indonesia reduces oil production when global oil consumption increases. We do not have an explanation for this negative correlation. We exclude Libya, Equatorial Guinea, and Indonesia from our analysis. We will be analyzing 11 OPEC countries only.

1.3.2 State-Owned Oil Industries

There is clear evidence that the oil- and gas-producing companies in OPEC are state-owned and behave like monopolies in the ways they set up production levels. We have been witnessing successive oil cuts in excess of the percentage stipulated by the Net Zero plan, clearly, in order to peg the price of oil. It is important to emphasize that all of the OPEC oil companies are state-owned monopolies or at least behave as such with no competition. We will consider OPEC oil companies as state-owned oil monopolies controlled by central governments.

The Algerian oil company Sonatrach is the national state-owned oil company. It was founded in 1963 and was effectively nationalized in 1967. Sonatrach controls all the processes of oil production, including exploration, extraction, refining, and marketing in Algeria. Group Sonangol (*Grupo Sonangol*) is a *parastatal (an organization or an industry that has some political authority and serves the state indirectly)* that formerly oversaw petroleum and gas production in Angola. It is one of the largest oil companies in Africa. In February 2019,

7 www.transparency.org/en/cpi/2022?gclid=EAIaIQobChMI4cup1um_gwMVPqRmAh0_HgxBEAAYASAAEgJnGfD_BwE&gad_source=1

the government of Angola transferred the industry's regulation functions of Sonangol to a new government agency, the National Oil, Gas, and Biofuel Agency (ANPG). The ANPG also gained from Sonangol the right to award fossil fuel exploration, development, and production contracts. The National Petroleum Company of the Congo (SNPC) is the national oil company of the Congo, DR. The company was established in 1998 after the closure of the public company Hydro-Congo. The company manages government-owned shares of production from oil fields in the country. Gabon is probably the fifth largest oil producer in Africa. In 1982, a petroleum law based on production-sharing contracts was in place, and it still is to date. Under this regime, the government is the owner of all oil production; the company acts as a service provider, for which it is rewarded with a production share. After the deduction of the royalties, contractors are paid to cover investment costs, and profit is shared by the state and the contractors. Iraq has a National Oil Company (in the North, the South, and other different locations in the country). Iraq's new oil laws, which were made after 2003, allowed production shares with foreign companies too. Under this regime, the government is the owner of all oil production; the company acts as a service provider, for which it is rewarded with a production share. After the deduction of the royalties, contractors are paid to cover investment costs, and profit is shared by the state and the contractors. It is unclear whether, or not, Nigeria's oil company Lekoil is a state-owned monopoly. It is reported that it is a Cayman-incorporated company, which is focused through its shareholding in Lekoil Nigeria on African oil exploration and production, with interests in Nigeria and offshore Namibia. The company was founded in 2010 by a former analyst from Alliance Bernstein and listed on the Alternative Investment Market of the London Stock Exchange in 2013. Petroleum of Venezuela is a Venezuelan state-owned oil and natural gas company. Iran has the Iranian National Oil Company. Kuwait has the Kuwait Oil Company. Saudi Arabia has ARAMCO, the Saudi Arabia Oil Group. Indonesia has two companies. Pertamina was founded as a state-owned oil monopoly in 1957 after the Royal Dutch/Shell's assets in Indonesia (trading as Bataafse Petroleum Maatschappij) were nationalized. The other one is PT Medco Energi Internasional Tbk or MedcoEnergi, which is an oil and gas company. It operates in trading and holding and related operations, as well as explorations for and production of oil and gas, power, services, chemicals, and rental properties.

1.3.3 OPEC Oil Richness

The second most important common feature of OPEC is that they are oil-rich. Figure 1.1 reports the proved oil reserves of the five founding countries of OPEC as of 2020. The data could be compared with those of Norway, Russia, and North America. OPEC makes up 70 percent of the world oil reserve. The five founding countries (Iran, Iraq, Kuwait, Saudi Arabia, and Venezuela) make up 58 percent of the world oil reserve. OPEC oil production makes up 38 percent of global crude oil production and 16 percent of global natural gas production. These numbers may indicate enormous wealth. However, these economies are not as healthy as they appear to be from their oil wealth and

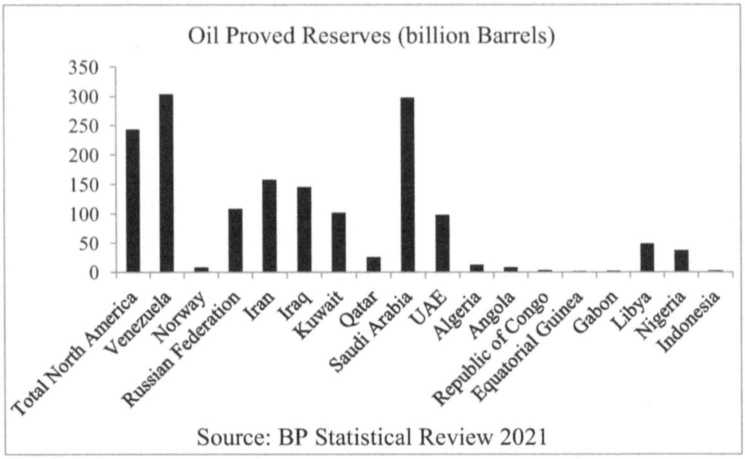

Figure 1.1 Proved Oil Reserves (Billion Barrels 2021)

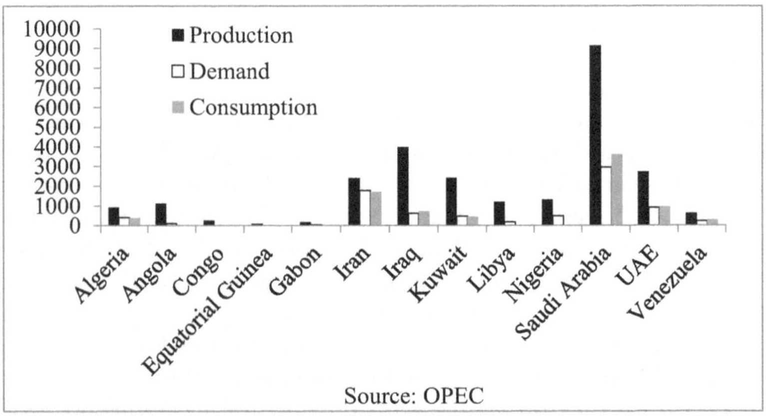

Figure 1.2 Oil Production and Estimated Oil Demand (1000 Barrels/Day, 2021)

production. Clearly, the Middle Eastern countries and Venezuela are much richer in oil than the African OPEC.

Figure 1.2 plots the amount of oil production and the estimated oil demand by OPEC in 2021. Not all consumption data are available, but differences between oil production and consumption suggest spare capacity and hence the ability to affect the supply of oil and affect global oil prices. Iraq, Kuwait, Saudi Arabia, and the UAE have tremendous advantages in that regard.

1.3.4 OPEC Are Rentier Economies

Oil rents to GDP ratios are relatively high. Table 1.1 reports the data for 2021. Venezuela data are unavailable. These figures are relatively high, double digits, compared with the entire world oil rent – GDP ratio, except for Indonesia, and Nigeria, which is difficult to explain and must be carefully interpreted.

Figure 1.3 plots the data presented in Table 1.1.

Table 1.1 Oil Rent as a Percent of GDP

Angola	28.3
Algeria	14.5
Gabon	15.6
Equatorial Guinea	14.9
Indonesia	0.8
Iran, Islamic Republic	18.3
Iraq	42.8
Kuwait*	27.6
Libya	56.4
Nigeria	6.2
Saudi Arabia	23.7
United Arab Emirates	15.7
Venezuela, RB	–
World	1.3

Source: World Bank. The asterisk denotes the year 2020.

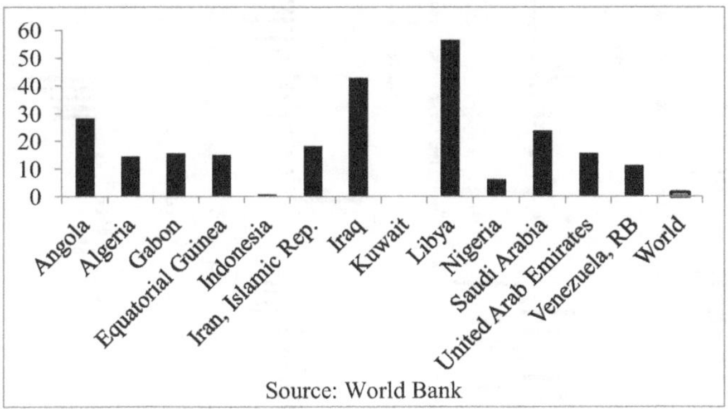

Figure 1.3 Oil Rent as a Percent of GDP

1.3.5 OPEC Has Low Productivity Growth

Total factor productivity growth is evidently low. Figure 1.4 plots the Conference Board estimates data. One should take these data with a grain of salt. The data are highly volatile and negative throughout the sample and across all countries. Iraq, Kuwait, Libya, Indonesia, and Venezuela have relatively the worst TFP growth.[8]

1.3.6 OPEC Is Oil-Dependent

1.3.6.1 Real GDP and Oil Prices Are Highly Correlated

Razzak (2023) shows evidence of oil dependency of the GCC, Kuwait, Saudi Arabia, and the UAE, which are also members of OPEC. The shares of oil in total output production are relatively high. We will test the correlation

8 It is arguable that low productivity could be due to (1) low level and growth of industrial output; (2) measurement issues with services output, which dominates most of the OPEC economies; and (3) estimation issues due to bad quality data. Explaining low productivity growth is beyond the scope of this book.

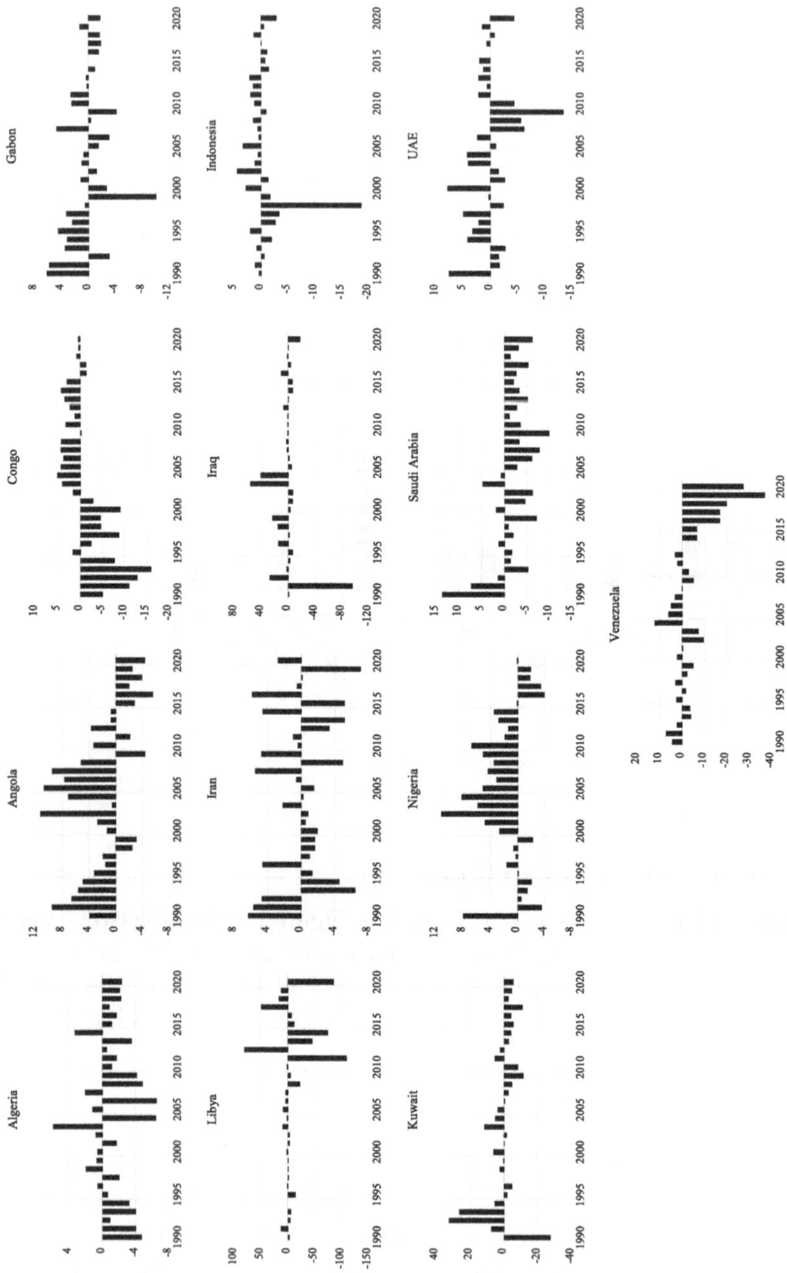

Figure 1.4 Total Factor Productivity Growth

Data Source: Conference Board.

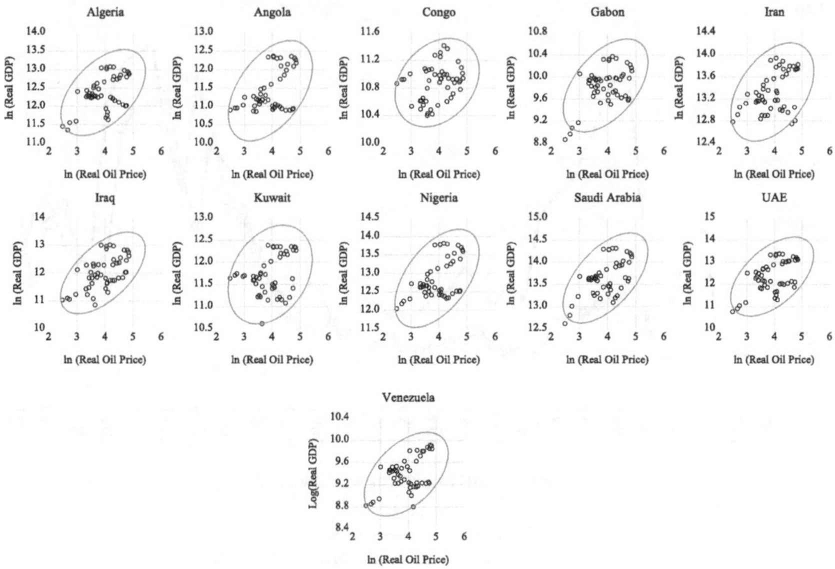

Figure 1.5 95-Percent Chi-Square Confidence Ellipse (1970–2019) Real GDP and Real Oil Price Correlated

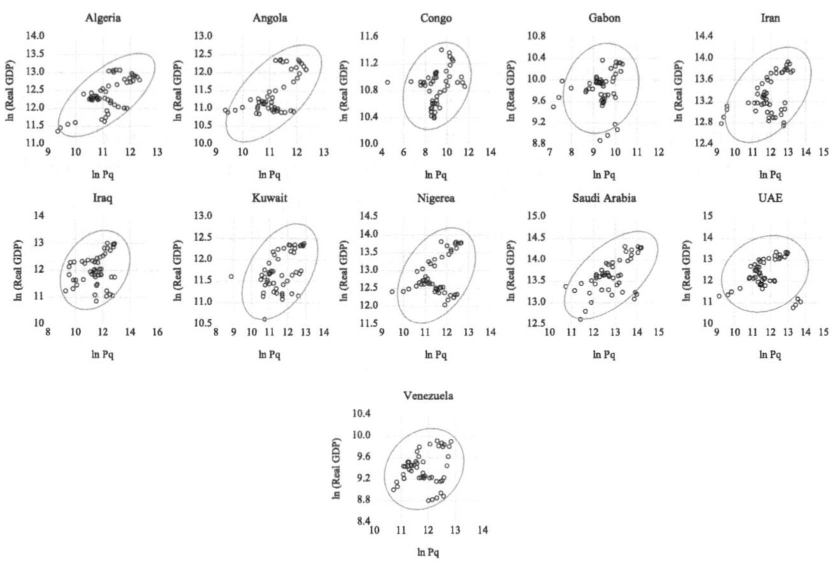

Figure 1.6 95-Percent Chi-Square Confidence Ellipse (1970–2019) Real GDP and the Value of Oil Production (in Real USD)

between real GDP, oil prices (in US dollars), and oil production (measured in real US dollars). Figures 1.5 and 1.6 plot the natural log of the *real* price of oil per barrel and real GDP – a 95 percent Chi-Squared Confidence Ellipse test (Johnson and Wichern 1992).

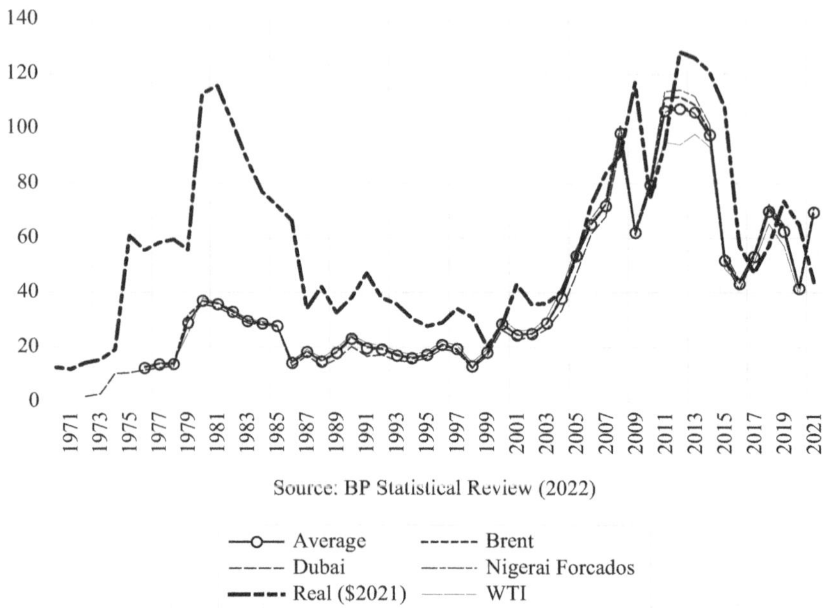

Figure 1.7 Different Measures of Crude Oil Prices Highly Correlated

In this analysis, we use the average *real* price of oil, which is the average of the Dubai oil price, the Brent oil price, the Nigeria Forcados, and the West Texas Intermediate oil price (source: BP Statistical Review) deflated by the US Consumer Price Index for 2021. The various prices of oil by country are highly correlated with this measure of the price of oil. Figure 1.7 plots the data.[9]

We will also test for cointegration, i.e., whether real GDP and oil prices share a common trend in the long run. Conditional on sharing a common trend in the long run, we also test whether real GDP and oil prices share common cycles.

1.3.6.2 Real GDP and Oil Share a Long-Run Common Trend

Trend is a very interesting issue in economics, but it is also a very complicated econometric problem. It is hard to model, identify, and predict; see, for example, Phillips (2003).

Before we analyze the trends, we plot the time series data for the natural logs of real GDP, lnY_t, the real oil price, lnP_t, and the oil production lnP_tq_t, where P_t is the price of oil in US dollars and q_t is the quantity of oil production in thousands of barrels/day in Figures 1.8–1.18.

9 Note that every OPEC country has its own oil price, which might be different and subject to more complicated conditions and trade deals. However, country-specific oil prices are highly correlated with Brent, Dubai, and Texas West Intermediary (TWI) prices.

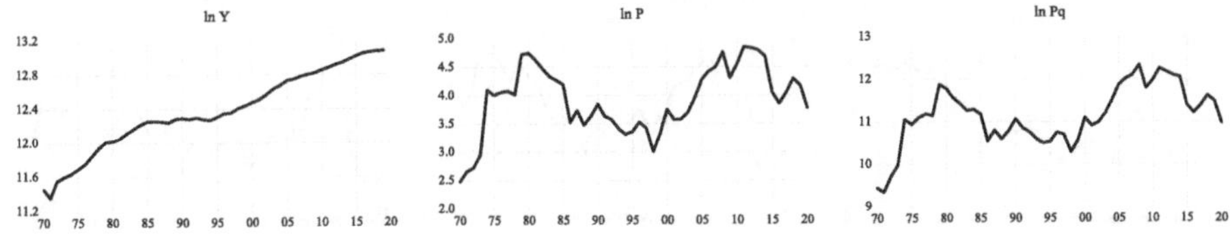

Figure 1.8 Algeria's Real GDP, Real Oil Price, and the Value of Oil Production (in Real USD)

Data Sources: Real GDP is from Penn World Table, and oil price and quantity are from BP Statistical Review.

Figure 1.9 Angola's Real GDP, Real Oil Price, and the Value of Oil Production (in Real USD)

Data Sources: Real GDP is from Penn World Table, and oil price and quantity are from BP Statistical Review.

Figure 1.10 Congo, DR's Real GDP, Real Oil Price, and the Value of Oil Production (in Real USD)

Data Sources: Real GDP is from Penn World Table, and oil price and quantity are from BP Statistical Review.

Figure 1.11 Gabon's Real GDP, Real Oil Price, and the Value of Oil Production (in Real USD)

Data Sources: Real GDP is from Penn World Table, and oil price and quantity are from BP Statistical Review.

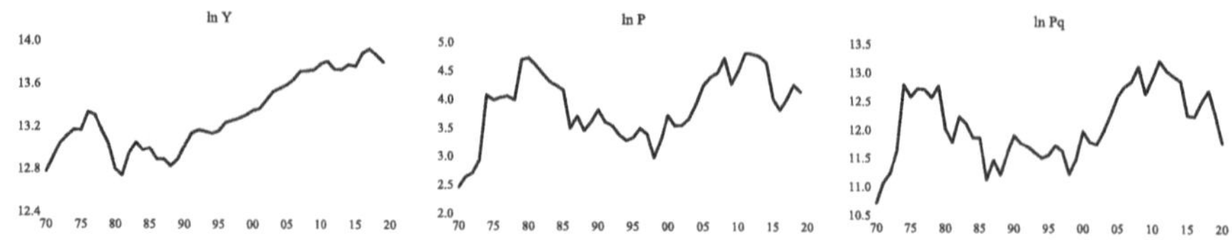

Figure 1.12 Iran's Real GDP, Real Oil Price, and the Value of Oil Production (in Real USD)

Data Sources: Real GDP is from Penn World Table, and oil price and quantity are from BP Statistical Review.

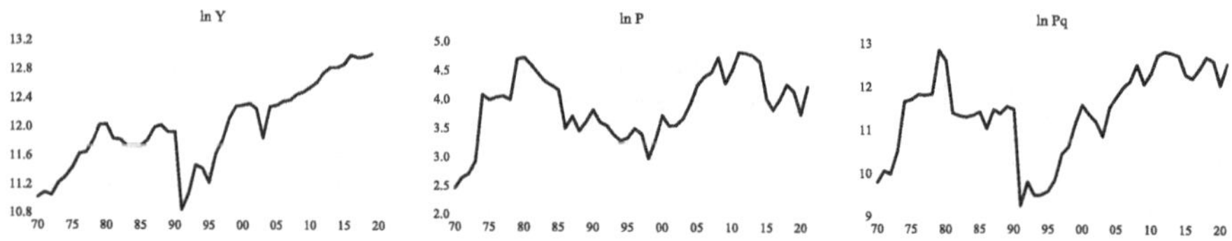

Figure 1.13 Iraq's Real GDP, Real Oil Price, and the Value of Oil Production (in Real USD)

Data Sources: Real GDP is from Penn World Table, and oil price and quantity are from BP Statistical Review.

Figure 1.14 Kuwait's Real GDP, Real Oil Price, and the Value of Oil Production (in Real USD)

Data Sources: Real GDP is from Penn World Table, and oil price and quantity are from BP Statistical Review.

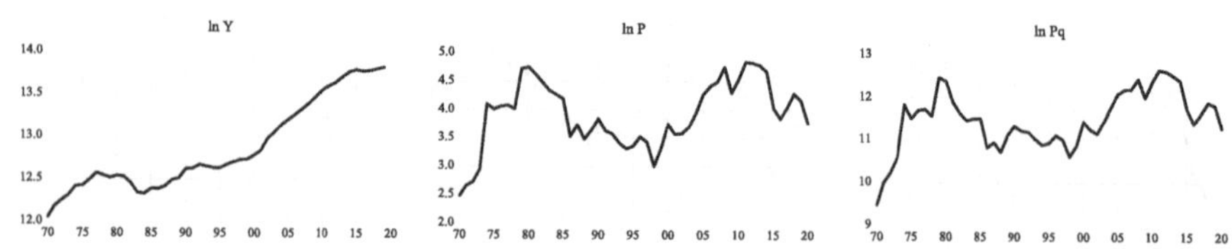

Figure 1.15 Nigeria's Real GDP, Real Oil Price, and the Value of Oil Production (in Real USD)

Data Sources: Real GDP is from Penn World Table, and oil price and quantity are from BP Statistical Review.

Figure 1.16 Saudi Arabia's Real GDP, Real Oil Price, and the Value of Oil Production (in Real USD)

Data Sources: Real GDP is from Penn World Table, and oil price and quantity are from BP Statistical Review.

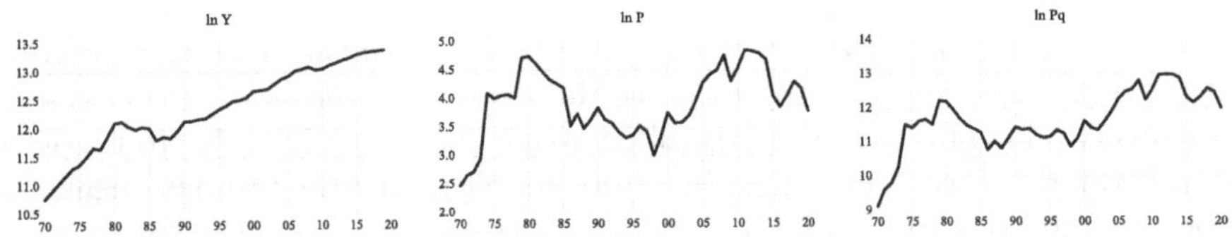

Figure 1.17 UAE Real GDP, Real Oil Price, and the Value of Oil Production (in Real USD)

Data Sources: Real GDP is from Penn World Table, and oil price and quantity are from BP Statistical Review.

Figure 1.18 Venezuela's Real GDP, Real Oil Price, and the Value of Oil Production (in Real USD)

Data Sources: Real GDP is from Penn World Table, and oil price and quantity are from BP Statistical Review.

All the data have trends. The real price of oil is volatile; oil prices behave like asset prices. Oil production is also volatile. There are breaks in the data, which are identified *ex-post* consistent with our earlier brief of the histories of these countries.

Before we test for cointegration, i.e., whether real GDP, lnY_t and oil measured in real US dollars lnP_tq_t, where P_t is the real price of oil and q_t is oil production, and also lnY_t and the real price of oil, lnP_t itself, share a long-run common trend, we examine the nature of trends in the data.

Determining the nature of the trends depicted in Figures 1.8–1.18 is crucial to our analysis. We are facing two types of trends in the data. Consider the following univariate time series:

$$x_t = \mu + e_t + \psi_1 e_{t-1} + \psi_2 e_{t-2} + \cdots = \mu + \psi(L)e_t, \tag{1.1}$$

whereby the sum of the absolute values of $\psi < \infty$. The roots of $\psi(.)$ are outside the unit circle. And, the error term e_t is a white noise sequence with mean zero and variance σ^2. It is important to understand that the unconditional expectation $E(x_t) = \mu$ is constant and independent of the date. It is also important to understand the forecast of x_t converges to the unconditional *mean* μ. Equation 1.1 is a representation of a *covariance stationary* process. The data in Figures 1.8–1.18 could not have been derived from such a process or under such assumptions. The data have visually recognizable trends. The question is what is the underlying model of this trend? There are two types. First,

$$x_t = \underbrace{\alpha + \delta t}_{mean} + \psi(L)e_t, \tag{1.2}$$

which is a *deterministic trend*. In equation (1.2), the mean is a linear function of the date t and replaces the mean of the *covariance stationary* process μ in equation (1.1). This time series is called *trend stationary*. In order to render it *stationary*, the linear trend must be removed. Note that the trend is linear, δt, not quadratic or exponential. Our plots above suggest that many of the time series might be best described as having exponential trends. In case $x_t = e^{\delta t}$, then $\frac{dx}{dt} = \delta x_t$. Thus, the trend exhibits *constant proportional growth*.

Such trend,

$$x_t - x_{t-1} = (1 - L)x_t = \Delta x_t = \delta + \psi(L)e_t, \tag{1.3}$$

is called *stochastic trend*, where $\psi(L) \neq 0$. The mean of Δx_t is δ. Setting $\psi(L) \neq 1$ means x_t is a unit root process. The meaning of this is that the time series x_t is integrated of order 1, or I(1). In plain language, it means that the shocks to such a process are very persistent. The moments of the time series are functions of time. The series x_t is *differenced-stationary*; i.e., it must be differenced in order to become stationary.

Rewriting (1.3), the process:

$$x_t = x_{t-1} + \delta + e_t, \tag{1.4}$$

which is also called *random walk with a drift* δ (or Brownian motion). If the time series has a unit root as in (1.3), $\psi(1)$ is $\neq 0$, whereby it is the polynomial:

$$\psi(z) = 1 + \psi_1 z^1 + \psi_2 z^2 + \cdots, \tag{1.5}$$

evaluated at $z = 1$. For further explanation, see Appendix 1.1.

Table 1.2 reports the test statistics for unit root (difference-stationary) and trend-stationary data. There are many tests for unit root, and this literature is quite big. We use a number of, *commonly used*, tests; the Dickey-Fuller (1979) – augmented Dickey-Fuller (ADF) (Said and Dickey 1984), the DF-GLS (Elliot, Rothenberg, and Stock 1996), and Phillips and Perron (1988). In applying these tests, we considered a specification (note that different

Table 1.2 The Data Have Unit Roots

H_0 : Unit Root $- \; \Delta x_t = \alpha + \beta \, Trend + \sum_{i=1}^{k} \delta_i \Delta x_{t-i} + \rho x_{t-1} + u_t$								
		ADF			DF-GLS		Phillips-Perron	
Country	*Sample*	x_t	*Lag i*	*P-Value ii*	*Lag i*	*t -Stat iii*	*Bandwidth Auto NW – Bartlett Kernel*	*P-Value ii*
Algeria	1970–2019	lnY_t	7	0.0012iv	8	–2.55	3	0.5949
		lnY_t	8	0.0592	8	–1.63	3	0.7958
	1980–2019	lnP_tq_t	0	0.4227	0	–1.85	1	0.4183
		lnP_t	0	0.2731	0	–2.01	1	0.2622
Angola	1970–2019	lnY_t	1	0.5560	1	–1.75	2	0.7933
		lnP_tq_t	0	0.3605	0	–1.97	0	0.3238
		lnP_t	0	0.3330	0	–1.93	1	0.3148
		lnY_t	1	0.9351	1	–1.47	4	0.9895
Congo, DR	1970–2019	lnP_tq_t	0	0.0000iv	1	–2.18	2	0.0000iv
		lnP_t	0	0.2731	0	–2.01	1	0.2622
	1985–2019	lnP_tq_t	0	0.2972	0	–2.36	1	0.2642
Gabon		lnY_t	9	0.0455	9	–2.93	4	0.1490
	1970–2019	lnP_tq_t	0	0.3652	0	–2.46	0	0.3652
		lnP_t	0	0.4784	0	–1.79	2	0.5055
	1970–2019	lnY_t	9	0.0100iv	9	–2.13	0	0.7550
Iran		lnY_t	9	0.7005	9	–2.92	1	0.3409
	1982–2019	lnP_tq_t	0	0.5010	0	–2.17	1	0.5049
		lnP_t	0	0.3709	0	–1.93	1	0.3619

(Continued)

Table 1.2 (Continued)

H_0 : *Unit Root* – $\Delta x_t = \alpha + \beta\, Trend + \sum_{i=1}^{k} \delta_i \Delta x_{t-i} + \rho x_{t-1} + u_t$

		ADF			DF-GLS		Phillips-Perron	
Country	*Sample*	x_t	*Lag i*	*P-Value ii*	*Lag i*	*t -Stat iii*	*Bandwidth Auto NW – Bartlett Kernel*	*P-Value ii*
Iraq	1970–2019	lnY_t	0	0.3396	0	–2.49	2	0.3250
		$lnP_t q_t$	0	0.4898	0	–2.08	2	0.4663
		lnP_t	0	0.2731	0	–2.08	1	0.2622
Kuwait	1970–2019	lnY_t	1	0.2618	1	–1.57	2	0.5195
		$lnP_t q_t$	0	0.2867	0	–2.60	1	0.3060
		lnP_t	0	0.2731	0	–2.02	1	0.2622
Nigeria	1970–2019	lnY_t	1	0.8045	2	–1.89	4	0.8734
		$lnP_t q_t$	0	0.1382	0	–2.05	2	0.1318
		lnP_t	0	0.2731	0	–2.02	1	0.2622
Saudi Arabia	1970–2019	lnY_t	6	0.3126	2	–2.53	4	0.1056
		$lnP_t q_t$	1	0.1767	1	–2.10	2	0.1676
		lnP_t	0	0.2731	0	–2.02	1	0.2622
UAE	1970–2019	lnY_t	10	0.0329iv	10	–1.92	2	0.1612
		$lnP_t q_t$	0	0.1263	0	–1.97	0	0.1181
		lnP_t	0	0.2731	0	–2.02	1	0.2622
Venezuela	1970–2011	lnY_t	1	0.1422	1	–2.80	0	0.4559
		$lnP_t q_t$	0	0.5823	0	–1.92	1	0.5711
		lnP_t	0	0.2731	0	–2.02	1	0.2622

Y is real GDP, *P* is the real price of oil, and *q* is the quantity of oil production. (i) Automatic based on AIC. (ii) P-values are (MacKinnon 1996) one-sided P-values. (iii) *t* -Stat 1, 5, and 10 percent critical values are –3.77, –3.19, and –2.89, respectively (Elliot, Rothenberg, and Stock (1996, Table 1). (iv) Rejects the unit root in favor of trend stationary. Note that lnP_t^o is the real price of oil for all countries.

specifications of the regressions have different distributions for unit root), where we fit an OLS regression with a constant and trend so we could test for a deterministic trend in the data. We used a variety of Information Criteria – e.g., the Akaike Information Criterion (AIC), Schwarz Information Criterion (SIC), and Hannan–Quinn Information Criterion (and some modified versions of these criteria) to determine the lag structure, but we only report the AIC because the results are the same.

There is evidence that the data have unit root particularly when the samples are adjusted to account for *ex-post* breaks. Sometimes, the sample matters for the results because real GDP and oil prices in OPEC have been subject to many big shocks such as the 1973 and 1979 first and second oil price shocks, wars such as the First and the Second Gulf Wars in 1990 and 2003, coup d'états, and so on. These unit root tests fit a linear line through the data (ordinary least squares (OLS) regressions); therefore, these tests could confuse a break in the data with unit root. Furthermore, we should always be cautious of the fact that these tests are weak – i.e., have low powers against stationary alternatives; in other words, they do not reject the null too often. There are differences in powers, however. The DF-GLS test for a unit root (Elliott, Rothenberg, and Stock 1996), has more power than the ADF test when the autoregressive root is large but less than one. There is a very large literature on the power of unit root tests, which is beyond the scope of this book, but it helps to be aware of these empirical facts. In addition, Stock (1991), Cochrane (1991), Rudebusch (1993), and Christiano and Eichenbaum (1990) argued that these tests could not distinguish between a root of 1 and 0.98 for example. We interpret the unit root as the shocks to real GDP and the oil price are highly persistent.

Cointegration is defined as follows: Let x_{1t} and x_{2t} be integrated processes $ARIMA(p,d,q)$ with $d \geq 1$. And, there exists a_1 and a_2 such that $Z_t = a_1x_{1t} + a_2x_{2t}$ is I(0) stationary linear combination. Thus, x_{1t} and x_{2t} are cointegrated. In other words, the two time series have stochastic trends, but they share a common trend. See more details in Appendix 1.1. We test the null hypothesis that the natural logs of real GDP and the oil production (measured in real US dollars) are *not* cointegrated, i.e., they do not share a long-run common trend. So, we are testing for the long-run common trend in real GDP with the real price of oil and with oil production (in real US dollars). Because this is a bivariate system, we use the Engle and Granger (1987) and the Phillips and Ouliaris (1990) tests. We report the results in Table 1.3. We compute both the tau-statistic (t-statistic) and normalized autocorrelation coefficient (z-statistic) for residuals obtained using each series in the group as the dependent variable in a cointegrating regression. Except in the case of Angola and one case in Congo, where the P-values are high, the null hypothesis of no cointegration is rejected at least at the 10 percent level. The real economy measured by real GDP and oil production (in real US dollars) share a long-run common trend.

Table 1.3 P-Values lnY_t and lnP_tq_t and lnY_t and lnP_t Cointegrated H_0 : No Cointegration

		Engle and Granger (1987)ii				*Phillips and Ouliaris (1990)iii*			
		lnY_t	lnP_tq_t	lnY_t	lnP_t	lnY_t	lnP_tq_t	lnY_t	lnP_t
Algeria	τ	0.1009	0.1032	0.0571	0.0644	0.0774	0.0787	0.0492	0.0543
	z	0.1606	0.1619	0.1476	0.1507	0.1205	0.1207	0.1275	0.1263
Angola	τ	0.0157	0.0222	0.0389	0.0448	0.0127	0.0199	0.0339	0.0382
	z	0.2822	0.2959	0.1290	0.1323	0.2938	0.2997	0.1122	0.1112
Congo, DR	τ	0.0000	0.0000	0.0363	0.0449	0.0001	0.0001	0.0328	0.0400
	z	0.0635	0.0694	0.1518	0.1578	0.0410	0.426	0.1380	0.1405
Gabon	τ	0.0220	0.0233	0.0815	0.0901	0.0185	0.0193	0.0723	0.0784
	z	0.0710	0.0722	0.1757	0.1787	0.0590	0.0585	0.1591	0.1576
Iran	τ	0.0411	0.0423	0.0498	0.0589	0.0329	0.0336	0.0422	0.0506
	z	0.0773	0.0781	0.1577	0.1607	0.0612	0.0612	0.1398	0.1366
Iraq	τ	0.1417	0.1454	0.0420	0.0466	0.1244	0.1633	0.0356	0.0390
	z	0.1819	0.1831	0.1130	0.1151	0.1271	0.1635	0.0954	0.0955
Kuwait	τ	0.0314	0.0326	0.0342	0.0418	0.0324	0.0338	0.0299	0.0359
	z	0.0549	0.0555	0.1385	0.1439	0.0648	0.0657	0.1171	0.1194
Nigeria	τ	0.0302	0.0314	0.0474	0.0533	0.0240	0.0248	0.0411	0.0460
	z	0.0758	0.0769	0.1358	0.1387	0.0583	0.0585	0.1193	0.1205
Saudi Arabia	τ	0.0416	0.0437	0.0601	0.0682	0.0372	0.0968	0.0538	0.0606
	z	0.0595	0.0606	0.1552	0.1587	0.0388	0.0972	0.1424	0.1443
UAE	τ	0.0660	0.0683	0.0888	0.0946	0.0419	0.0431	0.0760	0.0796
	z	0.1388	0.1403	0.1711	0.1720	0.0771	0.0775	0.1478	0.1454
Venezuela	τ	0.0802	0.0812	0.1352	0.1695	0.0728	0.0736	0.1205	0.1465
	z	0.0969	0.0973	0.2416	0.2565	0.0918	0.0920	0.2210	0.2253

The sample is 1970–2019. Y_t is the real GDP, P_t is the real oil price in US dollars, and q_t is the oil production in millions of barrels/day.

i. MacKinnon (1996) P-values of τ and z statistics.

ii. There is no intercept or trend in the regressions. Auto lag specification based on AIC, max lag = 10.

iii. There is no intercept and trend, long-run variance estimate pre-whitening with lags from AIC, max lag = –1, Bartlett kernel, Newey-West auto bandwidth, and NW auto lag length.

1.3.6.3 *Real GDP and Oil Production (in Real US Dollars) Share a Common Cycle*

It is perhaps necessary to ask whether real GDP and real oil prices also share a common cycle. We use the Vahid and Engle (1993) test. The results are reported in Table 1.4.

The sample is 1970–2019, number of observations $T = 50$; the number of lags, $k = 0$; λ is a canonical correlation; s is the smallest canonical correlation = 1.68 for all countries and it is the real price of oil; the system is bivariate $P = 2$; and the number of cointegration vectors $r = 1$.

All pairs of lnY_t and real oil prices lnP_t in all OPEC share a common cycle. Given the evidence we provided, we may conclude that the OPEC economies are significantly dependent on oil.

These facts presented earlier are consistent with the Resource Curse theory that resources could be more of an economic curse than a blessing, which has emerged in debates in the 1950s and the 1960s about the economic problems of low- and middle-income countries, e.g., Ross (1999). The term ***resource curse*** describes how resource-rich wealthy countries such as OPEC have been unable to have high productivity growth compared with relatively higher productivity growth countries that have little or no natural resources (e.g., Taiwan, Korea, Singapore, and Hong Kong). An influential Sachs and Andrew (1995) paper found a strong correlation between natural resource abundance and poor economic growth. This literature has grown enormously over time, where the effects of resource wealth on a wide range of economic outcomes have been examined and provided explanations for the types, the reasons, and the timing when a resource curse is likely to occur; see Frankel (2012) for example.

Table 1.4 Vahid and Engle (1993) Test for Common Cycles $c(k,s) = -(T-k-1)\sum_{i=1}^{s} ln(1-\lambda_i^2) \sim \chi^2_{s^2-spk+sr-sp}$ $H_0 : s = 0$, No Common Cycle

	Squared Canonical Correlation	$c(k,s)$	*P-Value*
Algeria	0.25	14.10	0.0002
Angola	0.23	12.81	0.0003
Congo, DR	0.08	4.09	0.0432
Gabon	0.25	14.10	0.0002
Iran	0.18	9.72	0.0018
Iraq	0.34	20.36	0.0000
Kuwait	0.09	4.62	0.0316
Nigeria	0.27	15.42	0.0001
Saudi Arabia	0.34	20.36	0.0000
UAE	0.29	16.78	0.0000
Venezuela	0.24	13.45	0.0002

The sample is 1970–2019, number of observations $T = 50$; the number of lags, $k = 0$; λ is canonical correlation; s is the smallest canonical correlation = 1.68 for all countries and it is the real price of oil's; the system is bivariate $P = 2$; and the number of cointegration vectors $r = 1$.

1.4 Global Emission, Global Oil Production, and Consumption Nexus

The Net Zero-Carbon 2050 is a legally binding agreement adopted by 196 countries (including OPEC countries) and ratified by 138 so far. Generally speaking, it aims at holding the increase in global average temperature below 2°C above pre-industrial levels and pursuing efforts to limit the temperature increase to 1.5°C above pre-industrial levels. The OPEC economies will be affected significantly because the production of fossil fuel (oil in particular), global CO_2 emission, and global oil consumption are highly correlated. Figure 1.19 plots the data. More rigorous analysis will show that they also share a common trend in the long run. Whether this UN goal is achievable or not, in 2050 or 2070, it has, nevertheless, serious economic consequences for the OPEC countries.

The question we try to answer in this book is whether the OPEC countries' oil market structure, which is a state-owned oil monopoly, whereby the state, largely, sets the production of oil to peg the price of oil, could survive the zero-carbon state of the world. The question arises because in microeconomic price theory, when faced with a negative demand shock, the monopolist cuts oil production (quantity) more than the producer in the competitive market does in order to prevent the, relatively higher, monopolist price from falling to the market's level. OPEC (also OPEC+, which is OPEC plus Russia) cuts oil production in 2022 and in April 2023 by 2 and 1.6 million barrels/day. Saudi Arabia announced a 1 million barrel/day cut in July 2023. These oil cuts were extended in September 2023.[10] Continuous reductions in oil production could reduce real GDP permanently in OPEC countries because real GDP

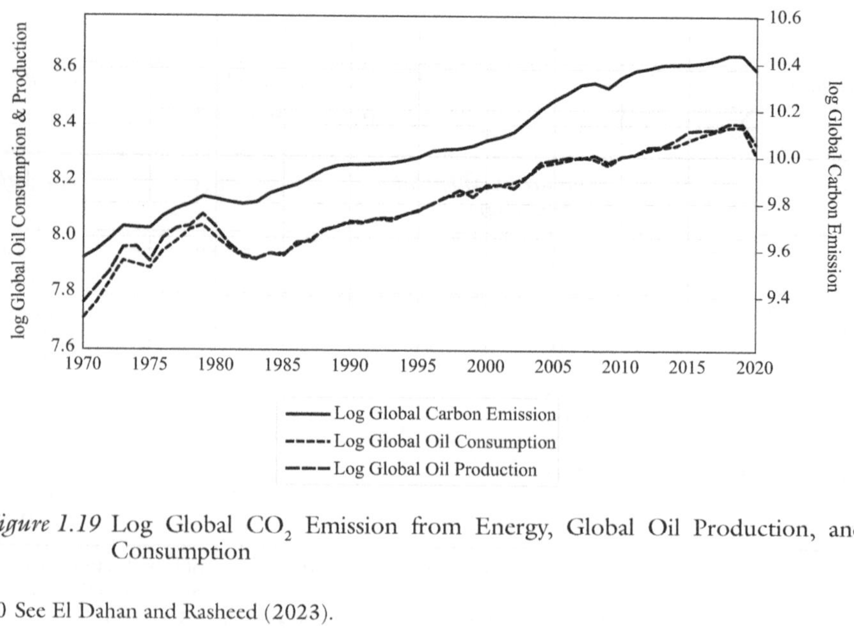

Figure 1.19 Log Global CO_2 Emission from Energy, Global Oil Production, and Consumption

10 See El Dahan and Rasheed (2023).

depends on oil, i.e., oil is a factor of production, and oil is the main component of GDP on the expenditure side.

Our objective is to use the stress test method in Razzak (2022) special case on Iraq. In the next chapters, we explain what stress test means in this context and detail the technical steps of the testing procedure. Essentially, we want to compare ***permanent income*** for the OPEC countries whose oil industries are state-owned, i.e., state monopolies, with hypothetical competitive oil industries.

Testing involves counterfactual scenarios and requires certain assumptions. To accomplish the test, we make strong assumptions, albeit supported by evidence. First, the global (governmental) commitment to drive emissions to zero by 2050 is binding. Some experts expect that the global demand for oil will decline permanently in the next 30 years or so (adverse demand shock). Global demand for hydrocarbon products is expected to fall between now and 2050. The US government introduced more than 4 trillion dollars in subsidies to sectors that are affected by the cut in hydrocarbon, International Renewable Energy Agency (*IRENA*). See the International Energy Agency (IEA)'s latest flagship report (2021), which says that by 2035, there will be no sales of new internal combustion engine passenger cars, and by 2040, the global electricity sector has already reached net-zero emissions.[11] Investments in alternative energy are also trending up, including in China, see Bloomberg NEF Clean Energy Investment Trends (2020). The Economist magazine's May 22, 2021 edition has a story entitled, *The Green Meme, a Green Bubble? We Dissect the Investment Boom*, where they show that since the start of 2020, our portfolio, when companies are equally weighted, has more than doubled; when firms are weighted by market capitalization, our portfolio has jumped by more than half. The reason for that difference is that many green firms are small – their median market capitalization is about $6 billion. The smallest 25 percent of the firms have risen by an average of 152 percent since January 2020. Firms that derive a greater share of their revenue from green activities, such as EV makers and fuel-cell companies, have also outperformed. The greenest 25 percent of firms saw their share prices rise by 110 percent. The most recent IEA report (2023) indicated that, and we quote, the scaling up of clean energy is the main factor behind a decline of fossil fuel demand of over 25 percent this decade in the Net Zero Emission (NZE) Scenario. However, well-designed policies, such as the early retirement or repurposing of coal-fired power plants, are key to facilitating declines in fossil fuel demand and creating additional room for clean energy to expand. In the NZE Scenario, strong growth in clean energy and other policy measures together lead to energy sector CO_2 emissions falling by 35 percent by 2030 compared with 2022. Second, we make assumptions about the quantity of oil production cuts by country. The assumptions are based on our estimated cut in oil production required to keep the price of oil at a ***certain breakeven price level*** with respect to the fall

11 For example, see Gillingham et al. (2023).

in global oil consumption by country. We found that in order to keep the price of oil unchanged at a certain breakeven level; a 1 percent decline in global oil consumption is met by more than 1 percent cut in oil production. These oil cuts translate to cuts that *exceed* the stipulated reductions by the Net Zero UN plan. Third, we assume that 80 US dollars/barrel is the breakeven price of oil for OPEC. We compute the average of the fiscal breakeven oil prices of Algeria, Iran, Iraq, Kuwait, Saudi Arabia and the UAE from 2000 to 2023 as published by the IMF, which is 84.2 US dollars. The average is 96.15 US dollars if 2024 IMF projections are included. The data for the rest of the OPEC countries are not readily available, therefore, we assume the breakeven price to 80 US dollar. These assumptions are used to construct a counterfactual time series for the price and quantity of oil, which we use to estimate *permanent income* under the state-owned oil monopoly scenario. Another set of assumptions is used to estimate *permanent income* under the competitive oil industry scenario. We will show that *permanent income* and, hence, *current* consumption fall significantly below baseline estimates under the monopolist's scenario than under the competitive scenario. OPEC's oil dependence and the current oil policy will have some adverse consequences when the world gradually but surely moves away from fossil fuels in the future. The oil dependence and the policy of cutting oil production in excess of Net Zero stipulated reductions in production to peg the price of oil will cause income and welfare loss, which requires OPEC to conduct severe-scenario stress tests and rethink the optimal institutional arrangements for the oil industries.

Appendix 1.1 – Unit Root Process

Hamilton (1994) provides a very good explanation for the unit root process. When I think of unit root I think of the simple solution of the quadratic equation and the standard formula to solve for the two roots.[12]

Consider the alternative to equation (1.3):

$$x_t = \alpha + \delta_t + u_t , \tag{A1.1.1}$$

where the error term u_t is a zero-mean $ARMA(p,q)$ process:

$$(1-\phi_1 L - \phi_2 L^2 - \cdots - \phi_p L^p)u_t = (1+\theta_1 L + \theta_2 L^2 + \cdots + \theta_q L^q)e_t , \tag{A1.1.2}$$

where the moving average operator $(1+\theta_1 L + \theta_2 L^2 + \cdots + \theta_q L^q)$ is invertible. The autoregressive operator $(1-\phi_1 L - \phi_2 L^2 - \cdots - \phi_p L^p)$ could be written as

$$(1-\phi_1 L - \phi_2 L^2 - \cdots - \phi_p L^p) = (1-\lambda_1 L)(1-\lambda_2 L)\cdots(1-\lambda_p L). \tag{A1.1.3}$$

If the roots (eigenvalues) λ_1, λ_2, $\cdots \lambda_p$ are inside the unit circle, then equation (A1.1.2) can be written as

$$u_t = \frac{1+\theta_1 L + \theta_2 L^2 + \cdots + \theta_q L^q}{(1-\lambda_1 L)(1-\lambda_2 L)\cdots(1-\lambda_p L)} e_t \equiv \psi(L)e_t , \tag{A1.1.4}$$

with $\sum_{i=0}^{\infty} |\psi| < \infty$ and the roots of $\psi(z) = 0$ outside the unit circle. Therefore, when $|\lambda_1| < 1$ for all i, the process (A1.1.1) becomes a special case of the trend-stationary process in equation (1.2). However, if $\lambda_1 = 1$ (i.e., unit root), and $\lambda_2, \lambda_3, \cdots \lambda_p$ are <1 in absolute value, then equation (A1.1.2) would suggest that

$$(1-L)(1-\lambda_2 L)(1-\lambda_3 L)\cdots(1-\lambda_p L)u_t = (1+\theta_1 L + \theta_2 L^2 + \cdots + \theta_q L^q)e_t \tag{A1.1.5}$$

Thus,

$$(1-L)u_t = \frac{1+\theta_1 L + \theta_2 L^2 + \cdots + \theta_q L^q}{(1-\lambda_2 L)(1-\lambda_3 L)\cdots(1-\lambda_p L)} e_t \equiv \psi(L)e_t , \tag{A1.1.6}$$

12 $ax^2 + bx + c = 0$ and $x = \dfrac{-b \mp \sqrt{b^2 - 4ac}}{2a}$.

where $\sum_{i=0}^{\infty}|\psi_i| < \infty$, and the roots $\psi(z) = 0$ outside the unit circle. Now let us go back to equation (A1.1.1) and take the first difference:

$$(1 - \mathrm{L})x_t = (1 - L)\alpha + [\delta t - \delta(t-1)] + (1 - L)u_t = 0 + \delta + \psi(L)e_t . \quad \text{(A1.1.7)}$$

Equation (A1.1.7) is a unit root process similar to equation (1.3). This difference-stationary process differs from the trend-stationary process in the forecasts, whereby that of the latter converges to a constant regardless of the value of x_t, while that of the former keeps changing with every new value of x_t. The mean square error (MSE) of the trend-stationary process reaches a finite bound as the forecast horizon gets larger, whereas the unit root difference stationary process's MSE grows linearly with the forecast horizon. Therefore, the standard deviation of the forecast error grows with the square root of the forecast horizon. If $\delta > 0$, then the forecast itself grows linearly in the forecast horizon. Data of a unit root process with a positive drift exhibit an upward trend if observed for a sufficiently long time. These issues are very important for the analysis of time series of the type we are dealing with in this book and that is why we have devoted a large space to it.

2 The Stress Test Strategy

Abstract

The stress test assesses hypothetical scenarios when a significant global oil consumption drop affects permanent income. Our eight-step strategy involves: assuming a microeconomic-based model for real GDP, testing data trends, estimating a VAR, generating dynamic stochastic GDP projections for 2020–2050 (baseline permanent income), re-estimating the model with OPEC reducing oil production but maintaining a breakeven price, producing new projections, computing deviations from baseline GDP, and repeating the same steps assuming OPEC is a competitive oil producer adjusting quantity and price to market demand shocks. This methodological approach elucidates the impact of different oil production models on economic outcomes.

2.1 Stress Testing?

Stress testing has been used in medical and engineering sciences for a long time. In coronary disease for example, where in very simple terms, patients are subjected to physical or exercise stress testing to measure the heart's performance; see Myrvin H. Ellestad (2003) for example. In structural engineering, for example, stress testing analyzes the structure (a building, a bridge, a metal structure, etc.) under a steady load to determine the stresses, strains, and deformations in the structure. Engineers use *static, dynamic, and fatigue analysis* to determine the design's strength to support the expected loads and ensure necessary safety requirements. For stress testing in civil engineering, see, for example, Megson (2019).

Although stress tests gained more attention in the economics literature as a tool to assess the financial systems vulnerabilities after the Global Financial Crisis, Andrew Crockett (1997) was a paper presented at the Jackson Hole central bankers meeting, where he spoke about techniques to assess financial vulnerabilities. Generally, stress tests encompass a number of techniques for assessing resilience to extreme events. They are used to determine the stability of a given financial (or economic) system.[1] The main objective of stress

1 Razzak (2013) provides a test for predicting instability in macroeconomic systems and markets.

DOI: 10.4324/9781003488125-2

testing financial markets is to test the reliance of the system beyond the normal operational capacity, i.e., very stressful situations, often to a breaking point. In financial literature, stress testing has traditionally referred to asset portfolios, but after the Global Financial Crisis, it has been applied to the entire banking and financial systems. Central banks produce periodical financial stability reports, where such analyses are reported. For a survey of stress tests, see, for example, the Committee on the Global Financial System CGFS (2005). For more on the issue, see papers produced by the IMF, for example, Cihak (2007) and Maino and Tintchev (2012). Demekas (2015) introduced a more sensible general equilibrium approach. Anderson et al. (2018) summarized the findings of the research, which aimed at presenting what they described as state-of-the-art approaches to macroprudential stress testing, including modeling and implementation challenges, providing a roadmap for future research, and discussing the potential uses of such tests to support policy.

Stress testing in economics literature focuses more on banking and financial markets although there are numerous stress tests' works on the effects of macroprudential, climate, and housing markets on the economy. We will not cite all the papers here, but a Google Scholar search will suffice. For example, see the September 2009 issue of the Journal of Central Banking on stress testing. For different methodologies, see Rebonato (2010) who provides a rather different approach for testing using a Bayesian method. A semi-parametric approach was used by Kanas and Molyneux (2018) and Orlov et al. (2023) who argued for sequential tests rather than one static test. There are compelling reasons to believe that stress tests must be conducted within a general equilibrium system or dynamic stochastic model. Single indicators are insufficient. Stochastic simulations and projections ***might be*** the only plausible way to deal with the Lucas critique (Lucas 1976).[2] Also, random shocks of various sources continuously affect the economy. Our method in this book emphasizes that any stress test should be based on (1) economic theory, (2) system estimation, and (3) dynamic stochastic projections.

2.2 Microeconomic Price Theory

The rest of the analyses in this book are based on Razzak (2022). Figure 2.1 illustrates the microeconomic theoretical foundation of the problem, which depicts the responses of the prices and quantities, under the monopolistic and competitive case scenarios, to an adverse demand shock.[3] Eventually, we will

2 Lucas famously argued that macro-econometric models with fixed estimated elasticities cannot capture the effects of policy (monetary, fiscal, etc.) on the parameters of the model because these elasticities are in fact not fixed but rather functions of policy parameters themselves. Whenever policy changes these elasticities change, thus forecasts of such macro-econometric models are uninformative.

3 Since the monopolist sets the price, where the marginal revenue curve intersects the marginal cost and cost is a function of quantity, the profit function is written in terms of quantity. $\pi = P(q).q - C(q)$. Maximized profit is $0 = \partial q = P(q) + qP'(q) - C'(q)$, where π is the profit, P is the price, and q is the quantity.

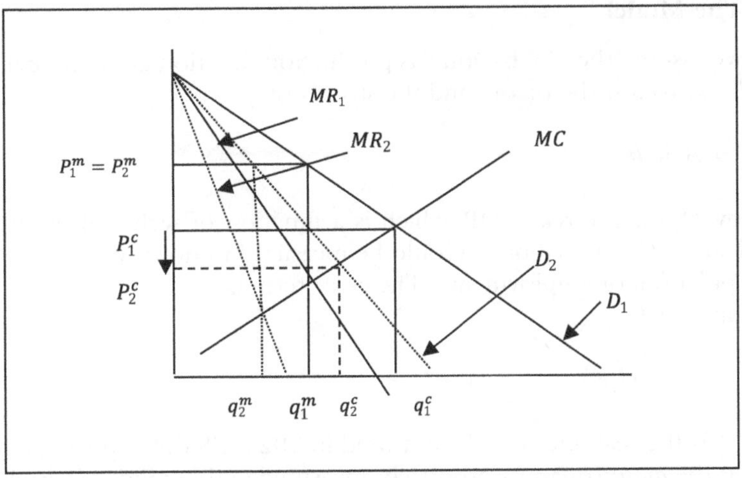

Figure 2.1 State-Owned Oil Producer (Monopoly and Competitive Oil Producer Responses to a Negative Demand Shock)

measure the effects of these two types of micro-level responses on ***permanent income***. The monopolist's price P_1^m and the quantity q_1^m are determined by the intersection of the marginal revenue curve (MR_1) with the marginal cost (MC). The competitive equilibrium occurs at the intersection of demand and the MC at a lower price P_1^c and quantity q_1^c. A sudden and severe decline in global oil consumption causes the demand curve, D_1 to shift down to D_2. Depending on the magnitude of the shift and the elasticity of the demand curve, the monopolist may be able to reduce the quantity of oil produced significantly, from q_1^m to q_2^m, in order to prevent the price of oil received before the shock from falling below P_1^m. Even if the monopolist price declines below P_1^m, it must remain above the market price; thus, $P_2^m > P_2^c$. The competitive producer, however, takes the lower market price P_2^c and produce q_2^c. Therefore, $P_1^m > P_2^c$ and $q_2^m < q_2^c$. Note that it is possible that the monopolist desires a higher price than q_2^m, which requires further reductions in output.

We seek to estimate the effects of the responses depicted in Figure 2.1 on the economy. Precisely, we want to measure (1) the effect of $P_1^m q_2^m$; the outcome of the monopolistic response to a sharp decline in global oil consumption, which is the manifestation of the Net Zero, on *expected* real GDP (2020–2050) and (2) the effect of $P_2^c q_2^c$, the outcome of the competitive producer's response to the shock, on *expected* real GDP. Expected real GDP is our measure of ***permanent income***. To do so, we have to construct a hypothetical time series for $P_{t1}^m, q_{t2}^m, P_{t2}^c$, and q_{t2}^c. Doing so will require some assumptions and information about the size of the response of the production of oil to the hypothetical decline in global oil consumption. We accomplish our objectives following eight steps, but, first, we need a model.

2.3 The Model

First, we assume the Cobb-Douglas production function as the model, which we will use to test the theory and the stress test:

$$Y_t = A_t K_t h_t e^{\varepsilon t}, \tag{2.1}$$

whereby (Y_t) is the real GDP, which is a function of technical progress A_t, capital stock K_t, and labor h_t (could be measured in hours worked, working-age population, or employment). The error term is ε_t.[4]

Assume that

$$A_t = (P_t q_t) H_t e^{vt}, \tag{2.2}$$

where P_t is the real price of oil (measured in 2021 US dollar prices per barrel) and q_t is the *actual* quantity produced (measured in thousands of barrels/day). $P_t q_t$, oil (measured in real US dollars) drives the OPEC economies. OPEC countries use oil revenues to finance education, training, health, infrastructure, and other aspects of technical progress. The variable H_t is the stock of human capital necessary to transform oil into technical progress. Human capital is an index based on average years of schooling and the rate of return to education.[5]

We will use the working-age population (15–64), *WAP*, as a measure of labor because hours-worked time series data are unavailable. The first two explanatory variables, i.e., capital and labor, need no further explanation; these factor inputs are the main explanatory variables of real GDP in the neoclassical growth model. Human capital is an intangible capital; e.g., Mankiw, Romer, and Weil (1992) explain the importance of the inclusion of human capital in the Solow model production function. The price and the quantity of oil play significant roles in the economic development of OPEC countries, especially in Iraq. Stiglitz (1974), for example, uses oil as a factor in the production function and measures it as the ratio of resource utilization to the stock of natural resources, while Solow and Wan (1976) only use the flow of oil. The error term is v_t.

The Cobb–Douglas production function (compared with other functions such as the CES) is very well-grounded in economic theory, is easy to estimate, and has a good empirical record (Miller 2008). For more on the use of the Cobb-Douglas in macroeconomic analysis, see Nickell (2003), Prescott (2004), and Christiano and Eichenbaum (1992) among others. Note that the shares of capital and labor are grounded in and recoverable from the Statistics of the National Account (SNA) directly, whereby the share of labor is simply

4 We ignore the shares in the Cobb-Douglas because we will not estimate them. Instead, we will estimate a VAR.

5 Human capital is a big research topic in economics. It is beyond the scope of this book to delve into this issue. There is no doubt that human capital belongs to this formula. However, it will be shown that the effect of human capital on real GDP varies across OPEC countries. In some countries, human capital has an insignificant effect in the sense that it accounts for a negligible amount of the variance of real GDP.

gross compensation to employees/nominal GDP ratio, and the share of capital is operating surplus/nominal GDP ratio.

Putting equations (2.1) and (2.2) together gives output production, which is equal to or less than output on the expenditure's side. Output on the expenditures' side is the sum of consumption C_t, investments I_t, government consumption (pure public consumption) G_t, and net exports X_t:[6]

$$Y_t = C_t + I_t + G_t + X_t \leq (P_t q_t) H_t e^{vt} K_t h_t e^{\varepsilon t} \tag{2.3}$$

Our objective is to estimate equation (2.3). We estimate the production side only because the price and quantity of oil are key variables in our stress test. Taking the natural log and combining the error terms in equation (2.3) give

$$lnY_t = f[ln(P_t q_t); lnH_t; lnK_t; lnh_t; u_t] \tag{2.4}$$

2.4 Estimation – Vector Autoregression (VAR)

Second, before we estimate the model, we test the time series properties of the data.

Third, we estimate a *baseline* VAR to summarize the dynamics of the variables in order to make dynamic stochastic projections of real GDP (Y_t), which would be our measure of ***permanent income, i.e., expected income.***

The VAR is given by

$$y_t = A_1 y_{t-1} \cdots A_p y_{t-p} + \varepsilon_t , \tag{2.5}$$

where $y_t = (y_1, y_{2t}, \cdots y_{kt})'$ is a $k \times 1$ vector of endogenous variables. There is also an exogenous constant term; $\varepsilon_t = (\varepsilon_1, \varepsilon_{2t}, \cdots \varepsilon_{kt})'$ is a $k \times 1$ vector of white-noise innovations with $(\varepsilon_t) = 0$; $E(\varepsilon_t \varepsilon_t') = \sum \varepsilon$; and $E(\varepsilon_t \varepsilon_s') = 0$ for $t \neq s$.

Let $(pk + d) \times 1$ be a vector

$$Z_t = (y'_{t-1} \cdots y'_{t-p})', \tag{2.6}$$

And write the VAR in a compact form:

$$Y_t = BZ_t + \epsilon_t . \tag{2.7}$$

6 A more general equilibrium model would not change our analysis; it could have a stand-in household with the textbook choices of labor leisure and consumption savings whose preferences are given by the expected utility function $E\left\{\sum_{i=0}^{\infty} \beta^t (lnC_t + \alpha ln(100 - h_t))\right\}$, where E denotes the expectations operator, C_t is consumption, and h_t is hours-worked, which is supplied to the market per worker per week for example. The assumption is that the worker has 100 hours a week, which he or she could supply. The discount factor $0 < \beta < 1$ measures the degree of patience, which increases as $\beta \to 1$. The parameter $\alpha > 0$ is the non-market productive time per household; therefore, $100 - h_t$ hours is simply leisure. The household owns the capital and rents it to the firm. The household would also have a typical budget constraint.

The vector y_t includes $(ln(P_tq_t), lnH_t, lnK_t, lnh_t, lnY_t)$ and ϵ is $(\varepsilon_{1t}, \varepsilon_{2t}, \varepsilon_{3t} \cdots \varepsilon_{5t})$; both are matrices of the endogenous variables that are the innovations, where P_t is the real oil price, q_t is the actual oil production, H_t is the human capital, h_t is the labor measured by working-age population (15–64 years), and Y_t is the real GDP. The matrices $B = (A_1, A_2, A_3, \cdots A_5, constant)$ and $Z = (Z_{1t}, Z_{2t}, Z_{3t} \cdots Z_{5t})$ are the matrix of coefficients and the matrix of regressors, respectively.

There are certain conditions that are required to estimate an unrestricted VAR. The time series must be unit root and cointegrated. A more challenging estimator would be a Vector Error Correction Model (VECM) in the sense that if the time series were to be cointegrated, we could impose some restrictions on the VAR. This is unnecessary in this case because we are not (1) interested in the short run and (2) we are not identifying any particular shock.

Fourth, we solve the baseline model and make baseline dynamic stochastic projections from 2020 to 2050. The solver will be described in detail later.

Fifth, we re-estimate the VAR under the monopolist's response to the hypothetical adverse demand shock. The monopolist responds by reducing q_t^m from q_1^m to q_2^m and keeping the price unchanged in response to severe decline in global oil consumption. There are a number of assumptions that we will discuss to quantify $P_{1t}^m q_{2t}^m$ to accomplish this step. Thus, we estimate a new VAR:

$$ln(P_{1t}^m q_{2t}^m),\ ln(H_t), ln(K_t),\ lnh_t,\ lnY_t. \tag{2.8}$$

Sixth, we solve this model and make new dynamic stochastic projections from 2020 to 2050 under the hypothetical specifications. Seventh, we compute the deviations of the dynamic stochastic projections of real GDP from the baseline projection. Eighth, we repeat all the aforementioned steps under certain assumptions we make to quantify $P_{2t}^c q_{2t}^c$ as shown in Figure 2.1, estimate the other new VAR:

$$ln(P_{1t}^c q_{2t}^c),\ ln(H_t), ln(K_t),\ lnh_t,\ lnY_t. \tag{2.9}$$

in the same order mentioned earlier, and compute the deviations of the dynamic stochastic projections from the baseline.

Next, we will execute our eight-step strategy to provide a stress test for OPEC.

3 The Time Series Properties of OPEC Data

Abstract

Real GDP is a function of technical progress proxied by oil and human capital, capital, and labor. The variables have trends, which require identification. We distinguish two types: a stochastic and a deterministic trend. The former means that the trend changes with time such that the all the moments are functions of time. Thus, the correlation between these variables is meaningless, unless these variables share a common trend in the long run, i.e., cointegrated. In a simple term, although each variable separately is a random process, together they are not. Those variables are cointegrated. We use a number of tests, albeit subject to all sorts of technical issues, they are adequate and informative about trend.

The reader, especially the econometricians, can look up the data plots and skip this chapter. Phillips (2003) argued that predicting trends is very difficult; however, it is crucial to understand the nature of trends in the data. The trends analysis, therefore, is a very necessary one for the rest of our analysis. It is necessary to determine the nature of the trend because the next step involves estimating the VAR model we presented earlier, and time series properties (i.e., unit root and cointegration) determine what estimator we use. We are concerned with identifying two types of trends, a stochastic trend, which is a unit root and indicates the persistence of economic shocks, and a deterministic trend (linear but could be something else, e.g., quadratic). Put it differently, statistically testing for the nature of the trend is not as simple as plotting and eyeballing the data. Distinguishing linear deterministic trend from stochastic (unit root) trend is not straightforward despite the fact that we have plenty of methods for testing. If the five variables of the model, oil, human capital, capital stock, working-age population, and real GDP have unit roots, then standard linear estimation methods such as OLS, VAR, and so on could not be used. If these unit root time series data are cointegrated, i.e., they share a common long-run trend, these estimators are valid for inference. There are also other estimators for such data, but picking the estimator is conditional on the time series properties of these variables. We begin executing our testing strategy by estimating a baseline model with baseline dynamic stochastic projections of real GDP, which we assume to be a reasonable measure of *permanent income*.

DOI: 10.4324/9781003488125-3

As explained earlier, we will use a VAR (k, p), where $k = 5$, namely, $[lnP_t q_t; lnH_t; lnK_t; lnWAP_t; lnY_t]$, in this order, where lnP_t is the natural log if the real price of oil in 2012 US dollar price (defined earlier), lnq_t is the actual amount of oil produced in million barrels per day, lnH_t is the human capital index based on average years of schooling and the returns to education, lnK_t is the real stock of capita in constant 2017 US dollar prices, $lnWAP_t$ is the working-age population (15–64) as a measure of labor, and lnY_t is the real GDP in constant 2017 US dollar prices, all measured in natural logs. In the VAR, p denotes the number of lags. The data appendix is at the end of this chapter. Plots of the data show that oil and GDP in particular have noticeable changes in the means and the slopes over the sample. Some data have highly questionable quality. The best example of unusable data is found in the case of Venezuela. In 2012, there was the beginning of a total collapse reflected in GDP, working-age population, the stock of capital, and the production of oil.

3.1 The Time Series Data

We plot the country data in Figures 3.1–3.11. The countries are Algeria, Angola, Congo DR, Gabon, Iran (The Islamic Republic), Iraq, Kuwait, Nigeria, Saudi Arabia, the UAE, and Venezuela. As explained earlier, the price of oil is the same for all countries even though they have different prices. All time series for all countries have trends with $lnP_t q_t$ most volatile because of the volatility of the price of oil. Angola's stock of capital has a visual change in the mean around 1999–2000 (Figure 3.2), and GDP has a dip in 1992–1994. Congo DR data are plotted in Figure 3.3. Human capital index and working-age population had a noticeable change in 1995. The slope of the stock of capital changed in in 1990, and real GDP plummeted sharply in 1989 and began increasing in 2001–2002. From 2002, the trend is positive and sharp. Gabon's data (Figure 3.4) are similar in the sense that they have trends, albeit human capital has a mild change in the slope in 1975; the stock of capital has a visible change in the slope in 1973, 1977, and 1987, respectively. Real GDP is highly volatile with a sharp rise from 1970 to 1976, followed by a number of dips and multiple changes in the mean and the slope. Figure 3.5 plots Iran's data. Iran has sharp positive trends in human capital, which is significantly higher than the human capital level in all African countries in our sample. Real GDP dipped sharply during the war with Iraq in 1980 and only recovered with a positive trend in 1995. The stock of capital has a slowly rising level. Iraq was in a war with Iran from 1980 to 1988; invaded Kuwait in 1990 and the First Gulf War started in 1991. Figure 3.6 shows that from 1992 to 2003, Iraq was subject to UN devastating sanctions. Then the Second Gulf War in 2003. One should not expect typical data, albeit the trends are positive with changes in the slopes. The level of human capital rose sharply then slowly; the stock of capital rose sharply then flattened and rose again after 2003. Real GDP did not dip as hard as Iran's in 1980; nevertheless, the economy was in a shallow and long lull. It is the First Gulf War that sends real GDP down sharply. Then it rose and fluctuated sharply from 1992 to 2003 with significant dips in 1995 and 2003 the Second Gulf War. Oil production is extremely volatile. Figure 3.7 plots Kuwait's data. Kuwait's economy was destroyed in 1990. However, human capital has a flat slope up to 1975 and then it rose up sharply and has a smaller slope from 1985 onward. The stock of capital, however, has a positive trend with a flatter slope between 1985 and 2003. Oil production collapsed in 1990–1992, and it is very volatile. Population plummeted during the First Gulf War in 1990 where most people left the country. Real GDP lnY_t is very similar to $lnP_t^o q_t^o$ because the Kuwaiti economy is highly dependent on oil production. One should be very cautious about the data of Iran-Iraq's interwar period 1980–1988 for Kuwait in 1991–1992. For example, the Kuwaiti economy was smashed and it is unclear how the data for real GDP, capital, human capital, and so on are computed.

Figure 3.8 plots the Nigerian data. Nigeria's data are more problematic than all other previous data. Human capital is relatively low and has a flat slope from 1970 to 1990. From 1990 onward, the slope rose sharply. The stock of capital has the opposite slope, a very sharp increase from 1970 to 1983, and then flattens to the end of the sample with a small slope. Oil production is highly volatile with various slopes. Real GDP is volatile with a mild upward slope up until 2001 and then it takes off.

The last three OPEC countries in our sample are Saudi Arabia, the UAE, and Venezuela. These are the richest producers in terms of oil reserves and production. Figure 3.9 plots the Saudi data. There are visually clear trends in human capital, working-age population, capital stock, and real GDP, albeit both the stock of capital and real GDP declined in 1980 after the second oil shock and then recovered. Volatility in the macro data must reflect the volatility of oil. Figure 3.10 presents the UAE data. Both the working-age population and human capital reached a plateau of about 2000. It is unclear what the reasons are, but the UAE population is mainly immigrants. The data look like the Saudi Data otherwise.

Figure 3.11 plots the Venezuelan data, which are significantly different from all OPEC data. The Venezuelan oil production, the stock of capital, and real GDP took a nosedive in 2012. The working-age population also declined from 2016 onward. There is only one possible explanation, which is the US sanctions. There are periods of changing slopes in human capital and the stock of capital despite the sharp positive slopes from 1970. From 1980 to 1990, human capital was flat. That said, the human capital level in Venezuela is the highest in OPEC.

3.2 The Nature of the Trends

As we explained in the previous chapter, the commonly used tests for unit root are weak, i.e., have low statistical powers, against stationary alternatives. Earlier, we cited important papers, which argued that the unit root tests have difficulty distinguishing a unit root from a root of 0.98. The ADF (Said and Dickey 1984) test and the Phillips and Perron (1988) test allow for different OLS regression specifications; hence, they have different distributions. We choose a specification similar to the one we used to test for unit root in lnY_t, lnP_t, and lnP_tq_t in Chapter 2, where the variable, e.g., Δx_t, is regressed on a constant term, linear trend, a number of lagged Δx_{t-i} where $i = 1 \cdots p$, and the lagged level x_{t-1}. Also, we choose this specification because we want to test the linear trend too. If, for example, we reject the null hypothesis of a unit root but the linear trend coefficient is statistically significant, the data might be trend-stationary. We have two more points to make regarding these tests. Rejection of the null hypothesis of unit root is very interesting because the power of the test is irrelevant when it rejects the null hypothesis. Thus, rejection of the null is a good indication that the data do not have unit root. Finally, these tests work by fitting a straight line through the data; they must confuse the break in the data, if any, with a unit root. See the mathematics of the unit root process in Chapter 1. The results of the unit root tests are reported in Appendix 3.1. We further test the data for unit root with a break and then we use (Kwiatkowski et al. 1992) the KPSS test, which has a different null hypothesis that the time series is I (0). We also test the data using different sample spans.

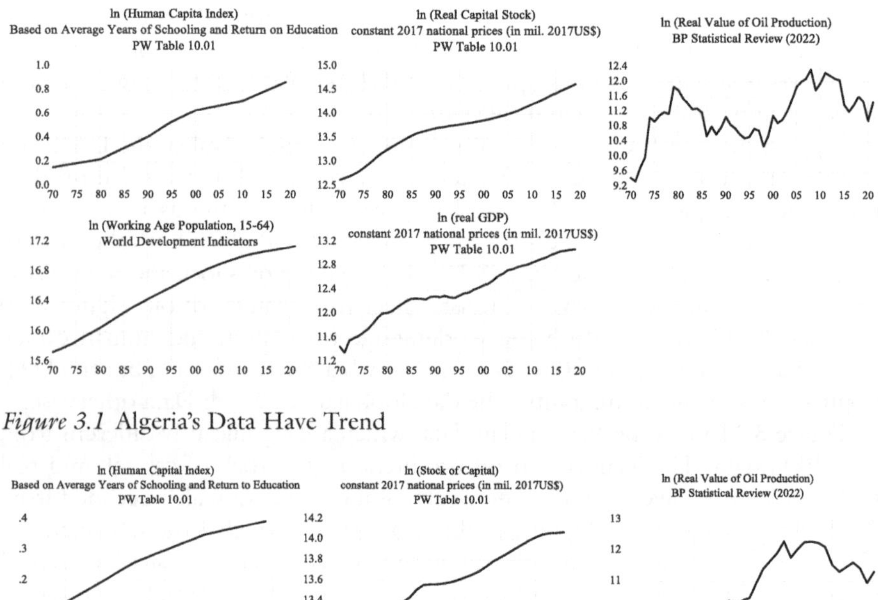

Figure 3.1 Algeria's Data Have Trend

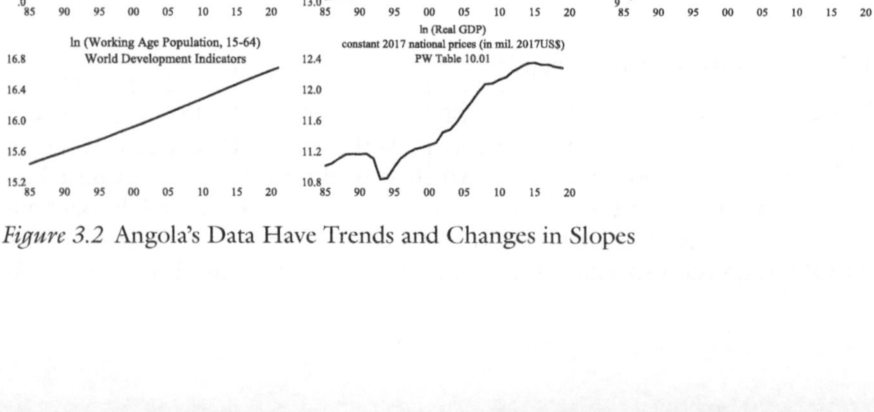

Figure 3.2 Angola's Data Have Trends and Changes in Slopes

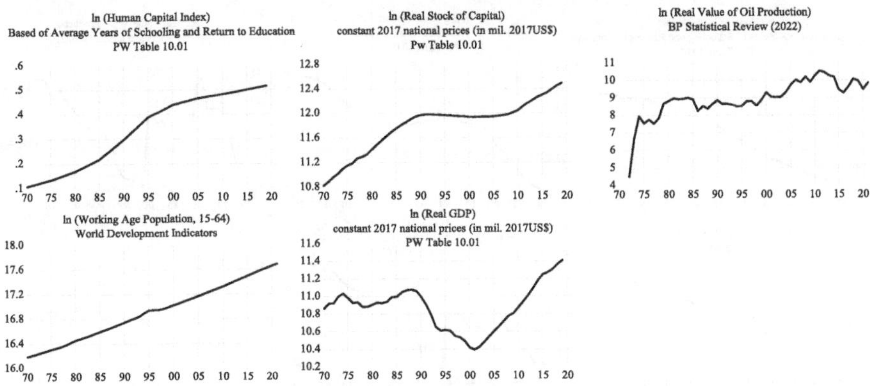

Figure 3.3 Congo DR Data Have More Changes in Slopes

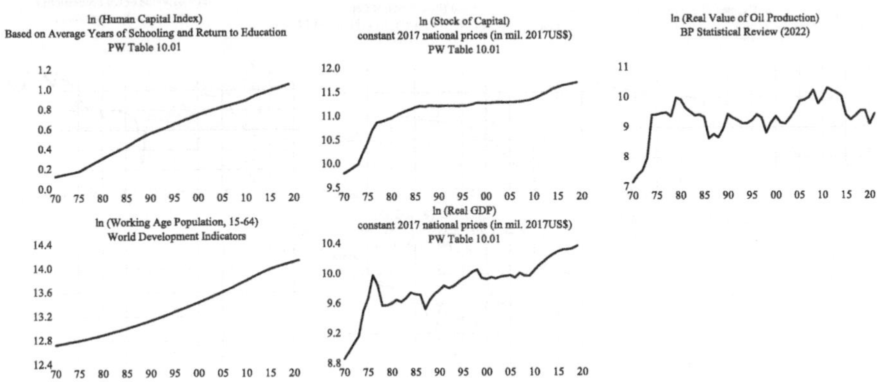

Figure 3.4 Gabon's Data Have Trends and Slope Changes

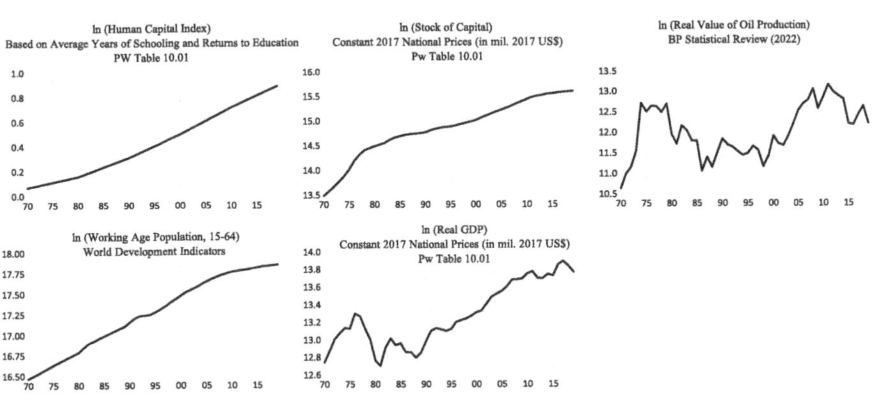

Figure 3.5 Iran's Data Have Trends and Few Changes in Slopes

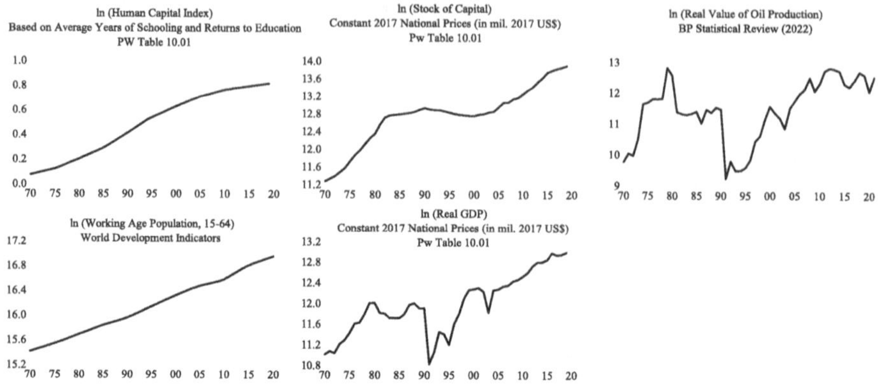

Figure 3.6 Iraq's Data Have Trends but They Are Very Volatile

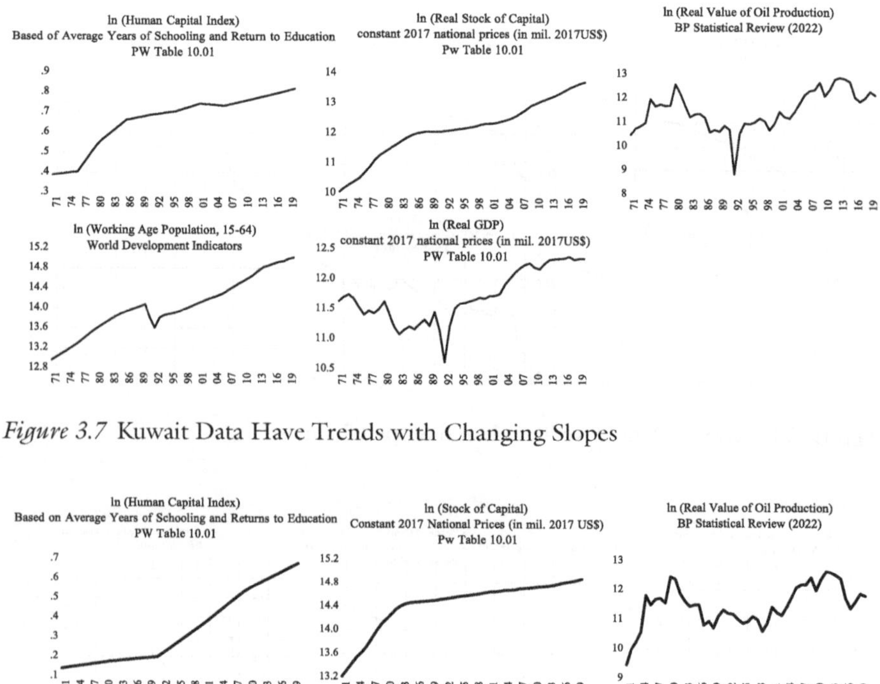

Figure 3.7 Kuwait Data Have Trends with Changing Slopes

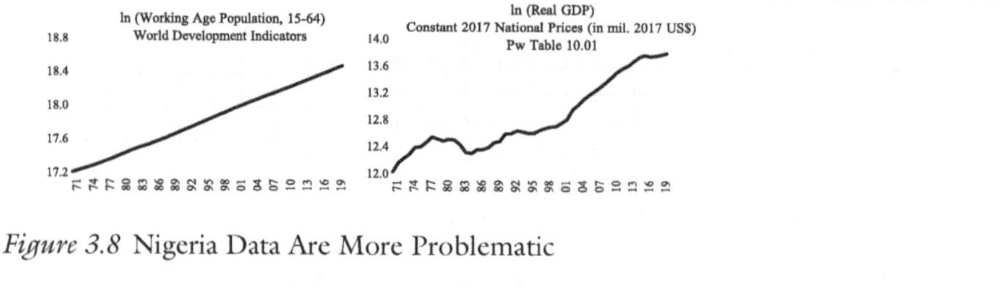

Figure 3.8 Nigeria Data Are More Problematic

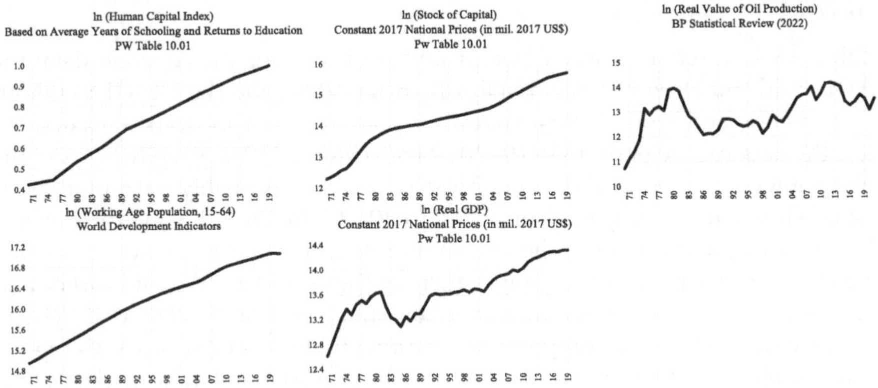

Figure 3.9 Saudi Arabia Trend Upward

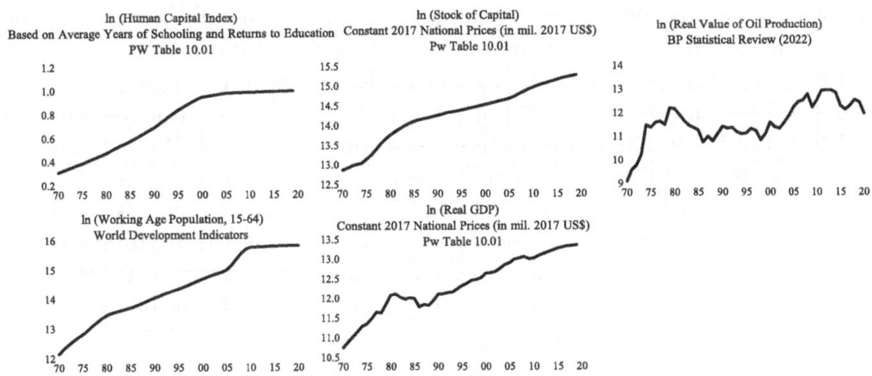

Figure 3.10 UAE Data Show Slow Trends Late in the Sample

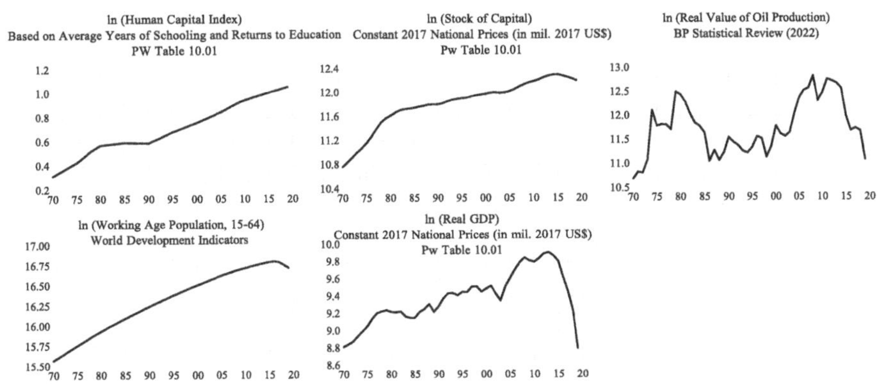

Figure 3.11 Venezuela Data Dominated by Downturns

Algeria

Table A3.1.1a reports three different unit root tests for the Algerian data: the ADF (Said and Dickey 1984), Phillips-Perron (1988), and the DF-GLS (Elliott, Rothenberg, and Stock 1996). We only report the unit root tests' P-values. We test the data for the periods 1970–2019 and 1980–2019 separately because the plot shows a change in the slope. Most of the data probably have unit roots, especially when the sample is from 1980 to 2019. The DF-GLS and the Phillips-Perron tests could not reject the unit root in all data. There is, however, a strong rejection of unit root in the capital stock by the ADF test. We said earlier that rejection ought to be taken seriously because the unit root tests are weak. Therefore, we test lnK_t again using the ADF test with breaks. Table A3.1.1b reports some results that still lean toward rejecting the unit root and indicate that capital stock is, probably, a trend-stationary capital stock with a break. The DF-GLS and the Phillips-Perron results indicate that lnK_t is probably a unit root series. Then we test for a unit root with a break for the sample 1980–2019. Table A3.1.1b reports the results. We still reject the unit root in the natural log of the stock of capital. Finally, because of the uncertainty of the results so far, we use one more test for lnK_t and lnY_t; the KPSS test (Kwiatkowski et al. 1992). The null is that x_t is a stationary process, not a unit root; thus, one cannot claim that the KPSS is more powerful than the three tests mentioned above because the null hypothesis of the KPSS is different. We use this test to test lnY_t and lnK_t over the two samples 1970–2019 and 1980–2019. Table A3.1.1c reports the results. The evidence we have from all these tests is that the Algerian five time series are best described as unit root processes from 1980 to 2019 not from 1970, but we are uncertain about the unit root in lnK_t because the results of the tests are not fully consistent. We have to bear in mind that this is the sample, which we ought to work with to the end of this analysis because the data from 1970 to 1979 are not useful for our purpose as it will become clear later when we consider the next step in the diagnosis of the trends, which is the test for cointegration.[1]

Angola

The results of the unit root tests for Angola are reported in Tables A3.1.2a and A3.1.2b. Like the Algerian data, the null hypothesis of unit root could not be rejected by the data, except for the stock of capital, which is only marginally significant in the ADF test. We explained earlier that the ADF rejection of the null hypothesis of unit root is very interesting and should be taken seriously. We repeat the ADF test for lnK_t over three sub-samples, which seem to have a visible change in the slope. The unit root hypothesis could not be rejected from

1 As explained earlier, exponential growth is a reasonable assumption in economics. For population, for example, proportional growth arises from the number of children being born that are a constant fraction of the current population. The same is true for prices and output. Taking the natural log of the exponential trend, in equation (3.2), the trend-stationary model, and similarly in equation (3.3), thus, when the natural log of a process is specified as a unit root process, the assumption is that the growth rate is a stationary process, e.g., is I(1) and is I(0).

1970 to 1990, 1991 to 2000, and 2001 to 2019. Then we tested the same time series using the ADF test with breaks in the intercept and the trend. We could not reject the null hypothesis of a unit root with breaks in the data. Finally, Table A3.1.2c reports the result of the KPSS test for the log capital stock of Angola, lnK_t. We interpret these tests to say that lnK_t for Angola is a unit root process with a break. The rest of the time series are probably unit root processes.

Congo, DR

Table A3.1.3 reports the unit root tests for Congo, DR. All the Data have unit roots from 1985 to 2019; the hypothesis of unit root in lnP_tq_t is rejected over the whole sample from 1970 to 2019.

Gabon

Table A3.1.4 reports the unit root tests' results for Gabon. The null hypothesis of a unit root could not be rejected for all variables except, where the ADF test suggests that lnY_t is trend-stationary. It marginally rejects the unit root with a P-value of 0.0455, but the trend is statistically significant in this regression. The ADF results notwithstanding, both DF-GLS and the Phillips-Perron suggest that it is a unit root.

Iran and Iraq

Iran and Iraq in particular have experienced multiple shocks from 1970 onward, including an eight-year war from 1980 to 1988, the First Gulf War involving Iraq in 1990–1992, UN sanctions on Iraq, and oil-for-food programs preventing Iraq from totally controlling its sales of oil from 1992 to 2033, and finally the Second Gulf War in 2003. Table A3.1.5 provides unit root tests for Iran's data. Turbulent periods from 1970 to 1980 do not seem suitable for unit root tests. The results indicate that the data have unit roots from 1980 to 2019. The Phillips-Perron suggests that human capital might be, marginally, trend-stationary.

Iraq's data seem different from Iran's. Table A3.1.6a reports the results of the unit root tests. The ADF test rejects the unit root in the stock of capital, just like in the cases of Algeria and Angola. The DF-GLS and the Phillips-Perron tests do not. In the ADF test regression, the linear trend is statistically significant with a P-value of 0.0005. The plot of the data in Figure 3.6 clearly shows different slopes and means over the samples from 1970 to 1981, 1982 to 2003, and 2004 to 2019. We test the stock of capital for a unit root with a break. We could not reject the unit root with a break.

Kuwait

Kuwait is yet another country with many, *exp-post*, breaks. Table A3.1.7 reports the results of the tests. Surprisingly, all the Kuwaiti data have unit roots without a break. One must be suspicious of Kuwait's data for the period

1990–1992 when the economy was fully destroyed and all government institutions were suspended.

Nigeria

Nigeria is an African country whose human capita and the stock of capital data in Figure 3.8 show visible changes in the slope. Table A3.1.8a reports the tests for unit roots. The ADF and the Phillips-Perron tests rejected the unit root in the stock capital only. Again, the tests' results for lnK_t are similar to Algeria, Angola, and Iraq. We test for the unit root with a break in the stock of capital data. Table A3.1.8b tests the stock of capital for a unit root with a break using the ADF test. We reject the unit root with a break in the model with an innovational outlier break; however, the linear trend break in the regressions is statistically significant too. In the additive outlier break model, there is a unit root. Therefore, we cannot really find a consistent diagnosis of the trend in the Nigerian stock of capital. Table A3.1.8c reports the KPSS test results for the stock of capital. We test the data for the sample 1970–2019. We reject the null hypothesis that lnK_t is stationary in favor of the alternative of a unit root at the 5 percent level (not at the 1 percent). Taken together, these tests suggest that lnK_t is trend-stationary. The linear deterministic trend in the regression is significant in all these tests. The implication is that the variables lnP_tq_t, lnH_t, $lnWAP_t$, and lnY_t could be tested for cointegrated without lnK_t.

The remaining OPEC countries are among the richest in the world in terms of oil reserves, Saudi Arabia, the UAE, and Venezuela, albeit the data are very peculiar, especially the Venezuelan data.

Saudi Arabia

Table A3.1.9 reports the unit root test results for Saudi Arabia. There are two observations about the results for Saudi Arabia. First, the stock of capital, just like Algeria, Angola, Iraq, and Nigeria, seems to be different from the rest of the data. Here the ADF, again, is the only test rejecting the null hypothesis of unit root. We cannot ignore such results as we explained earlier. Second, the t-statistics of the DF-GLS for the working-age population is positive, which should be negative. In the ADF test, a positive τ indicates that the root is explosive. It is difficult to explain why the population has an explosive root. Therefore, we change the sample to 1980–2019 and test again. This time, the test statistics indicate unit root in the stock of capital and working-age population. Therefore, the sample size seems to affect the results of the unit root tests, but not in a straightforward way. If the oil shocks in the 1970s have some important persistence to add to the data, one would expect the unit root to show up in the sample from 1970 to 2019, which is not the case. The tests find a unit root from 1980 and 1982 to 2019.

UAE

Table A3.1.10 reports the results of the unit root tests for the UAE data. We encountered a similar issue with the sample span, where the ADF rejects the null of unit root; it does so with respect to lnY_t over the sample 1970–2019. This is again a very interesting result.

It suggests that a weak test, which fails to reject the null often, rejects it now. When we tested the data over the sample from 1985 to 2019, the ADF failed to reject the null of unit root in real GDP. The trend must have been changing over the sample as the nature of the shocks to these unique economies changed.

Venezuela

Venezuela has very unusual data. The plots in Figure 3.11 show the anomalies clearly. Therefore, we test the data over the period 1970–2011. *Ex-post*, we know what happened in 2012 onward that might have caused the Venezuelan economy to crash. Table A3.1.11 reports the results of the unit root tests for Venezuela. Again, lnK_t is the variable, where the unit root is mostly rejected by the ADF test. In all the previous cases similar to this, the coefficient of linear trend β is statistically significant, which indicates that the time series is probably trend-stationary and not difference-stationary. The data appendix explains the Penn World Table construction of the stock of capital time series.

The next necessary step in this analysis, prior to estimation, is to test the null hypothesis that the variables, lnP_tq_t, lnH_t, lnK_t, $lnWAP_t$, and lnY_t are *not* cointegrated or test the four variables lnP_tq_t, lnH_t, $lnWAP_t$, and lnY_t since lnK_t might be trend-stationary and not a unit root. If they are cointegrated, we would be able to estimate the VAR in log levels using least squares, which is our preferred method because our objective is to generate a dynamic summary of the data to capture the *long-run* relationships between oil and the other macro fundamentals. A VECM is also applicable, but we are not concerned with the dynamic short-run behavior. We will estimate an unrestricted VAR in log levels because if we choose VECM instead, we have to estimate at least five different specifications; (no trend in the data, no intercept – no trend), (no trend in the data, intercept – no trend), (linear trend in the data, intercept no trend), (linear trend in the data, intercept – trend), and (quadratic trend in the data, intercept – trend), and imposing restrictions about the number of cointegrated vectors. This is unnecessary for our purpose, which focuses on the long run and uses the VAR as a summary of the dynamics of the data to generate dynamic stochastic projections for 2020–2050.

3.3 Cointegration

We will test for cointegration in the OPEC countries. Note that the null hypothesis is no cointegration, and we will also adjust the samples for some countries because of the *ex-post* breaks in the data. For multivariate analysis, we use the Johansen test (1988, 1991, 1995) and the Johansen-Juselius (1995) test.[2] Because the test involves fitting a number of specifications of the trend,

2 Because this is a multivariate case, we use the Johansen's maximum likelihood test, Johansen (1988, 1991,1995) and Johansen and Juselius (1990), $\lambda -$ max (or maximum eigenvalue test), and the Trace statistics. See also Cheung and Lai (1993) degree-of-freedom corrections.

the output is very large, and for this reason, we will only provide a summary of the results rather than repeating all the results. This test is a reduced-rank residuals-based test. See Gonzalo (1994) for example on the comparison of power of five different residuals-based tests for cointegration among a very large literature on this issue. Appendix 3.2 includes Tables A3.2.1–A3.2.11, which report the Trace and the Maximum Eigenvalue Johansen tests and the estimated number of significant cointegration relationships in the OPEC countries.

There are zero to five estimated cointegration relationships in every country, depending on the VAR specification. We have to conclude that the variables of the model, the natural logs of the real value of oil production, human capital, stock of capital, working-age population (age 15–64 years), and real GDP share a long-run common trend. We also tested the null hypothesis without including lnK_t. The other four variables are cointegrated. Therefore, we will estimate the baseline VAR model presented earlier in log-levels next.

Technical Appendix 3.1 – Tables for the Unit Root Tests

Table A3.1.1a Algeria – Most of the Data Have Unit Roots H_0 : Unit Root – $\Delta x_t = \alpha + \beta Trend + \sum_{i=1}^{k} \delta_i \Delta x_{t-i} + \rho x_{t-1} + u_t$

ADF				*DF-GLS*		*Phillips-Perron*	
Sample	x_t	*Lag*	*P-Value*	*Lag*	*t-Stat*	*Bandwidth Auto NW – Bartlett Kernel*	*P-Value*
1970–2019	lnY_t	7	0.0012*	8	−2.55	3	0.5949
	lnH_t	1	0.0912	1	−3.05	5	0.5667
	lnK_t	10	0.0082*	9	−3.20	5	0.6404
	$lnWAP_t$	10	0.9934	10	−1.95	4	1.0000
1980–2019	lnY_t	8	0.0592	8	−1.63	3	0.7958
	lnP_tq_t	0	0.4227	0	−1.85	1	0.4183
	lnH_t	1	0.2256	1	−2.64	5	0.8796
	lnK_t	7	0.0003*	9	−3.20	5	0.8236
	$lnWAP_t$	9	0.9914	5	−2.57	4	1.0000

- Lags are automatic based on AIC.
- Asterisk (*) means rejection of the null hypothesis that the time series has a unit root at the 1 percent level; MacKinnon (1996) one-sided P-values.
- The DF-GLS critical value at the 1 percent level is −3.77.

Table A3.1.1b Algeria, ADF with Break, lnK_t in Intercept and Trend Sample 1980–2019 H_0 : Unit Root with a Break

Innovational Outlier Break				*Additive Outlier Break*		
Break Selection	*Lag (AIC)*	*P-Value*	*Break*	*Lag (AIC)*	*P-Value*	*Break*
Min. DF t	7	0.0180*	1999	1	0.0325*	2007
Min trend break t-stat	5	0.0654	1986	0	>0.99	1989
Max trend break t-stat	8	0.0000*	2007	1	<0.01*	2004

- AIC denotes the Akaike Information Criterion;
- Vogelsang (1993) one-sided P-value;
- Break Specifications: intercept and trend;
- Trend Specifications: intercept and trend.

Table A3.1.1c Algeria KPSS LM-Statistic for lnY_t and $lnK_t - H_0 : I(0)$

		Lags	*LM-Stat*	
lnY_t	1970–2019	5	0.104904	Cannot reject H_0
	1980–2019	5	0.145314	Reject H_0 marginally at the 5 percent level and rejects it at the 10 percent level
lnK_t	1970–2019	5	0.155260	Reject H_0 at the 5 percent level
	1980–2019	5	0.143688	Reject H_0 at the 10 percent level

- Lags are from Newey-West automatic using Bartlett kernel.
- Kwiatkowski et al. (1992, Table 1), critical values at the 1 percent level is 0.216000, at the 5 percent level 0.146000, and at the 10 percent level 0.119000.

Table A3.1.2a Angola's Data Have Unit Roots

		ADF		*DF-GLS*		*Phillips-Perron*	
Sample	x_t	*Lag*	*P-Value*	*Lag*	*t-Stat*	*Bandwidth Auto NW – Bartlett Kernel*	*P-Value*
1970–2019	lnY_t	1	0.5560	1	−1.75	2	0.7933
	lnP_tq_t	0	0.3605	0	−1.97	0	0.3238
	lnH_t	1	0.2983	1	−2.75	5	0.4363
	lnK_t	1	0.0407*	1	−3.37	4	0.2829
	$lnWAP_t$	10	0.8824	7	−2.83	5	0.8668
1970–1990	lnK_t	0	0.9557				
1991–2000	lnK_t	0	0.5685				
2001–2019	lnK_t	1	0.2337				

- Lags are automatic based on AIC.
- Asterisk (*) means rejection of the null hypothesis that the time series has a unit root at the 5 percent level; MacKinnon (1996) one-sided P-values.
- The DF-GLS critical value at the 1 percent level is −3.77.

Table A3.1.2b Angola, ADF with Break, lnK_t in Intercept and Trend Sample 1970–2019 H_0 : Unit Root with a Break

Innovational Outlier Break				*Additive Outlier Break*		
Break Selection	*Lag (AIC)*	*P-Value*	*Break*	*Lag (AIC)*	*P-Value*	*Break*
Min. DF t	10	0.2214	2003	1	0.2901	1983
Min trend break t-stat	1	0.3256	2010	1	0.3256	2010
Max trend break t-stat	3	0.5209	1991	6	0.6816	1993

- AIC denotes the Akaike Information Criterion;
- Vogelsang (1993) one-sided P-value;
- Break specifications: intercept and trend;
- Trend specifications: intercept and trend;

Table A3.1.2c Angola KPSS LM Statistic for lnK_t $H_0 : I(0)$

		Lags	*LM-Stat*	
lnK_t	1970–2019	5	0.064507	Cannot reject H_0
	1970–1990	3	0.177469	Reject H_0 at the 5 percent level
	1991–2000	5	0.336815	Reject H_0 at the 1 percent level
	2001–2019	2	0.195409	Reject H_0 at the 5 percent level

-Lags are from Newey-West automatic using Bartlett kernel.
-Kwiatkowski et al. (1992, Table 1), critical values at the 1 percent level is 0.216000, at the 5 percent level 0.146000, and at the 10 percent level 0.119000.

Table A3.1.3 Congo's Data Have Unit Roots

$$H_0 : \textit{Unit Root} - \Delta x_t = \alpha + \beta\, \textit{Trend} + \sum_{i=1}^{k} \delta_i \Delta x_{t-i} + \rho x_{t-1} + u_t$$

			ADF	*DF-GLS*		*Phillips-Perron*
Country	*Sample*	x_t	*Lag*	*P-ValueLag*	*t-Stat*	*Bandwidth Auto NW – Bartlett Kernel P-Value*
1970–2019	lnY_t	1	0.9351	1−1.47	4	0.9895
	lnP_tq_t	0	0.0000*	1−2.18	2	0.0000
	lnH_t	1	0.4520	1−2.74	5	0.9859
	lnK_t	1	0.4306	1−1.92	5	0.5343
	$lnWAP_t$	5	0.5812	5−1.93	3	0.5727
1985–2019	$lnP_t^oq_t^o$	0	0.2972	0−2.36	1	0.2642

- Lags are automatic based on AIC.
- Asterisk (*) means rejection of the null hypothesis that the time series has a unit root at the 1 percent level; MacKinnon (1996) one-sided P-values.
- The DF-GLS critical value at the 1 percent level is −3.77.

Table A3.1.4 Gabon's Data Have Unit Roots

$$H_0 : \textit{Unit Root} - \Delta x_t = \alpha + \beta\, \textit{Trend} + \sum_{i=1}^{k} \delta_i \Delta x_{t-i} + \rho x_{t-1} + u_t$$

		ADF		*DF-GLS*		*Phillips-Perron*	
Sample	x_t	*Lag*	*P-Value*	*Lag*	*t-Stat*	*Bandwidth Auto NW – Bartlett Kernel*	*P-Value*
1970–2019	lnY_t	9	0.0455#	9	−2.93	4	0.1490
	lnP_tq_t	0	0.3652	0	−2.46	0	0.3652
	lnH_t	2	0.7973	1	−2.05	4	0.9646

(*Continued*)

Table A3.1.4 (Continued)

H_0 : *Unit Root* – $\Delta x_t = \alpha + \beta Trend + \sum_{i=1}^{k} \delta_i \Delta x_{t-i} + \rho x_{t-1} + u_t$

		ADF		DF-GLS		Phillips-Perron	
Sample	x_t	*Lag*	*P-Value*	*Lag*	*t-Stat*	*Bandwidth Auto NW – Bartlett Kernel*	*P-Value*
	lnK_t	10	0.4081	10	−1.41	2	0.1056
	$lnWAP_t$	8	0.1482	7	−3.20	5	0.1838

- Lags are automatic based on AIC.- Hash (#) means rejection of the null hypothesis that the time series has a unit root at the 5 percent level; MacKinnon (1996) one-sided P-values.- The DF-GLS critical value at the 1 percent level is −3.77.

Table A3.1.5 Most of Iran's Data Have Unit Roots, Albeit from 1980 Onward

H_0 : *Unit Root* – $\Delta x_t = \alpha + \beta Trend + \sum_{i=1}^{k} \delta_i \Delta x_{t-i} + \rho x_{t-1} + u_t$

		ADF		DF-GLS		Phillips-Perron	
Sample	x_t	*Lag*	*P-Value*	*Lag*	*t-Stat*	*Bandwidth Auto NW – Bartlett Kernel*	*P-Value*
1970–2019	lnY_t	9	0.0100*	9	−2.13	0	0.7550
	lnP_tq_t	0	0.3164	1	−2.15	3	0.2651
	lnH_t	1	0.0782#	1	−2.04	4	0.0056*
	lnK_t	1	0.0046*	1	−2.40	4	0.0489*
	$lnWAP_t$	3	0.9991	3	−1.10	0	1.0000
1982–2019	lnY_t	9	0.7005	9	−2.92	1	0.3409
	lnP_tq_t	0	0.5010	0	−2.17	1	0.5049
	lnH_t	1	0.5624	1	−1.21	4	0.0403*
	lnK_t	1	0.3074	1	−2.71	4	0.7744
	$lnWAP_t$	3	0.9971	3	−1.26	1	0.9997

- Lags are automatic based on AIC.
- Asterisk (*) means rejection of the null hypothesis that the time series has a unit root at the 1 percent level. Hash (#) means rejection of the null hypothesis that the time series has a unit root at the 10 percent level; MacKinnon (1996) one-sided P-values.
- The DF-GLS critical value at the 1 percent level is −3.77.

Table A3.1.6a Iraq's Data Have Unit Roots

H_0 : *Unit Root* $- \Delta x_t = \alpha + \beta\, Trend + \sum_{i=1}^{k} \delta_i \Delta x_{t-i} + \rho x_{t-1} + u_t$

		ADF		DF-GLS		Phillips-Perron	
Sample	x_t	*Lag*	*P-Value*	*Lag*	*t-Stat*	*Bandwidth Auto NW – Bartlett Kernel*	*P-Value*
1970–2019	lnY_t	0	0.3396	0	−2.49	2	0.3250
	lnP_tq_t	0	0.4898	0	−2.08	2	0.4663
	lnH_t	1	0.7677	1	−2.72	5	0.9981
	lnK_t	7	0.0184*	1	−1.96	5	0.6092
	$lnWAP_t$	7	0.5808	7	−1.34	4	0.4694

- Lags are automatic based on AIC.
- Asterisk (*) means rejection of the null hypothesis that the time series has a unit root at the 1 percent level; MacKinnon (1996) one-sided P-values.
- The DF-GLS critical value at the 1 percent level is −3.77.

Table A3.1.6b Iraq, ADF with Break, lnK_t in Intercept and Trend Sample 1970–2019

	Innovational Outlier Break			*Additive Outlier Break*		
Break Selection	*Lag (AIC)*	*P-Value*	*Break*	*Lag (AIC)*	*P-Value*	*Break*
Min. DF t	7	0.3995	2013	7	0.9697	2003
Min trend break t-stat	0	>0.99	1982	1	0.8338	1987
Max trend break t-stat	9	0.4711	1985	3	0.5283	2004

- AIC denotes the Akaike Information Criterion;
- Vogelsang (1993) one-sided P-value;
- Break Specifications: intercept and trend;
- Trend Specifications: intercept and trend.

Table A3.1.7 Kuwait – The Data Have Unit Roots

H_0 : *Unit Root* $- \Delta x_t = \alpha + \beta\, Trend + \sum_{i=1}^{k} \delta_i \Delta x_{t-i} + \rho x_{t-1} + u_t$

		ADF		DF-GLS		Phillips-Perron	
Sample	x_t	*Lag*	*P-Value*	*Lag*	*t-Stat*	*Bandwidth Auto NW – Bartlett KERNEL*	*P-Value*
1970–2019	lnY_t	1	0.2618	1	−1.57	2	0.5195
	lnP_tq_t	0	0.2867	0	−2.60	1	0.3060

(*Continued*)

Table A3.1.7 (Continued)

H_0 : *Unit Root* $-\Delta x_t = \alpha + \beta Trend + \sum_{i=1}^{k}\delta_i\Delta x_{t-i} + \rho x_{t-1} + u_t$							
		ADF		*DF-GLS*		*Phillips-Perron*	
Sample	x_t	*Lag*	*P-Value*	*Lag*	*t-Stat*	*Bandwidth Auto NW – Bartlett KERNEL*	*P-Value*
	lnH_t	1	0.2187	1	−2.23	4	0.8631
	lnK_t	1	0.1089	1	−2.45	5	0.3599
	$lnWAP_t$	3	0.5209	3	−1.90	1	0.6274

- Lags are automatic based on AIC.
- Asterisk (*) means rejection of the null hypothesis that the time series has a unit root at the 1 percent level; MacKinnon (1996) one-sided P-values.
- The DF-GLS critical value at the 1 percent level is −3.77.

Table A3.1.8a Nigeria – The Data Have Unit Roots

H_0 : *Unit Root* $-\Delta x_t = \alpha + \beta Trend + \sum_{i=1}^{k}\delta_i\Delta x_{t-i} + \rho x_{t-1} + u_t$							
		ADF		*DF-GLS*		*Phillips-Perron*	
Sample	x_t	*Lag*	*P-Value*	*Lag*	*t-Stat*	*Bandwidth Auto NW – Bartlett Kernel*	*P-Value*
1970–2019	lnY_t	1	0.8045	2	−1.89	4	0.8734
	lnP_tq_t	0	0.1382	0	−2.05	2	0.1318
	lnH_t	1	0.2529	1	−2.28	5	0.6716
	lnK_t	1	0.0352*	10	−2.47	5	0.0055*
	$lnWAP_t$	7	0.2727	2	−1.48	5	0.0958#

- Lags are automatic based on AIC.
- Asterisk (*) means rejection of the null hypothesis that the time series has a unit root at the 1 percent level; MacKinnon (1996) one-sided P-values.
- The DF-GLS critical value at the 1 percent level is −3.77.

Table A3.1.8b Nigeria, ADF with Break, lnK_t in Intercept and Trend Sample 1970–2019

Innovational Outlier Break				*Additive Outlier Break*		
Break Selection	*Lag (AIC)*	*P-Value*	*Break*	*Lag (AIC)*	*P-Value*	*Break*
Min. DF t	0	<0.01	1976	5	<0.01	1991
Min trend break t-stat	0	<0.01	1979	4	0.5787	1982
Max trend break t-stat	0	<0.01	1979	1	0.5286	2015

- AIC denotes the Akaike Information Criterion;
- Vogelsang (1993) one-sided P-value;
- Break Specifications: intercept and trend;
- Trend Specifications: intercept and trend.

Table A3.1.8c Nigeria KPSS LM-Statistic for lnK_t $H_0 : I(0)$

		Lags	*LM-stat*	
lnK_t	1970–2019	5	0.197601	Reject H_0 at the 5 percent level
	1985–2019	4	0.088738	Cannot reject H_0

- Lags are from Newey-West automatic using Bartlett kernel.
- Kwiatkowski et al. (1992, Table 1), critical values at the 1 percent level is 0.216000, at the 5 percent level 0.146000, and at the 10 percent level 0.119000.

Table A3.1.9 Saudi Arabian – Most of the Data Have Unit Roots

H_0 : *Unit Root* $- \Delta x_t = \alpha + \beta\, Trend + \sum_{i=1}^{k} \delta_i \Delta x_{t-i} + \rho x_{t-1} + u_t$

		ADF		*DF-GLS*		*Phillips-Perron*	
Sample	x_t	*Lag*	*P-Value*	*Lag*	*t-Stat*	*Bandwidth Auto NW – Bartlett Kernel*	*P-Value*
1970–2019	lnY_t	6	0.3126	2	–2.53	4	0.1056
	lnP_tq_t	1	0.1767	1	–2.10	2	0.1676
	lnH_t	6	0.9699	6	–1.61	4	0.9561
	lnK_t	1	0.0076*	1	–2.97	5	0.4589
	$lnWAP_t$	2	0.9999	2	0.09!	4	0.9996
1980–2019	lnK_t	3	0.1801	2	–2.70	4	0.9429
	$lnWAP_t$	4	0.9336	5	–0.87	4	0.8221

- Lags are automatic based on AIC.
- Asterisk (*) means rejection of the null hypothesis that the time series has a unit root at the 1 percent level; MacKinnon (1996) one-sided P-values.
- The DF-GLS critical value at the 1 percent level is –3.77.
- The exclamation mark (!) denotes a result that we do not have an explanation for.

Table A3.1.10 UAE – The Data Have Unit Roots

H_0 : *Unit Root* $- \Delta x_t = \alpha + \beta\, Trend + \sum_{i=1}^{k} \delta_i \Delta x_{t-i} + \rho x_{t-1} + u_t$

			ADF	*DF-GLS*		*Phillips-Perron*	
Sample	x_t	*Lag*	*P-Value*	*Lag*	*t-Stat*	*Bandwidth Auto NW – Bartlett Kernel*	*P-Value*
1970–2019	lnY_t	10	0.0329*	10	–1.92	2	0.1612
	lnP_tq_t	0	0.1263	0	–1.97	0	0.1181
	lnH_t	6	0.9621	6	–1.74	5	0.9996

(*Continued*)

Table A3.1.10 (Continued)

$$H_0: \ Unit \ Root - \Delta x_t = \alpha + \beta \ Trend + \sum_{i=1}^{k} \delta_i \Delta x_{t-i} + \rho x_{t-1} + u_t$$

		ADF		*DF-GLS*		*Phillips-Perron*	
Sample	x_t	*Lag*	*P-Value*	*Lag*	*t-Stat*	*Bandwidth Auto NW – Bartlett Kernel*	*P-Value*
	lnK_t	1	0.0526	1	−2.54	5	0.7026
	$nWAP_t$	10	0.6303	10	−0.77	4	0.6659
1985–2019	lnY_t	1	0.0628	1	−2.56	2	0.1051

- Lags are automatic based on AIC.
- Asterisk (*) means rejection of the null hypothesis that the time series has a unit root at the 1 percent level; MacKinnon (1996) one-sided P-values.
- The DF-GLS critical value at the 1 percent level is 3.77.

Table A3.1.11 Venezuela's – The Data Have Unit Roots

$$H_0: \ Unit \ Root - \Delta x_t = \alpha + \beta \ Trend + \sum_{i=1}^{k} \delta_i \Delta x_{t-i} + \rho x_{t-1} + u_t$$

		ADF		*DF-GLS*		*Phillips-Perron*	
Sample	x_t	*Lag*	*P-Value*	*Lag*	*t -Stat*	*Bandwidth Auto NW – Bartlett Kernel*	*P-Value*
1970–2011	lnY_t	1	0.1422	1	−2.80	0	0.4559
	lnP_tq_t	0	0.5823	0	−1.92	1	0.5711
	lnH_t	1	0.0691	1	−3.19	5	0.6106
	lnK_t	3	0.0163*	3	−2.40	4	0.1290
	$lnWAP_t$	8	1.0000	3	−0.33	5	1.0000

- Lags are automatic based on AIC.
- Asterisk (*) means rejection of the null hypothesis that the time series has a unit root at the 1 percent level; MacKinnon (1996) one-sided P-values.
- The DF-GLS critical value at the 1 percent level is −3.77.

Technical Appendix 3.2 – Summary Tables for Testing for Common Trend (Cointegration)

Table A3.2.1 Summary of the Johansen's Test Results, Algeria lnP_tq_t, lnH_t, lnK_t, $lnWAP_t$, and lnY_t – Cointegrated Number of Cointegration Relationships by Different Specifications 1980–2019

Data Trend:	*None*	*None*	*Linear*	*Linear*	*Quadratic*
Test type	No intercept No trend	Intercept No trend	Intercept No trend	Intercept Trend	Intercept Trend
Trace	5	5	4	5	4
Max-λ	5	5	4	3	4

- Critical values are based on the 5 percent level (MacKinnon, Haug, and Michelis 1999).
- The number of lags is 2.
- AIC by Rank (rows) and Model (columns).
- Schwarz Information Criteria by Rank (rows) and Model (columns).
- Dummy variables for 1990 and 2015 are included as exogenous variables.

Table A3.2.2 Summary of the Johansen's Test Results, Angola lnP_tq_t, lnH_t, lnK_t, $lnWAP_t$, and lnY_t – Cointegrated Number of Cointegration Relationships by Different Specifications 1970–2019

Data Trend:	*None*	*None*	*Linear*	*Linear*	*Quadratic*
Test type	No intercept No trend	Intercept No trend	Intercept No trend	Intercept Trend	Intercept Trend
Trace	2	3	3	4	5
Max-λ	2	3	3	2	2

- Critical values are based on the 5 percent level (MacKinnon, Haug, and Michelis 1999).
- The number of lags is 2.
- AIC by Rank (rows) and Model (columns).
- Schwarz Information Criteria by Rank (rows) and Model (columns).

Table A3.2.3 Summary of the Johansen's Test Results, Congo lnP_tq_t, lnH_t, lnK_t, $lnWAP_t$, and lnY_t – Cointegrated Number of Cointegration Relationships by Different Specifications 1985–2019

Data Trend:	*None*	*None*	*Linear*	*Linear*	*Quadratic*
Test type	No intercept No trend	Intercept No trend	Intercept No trend	Intercept Trend	Intercept Trend

(*Continued*)

Table A3.2.3 (Continued)

Data Trend:	*None*	*None*	*Linear*	*Linear*	*Quadratic*
Trace	5	4	3	4	3
Max-λ	2	3	3	3	3

- Critical values are based on the 5 percent level (MacKinnon, Haug, and Michelis 1999).
- The number of lags is 2.
- AIC by Rank (rows) and Model (columns).
- Schwarz Information Criteria by Rank (rows) and Model (columns).

Table A3.2.4 Summary of the Johansen's Test Results, Gabon lnP_tq_t, lnH_t, lnK_t, $lnWAP_t$, and lnY_t – Cointegrated Number of Cointegration Relationships by Different Specifications 1975–2019

Data Trend:	*None*	*None*	*Linear*	*Linear*	*Quadratic*
Test Type	No intercept No trend	Intercept No trend	Intercept No trend	Intercept Trend	Intercept Trend
Trace	4	5	4	5	5
Max-λ	4	3	2	3	3

- Critical values are based on the 5 percent level (MacKinnon, Haug, and Michelis 1999).
- The number of lags is 2.
- AIC by Rank (rows) and Model (columns).
- Schwarz Information Criteria by Rank (rows) and Model (columns).

Table A3.2.5 Summary of the Johansen's Test Results, Iran lnP_tq_t, lnH_t, lnK_t, $lnWAP_t$, and lnY_t – Cointegrated Number of Cointegration Relationships by Different Specifications 1982–2019

Data Trend:	*None*	*None*	*Linear*	*Linear*	*Quadratic*
Test type	No intercept No trend	Intercept No trend	Intercept No trend	Intercept Trend	Intercept Trend
Trace	5	2	2	3	3
Max-λ	2	2	2	2	3

-Critical values are based on the 5 percent level (MacKinnon, Haug, and Michelis 1999).
-The number of lags is 2.
-AIC by Rank (rows) and Model (columns).
-Schwarz Information Criteria by Rank (rows) and Model (columns).

Table A3.2.6 Summary of the Johansen's Test Results, Iraq lnP_tq_t, lnH_t, lnK_t, $lnWAP_t$, and lnY_t – Cointegrated Number of Cointegration Relationships by Different Specifications 1972–2019

Data Trend:	*None*	*None*	*Linear*	*Linear*	*Quadratic*
Test type	No intercept No trend	Intercept No trend	Intercept No trend	Intercept Trend	Intercept Trend
Trace	5	5	3	3	2
Max-λ	2	2	1	2	2

- Critical values are based on the 5 percent level (MacKinnon, Haug, and Michelis 1999).
- The number of lags is 2.
- AIC by Rank (rows) and Model (columns).
- Schwarz Information Criteria by Rank (rows) and Model (columns).
- Dummy variables that take a value of 1 in 1980, 1990, 1995, and 2003, and 0 elsewhere are included.

Table A3.2.7 Summary of the Johansen's Test Results, Kuwait lnP_tq_t, lnH_t, lnK_t, $lnWAP_t$, and lnY_t – Cointegrated Number of Cointegration Relationships by Different Specifications 1981–2019

Data Trend:	*None*	*None*	*Linear*	*Linear*	*Quadratic*
Test type	No intercept No trend	Intercept No trend	Intercept No trend	Intercept Trend	Intercept Trend
Trace	1	2	1	2	5
Max-λ	1	1	1	1	1

- Critical values are based on the 5 percent level (MacKinnon, Haug, and Michelis 1999).
- The number of lags is 2.
- AIC by Rank (rows) and Model (columns).
- Schwarz Information Criteria by Rank (rows) and Model (columns).
- Dummy variable that takes a value of 1 in 1991 and 0 elsewhere is included.

Table A3.2.8 Summary of the Johansen's Test Results, Nigeria lnP_tq_t, lnH_t, lnK_t, $lnWAP_t$, and lnY_t – Cointegrated Number of Cointegration Relationships by Different Specifications 1985–2019

Data Trend:	*None*	*None*	*Linear*	*Linear*	*Quadratic*
Test type	No intercept No trend	Intercept No trend	Intercept No trend	Intercept Trend	Intercept Trend
Trace	5	4	2	3	2
Max-λ	3	4	2	2	2

- Critical values are based on the 5 percent level (MacKinnon, Haug, and Michelis 1999).
- The number of lags is 2.
- AIC by Rank (rows) and Model (columns).
- Schwarz Information Criteria by Rank (rows) and Model (columns).

Table A3.2.9 Summary of the Johansen's Test Results, Saudi Arabia lnP_tq_t, lnH_t, lnK_t, $lnWAP_t$, and lnY_t – Cointegrated Number of Cointegration Relationships by Different Specifications 1980–2019

Data Trend:	*None*	*None*	*Linear*	*Linear*	*Quadratic*
Test type	No intercept No trend	Intercept No trend	Intercept No trend	Intercept Trend	Intercept Trend
Trace	3	3	4	4	5
Max-λ	3	4	4	3	3

- Critical values are based on the 5 percent level (MacKinnon, Haug, and Michelis 1999).
- The number of lags is 2.
- AIC by Rank (rows) and Model (columns).
- Schwarz Information Criteria by Rank (rows) and Model (columns).
- Dummy variables that take a value of 1 in 1991 and 2009 and 0 elsewhere are included.

Table A3.2.10 Summary of the Johansen's Test Results, UAE lnP_tq_t, lnH_t, lnK_t, $lnWAP_t$, and lnY_t – Cointegrated Number of Cointegration Relationships by Different Specifications 1985–2019

Data Trend:	*None*	*None*	*Linear*	*Linear*	*Quadratic*
Test Type	No intercept No trend	Intercept No trend	Intercept No trend	Intercept Trend	Intercept Trend
Trace	5	5	5	4	3
Max-λ	1	2	1	2	3

- Critical values are based on the 5 percent level (MacKinnon, Haug, and Michelis 1999).
- The number of lags is 2.
- AIC by Rank (rows) and Model (columns).
- Schwarz Information Criteria by Rank (rows) and Model (columns).

Table A3.2.11 Summary of the Johansen's Test Results, Venezuela lnP_tq_t, lnH_t, lnK_t, $lnWAP_t$, and lnY_t – Cointegrated Number of Cointegration Relationships by Different Specifications 1972–2011

Data Trend:	*None*	*None*	*Linear*	*Linear*	*Quadratic*
Test type	No intercept No trend	Intercept No trend	Intercept No trend	Intercept Trend	Intercept Trend
Trace	4	5	5	4	3
Max-λ	4	5	5	3	2

- Critical values are based on the 5 percent level (MacKinnon, Haug, and Michelis 1999).
- The number of lags is 2.
- AIC by Rank (rows) and Model (columns).
- Schwarz Information Criteria by Rank (rows) and Model (columns).

Appendix 3.3 – Data Sources

The data source of real GDP, the human capital index, and the stock of capital are the Penn World Table 10.01. The price of oil and oil production are from BP Statistical Reviews 2022, and the working-age population is from the World Development Indicators of the World Bank.

Previous Penn World Tables used asset-specific investment data based on National Accounts statistics, derived from the Conference Board's (TCB) Total Economy Database, and estimates using the commodity-flow method (CFM). PWT 10.0 adjusted the linking procedure between both sources. Initially, it only linked at the final nine-asset level; it only used investment shares from TCB at the most detailed, nine-asset level. For 10.01, it also incorporated TCB investment data if it was only available for higher-level assets, for example, total construction. They define a tree-like structure of assets, where the nine lowest-level assets (children) are assigned to several higher-level assets (parents, grandparents, etc.). Investment shares are expressed relative to the direct parent, and TCB data are extrapolated using CFM data or fixed shares for years where data are missing for that child or any of its siblings. This means that even though the share of 'Residential structures' and 'Other construction' relative to 'Total construction' may be based on fixed shares for a given year, the share of 'Total construction' in Gross Fixed Capital Formation' can still be based directly on TCB data for that year. According to the PWT documentation, this ensures that *broad trends* reported in the National Accounts' investment series are also incorporated in this release of PWT. In the previous table, PWT 9.1 only TCB nominal investment data from 1993 onward are used. Prior to 1993, the shares were extrapolated at the nine-asset level using estimates from the CFM. Even though information on investment in 'Total construction' (Struc) was available from TCB, the trend is based solely on (volatile) CFM data. In PWT 10.0, all available primary information is used. The trend in 'Total construction' from 1950 to 2018 is based on TCB investment data. Prior to 1993, they relied on CFM data to break this aggregate further down into two assets: 'Residential structures' and 'Other construction.' The new investment data have a marked impact on the estimates of"capi'al stock and services for about 30 countries, where TCB offers only a partial time series of nominal investments. For references, see Feenstra, Inklaar, and Timmer (2015), Hsieh and Klenow (2010), and Inklaar, Robert, Woltjer, and Albarran (2019).

4 Estimating Baseline Permanent Income for OPEC

Abstract

The analysis in this chapter uses OPEC data to estimate an unrestricted VAR model to summarize the dynamics of real GDP and its drivers (oil, human capital, labor, and capital). Cointegration of these variables suggests a common long-term trend; hence the VAR is estimated in log-level. The VAR model is used to generate dynamic stochastic projections of real GDP's up to 2050, which is our baseline estimate of permanent income.

4.1 The Methodology

We have tested the OPEC data and found that the five variables in the model, $lnP_t q_t$, lnH_t, lnK_t, $lnWAP_t$, and lnY_t are cointegrated (i.e., share a long-run common trend), albeit the sample span varies across countries. Therefore, we could estimate the VAR described earlier either in log levels or as a VECM. The VAR in log levels is sufficient for our purpose because it provides the dynamics needed to generate baseline dynamic stochastic projections to 2050 for real GDP, and it would be consistent with, and satisfies the time series econometrics requirements of the data. It would also be consistent with our objective to estimate *permanent income*, which is the *expected income* over the period 2020–2050 (Friedman 1957). The VAR in log-levels would be used to generate dynamic stochastic projections over the period 2020 to 2050. VECM, however, is slightly more challenging because we have to pay a lot more attention to restrictions such as the number of cointegration vectors, which vary across different specifications as we reported earlier. In addition, the data are problematic and very difficult to fit because of breaks, missing observations, and high volatility.

We report a number of diagnostic tests for serial correlation in the residuals, e.g., the LM test – the Lagrange Multiplier, the White (1980) test for heteroskedasticity, and a number of tests for normality. All tables are reported in Appendix 4.1. The model is then solved, and a baseline dynamic stochastic projection for lnY_t over the period 2020–2050 is produced. The method is described in Eviews software 10.0. We solve the VAR using Broyden's method, which is a modified Newton's method. It uses an *approximation* instead of the true Jacobian when linearizing the

DOI: 10.4324/9781003488125-4

model. We update the approximation at every iteration of the 5000 iterations by comparing the residuals from the new trial values of the endogenous variables with the residuals predicted by the linear model based on the current Jacobian approximation. In addition, we use analytic derivatives with the starting values being the actual values. Then we solve the model in both directions (forward and backward). We stop solving when we hit a missing value. In a stochastic simulation, we solve the equations of the model such that the residuals (10,000 iterations bootstrapped innovations) match to randomly drawn errors, and the coefficients and exogenous variables of the model change randomly. The solution generates a distribution of outcomes for the endogenous variables in every period. We approximate the distribution by solving the model many times using different draws or the random components in the model then calculating statistics over all the different outcomes. Only values of the endogenous variables from before the solution sample are used in the dynamic solution of the projections. Lagged endogenous variables are calculated using the solutions calculated in previous periods, i.e., not from actual historical values. A series for the mean is calculated. We consider 10,000 repetitions reasonable to capture the true values; however, some random variation may be present between adjacent observations. The 95 percent confidence intervals are computed using an updating algorithm. For the diagonal covariance matrix, the diagonal elements are set to zero. We do not scale the variances.

4.2 Estimation

4.2.1 Algeria – Baseline Permanent Income Estimate

We fit an unrestricted VAR in log levels for the period 1980–2019 with a constant term and two dummy variables as exogenous variables, one takes a value of 1 in 1991 and zero elsewhere to account for the Algerian civil war and another for 2015 to account for the fall in oil and gas prices a year earlier in 2014. Note that the actual data are only available to the year 2019. Table A4.1 reports the Information Criteria we used. The Information Criteria suggest two to three lags. We tried both, but the third lag is not always significant. We decided that a VAR ($k = 5, p = 2$) is a reasonable summary of the dynamics of the data. Table A4.2 reports the lag-exclusion Wald test. The two lags are statistically significant. The diagnosis includes testing the residuals. Table A4.3 reports the autocorrelation LM test statistics, where the null hypothesis H_0 : no serial correlation. That implies that two lags were sufficient to soak up the serial correlation. Table A4.4 reports the White Heteroskedasticity test statistics; White's (1980) test is a test of the null hypothesis of no heteroskedasticity against heteroskedasticity of unknown, general form. H_0 : no heteroskedasticity in the residuals (with no cross terms). Table A4.5 reports the test for normality of the residuals. The null hypotheses could not be rejected at all lags. The residuals of the Algerian's baseline VAR pass all diagnosis tests.

The variance decomposition of the data is plotted in Figure 4.1, which has the same information provided by the impulse response functions but is more useful in our case because we want to show the variance of real GDP due to

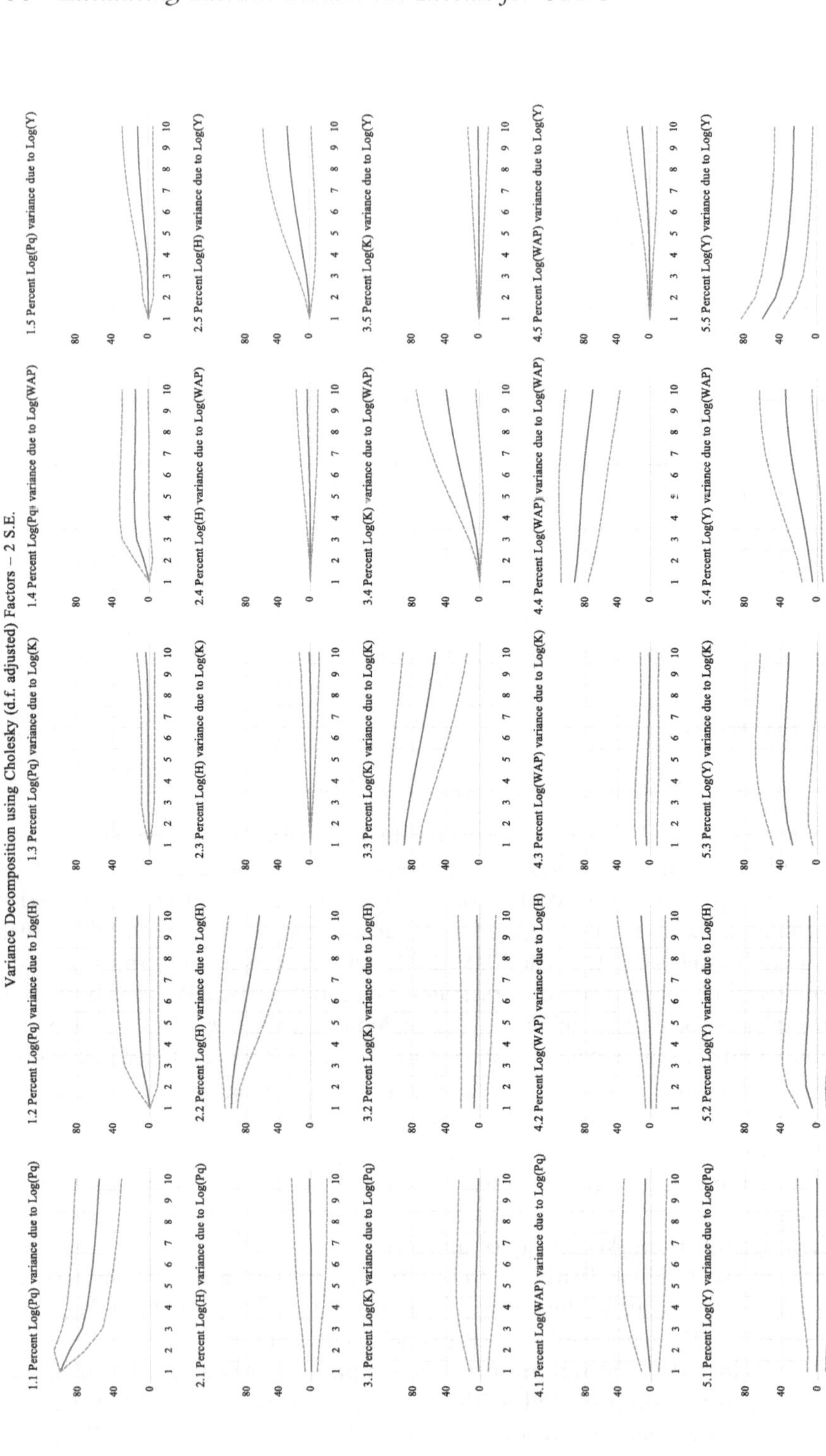

Figure 4.1 Algeria's Baseline VAR Variance Decomposition

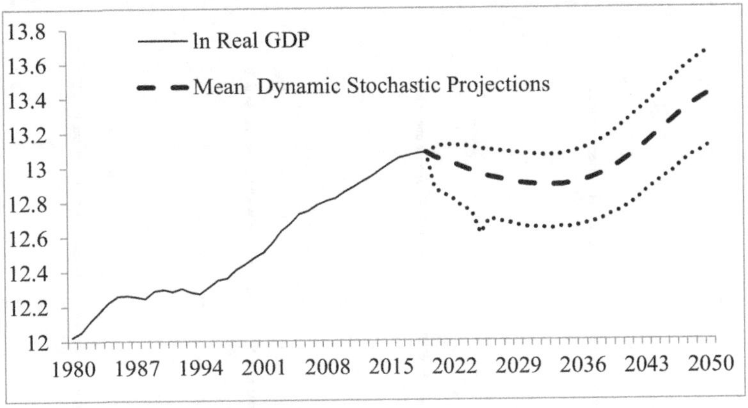

Figure 4.2 Algeria's Estimated Baseline Permanent Income

variations in each of the explanatory variables in our model, especially oil.[1] Figure 4.1 is a 5 by 5 matrix, where the plots are numbered accordingly. We focus on the last row (Plots 5.1–5.5). Oil does not seem to explain much of the real GDP in Algeria. We could only speculate that Algeria is a major gas producer; thus, oil has a smaller effect on real GDP. The variance of human capital explains about 20 percent of the variance of real GDP (Plot 5.2); the stock of capital's variance explains about 40 percent of the variance of real GDP (Plot 5.3); and the variance of real GDP due to working-age population increases until it reaches 40 percent (Plot 5.4). So, human capital, the stock of capital, and labor eventually explain all of the variations in real GDP. Finally, we solve the model as described earlier. Then we generate dynamic stochastic projections of real GDP from 2020 to 2050, which is a measure of expected real GDP or *permanent income* for Algeria. Figure 4.2 plots the data. The baseline estimate of permanent income for Algeria shows an upward trend, and the standard errors, which we generated by 10,000 bootstraps, are reasonably estimated.

4.2.2 *Angola – Baseline Permanent Income Estimate*

Keep in mind that the data are challenging. We fit the baseline VAR ($k = 5, p = 2$) from 1982 to 2019 with a constant term and without dummy variables. Tables A4.6 and A4.7 report test results for the number of lags. The residuals of Angola's VAR are serially uncorrelated and homoskedastic. The residuals are normal in three equations. There are Skewness and Kurtosis in the human capital and real GDP equations. Keep in mind again that we use 1000-iteration Monte Carlo to calculate the standard errors of the variance decomposition. Nonetheless, one must be cautious and

1 For all countries, we use different orders of the variables in the VAR and found no significant changes in the results. Furthermore, Koop, Pesaran, and Potter (1996) and Isakin and Ngo (2020) show that when models are linear, traditional Impulse Response Functions and Variance Decomposition are valid.

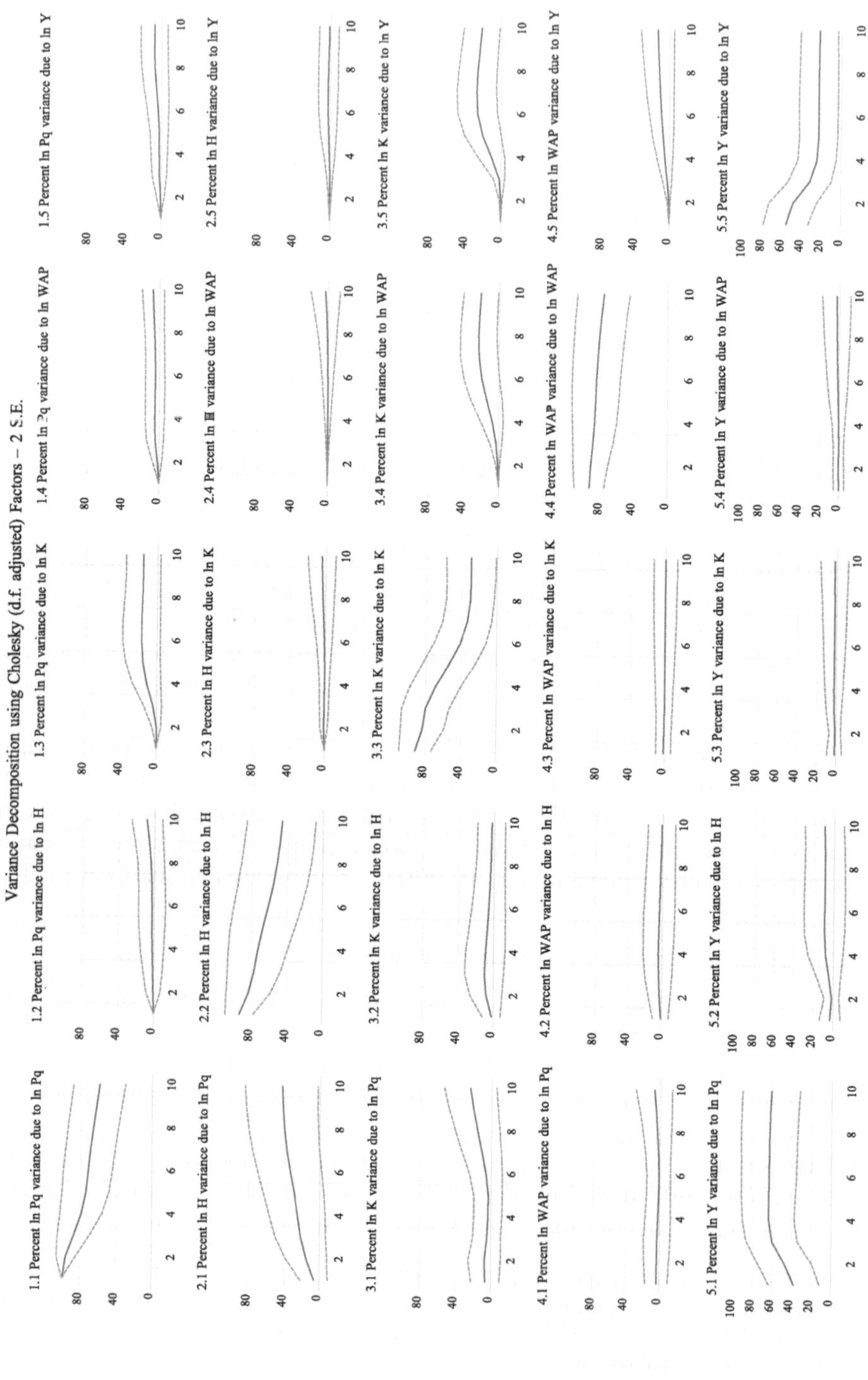

Figure 4.3 Angola's Baseline VAR Variance Decomposition

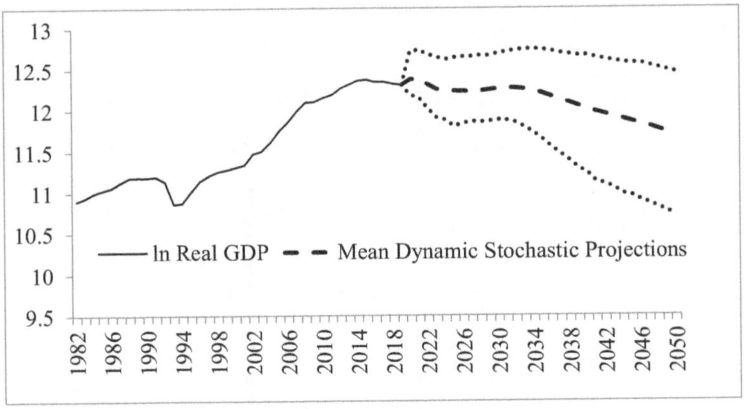

Figure 4.4 Angola's Estimated Baseline Permanent Income

take the final dynamic stochastic projections with a large grain of salt in all cases where the non-normality of the residuals is present, especially in the GDP equation. Figure 4.3 plots the variance decomposition. Unlike Algeria, 60 percent of the variations in real GDP are due to oil (Plot 5.1). Oil also increasingly explains the variance of human capital (Plot 2.1). Human capital, however, does not explain the variance of real GDP as one would expect. None of the other explanatory variables explain any of the variation in real GDP. Angola's GDP is largely oil.

Figure 4.4 plots the dynamic stochastic projection of real GDP, i.e., our estimated permanent income. The baseline estimate of *permanent income* for Angola South declines as the forecast horizon increases.

4.2.3 Congo, DR – Baseline Permanent Income Estimate

These data are problematic. We estimate a VAR ($k = 5, p = 2$) with a constant term from 1985 to 2019. The sample is chosen to deal with significant anomalies in the data from 1970 to 1985 as explained earlier. The diagnostic statistics are reported in the appendix in Tables A4.11–A4.15. Three lags are significant in Table A4.11; however, the lag exclusion test in Table A4.12 finds two lags only. So, we fit a VAR with two lags. The residuals test for serial correlation is reported in Table A4.13, which indicates some serial correlation at lags 1 and 2. There is a serial correlation at lags 1 and 2, but there is no heteroskedasticity in Congo's baseline model's residuals. Fitting more lags removes the serial correlation, but fitting more lags increases the volatility in the dynamic stochastic projections, which is a larger problem for the objective of this analysis. We have to juggle this tradeoff. Non-normality is also present in the system's residuals. The joint tests are significant, i.e., non-normality; however, the real GDP equation has normal residuals. We could not possibly improve these diagnostics without trading off more instability in the estimated baseline permanent income. Figures 4.5 and 4.6 plot the variance decomposition and the estimated baseline permanent income.

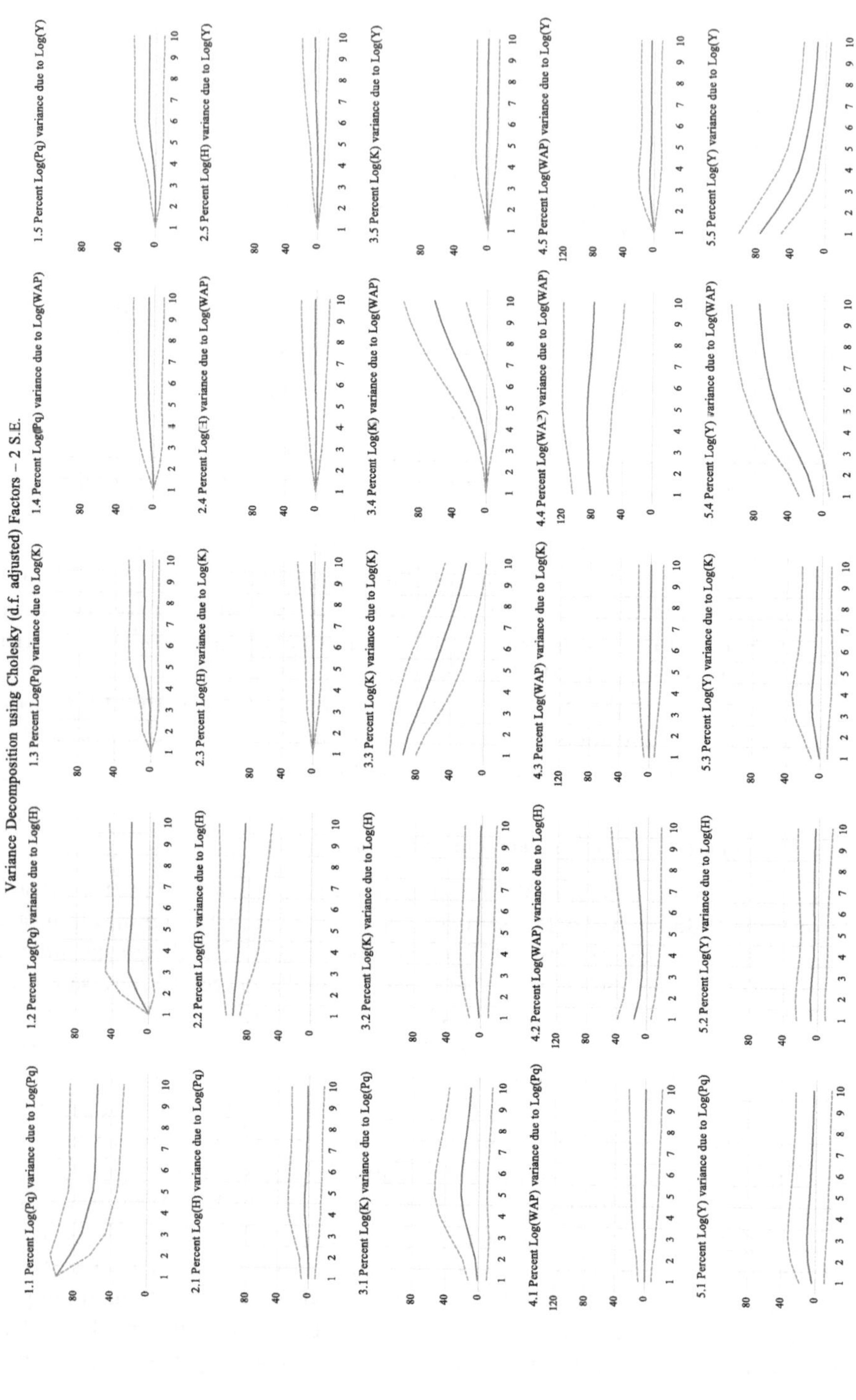

Figure 4.5 Congo's Baseline VAR Variance Decomposition

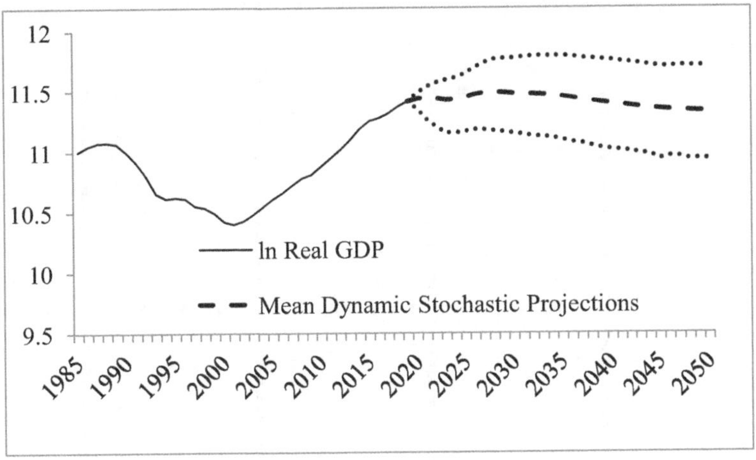

Figure 4.6 Congo's Estimated Baseline Permanent Income

Unlike Angola but similar to Algeria, oil does not seem to explain the variance of real GDP of the Congo, DR. Real GDP variance is almost entirely due to labor – working-age population (15–64 years). Labor (Plot 5.4) explains about 80 percent of the variance of real GDP. Labor also explains up to 80 percent of the variance of the stock of capital (Plot 3.4). Note also that contrary to the prediction of economic theory, human capital explains nothing in these three African countries (Algeria, Angola, and Congo, DR). Finally, we solve this VAR and generate baseline dynamic stochastic projections of real GDP, i.e., our estimate of permanent income for Congo, DR. We plot the data in Figure 4.6. It looks flat.

4.2.4 Gabon – Baseline Permanent Income Estimate

Gabon is the fourth African country in our sample. We estimate a VAR ($k = 5, p = 2$) with a constant term from 1985 to 2019. The sample is chosen to deal with significant anomalies in the data from 1975 to 1985 as explained earlier. The diagnostic statistics are reported in Tables A4.16–A4.20. We examined the significance of these lags using the Wald lag exclusion test, and we could only find two lags to be statistically significant. There is some serial correlation at lag 1, but less so at lag 2. Fitting more lags could soak up the serial correlation; however, when we did that it increased the volatility of the dynamic stochastic projections. Unfortunately, there is a significant joint heteroskedasticity. The residuals of the real GDP equation, which is our primary concern, seem to be normal. Again, we use 1000-iteration Monte Carlo to compute the standard errors of the variance decomposition; nonetheless, these are not the best statistics we hope for. Figure 4.7 plots the variance decomposition for Gabon. Oil does not explain the variations in real GDP. The stock of capital (Plot 5.3) explains most of the variations in real GDP. The variance of real GDP due to variations in the stock of capital is about 60 percent. The

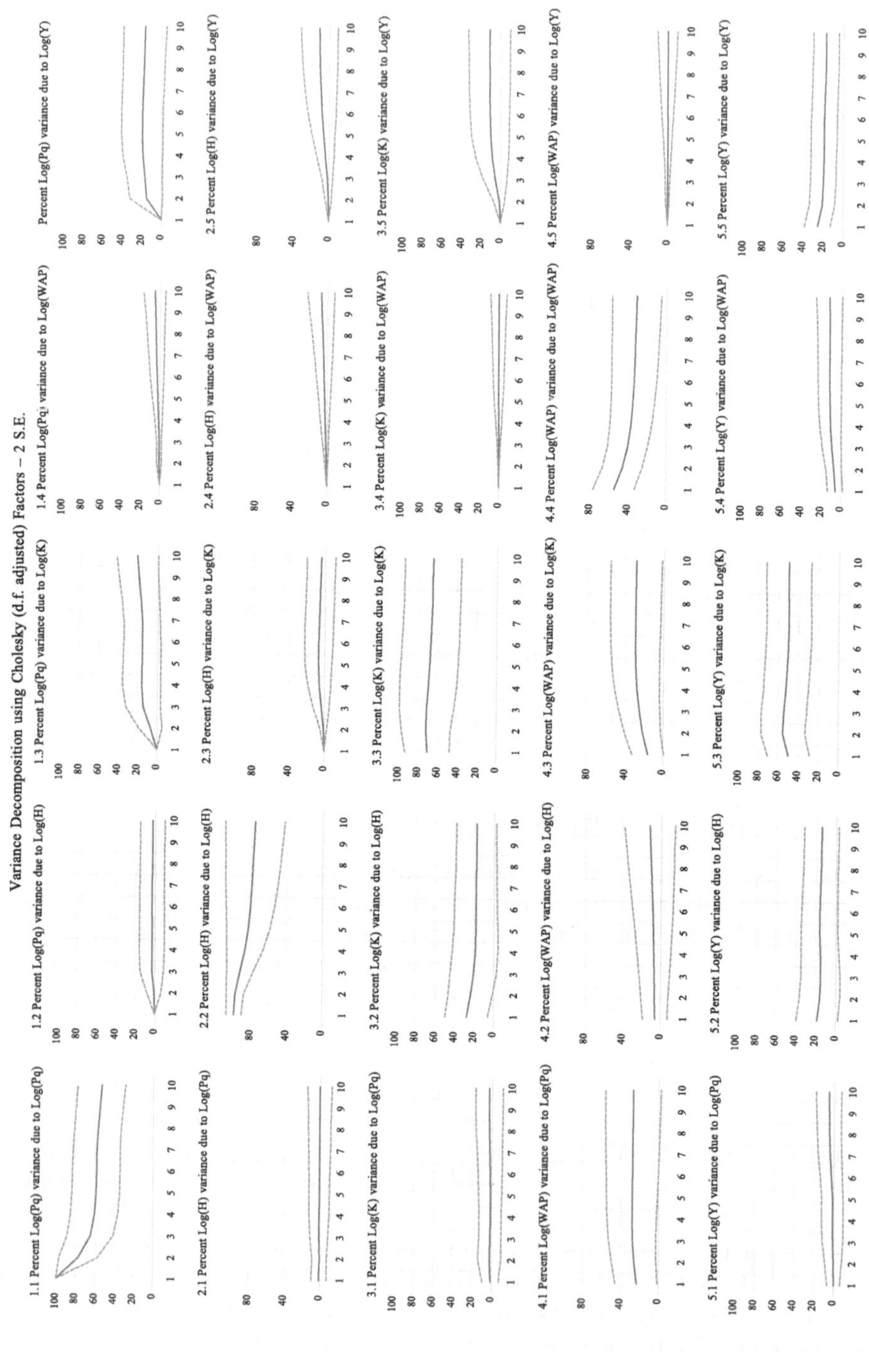

Figure 4.7 Gabon's Baseline VAR Variance Decomposition

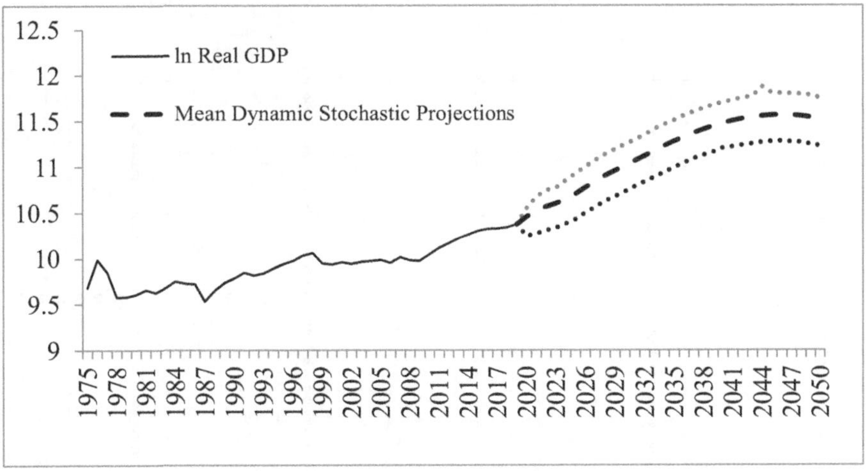

Figure 4.8 Gabon's Estimated Baseline Permanent Income

variance of real GDP due to variations in human capital is about 20 percent (Plot 5.2). Therefore, Gabon's real GDP drivers are different from those of the Congo's, Angola's, and Algeria's. In Algeria, variations in human capital, stock of capital, and labor explain the variation in real GDP; it was oil in Angola; and labor only in Congo, DR.

We solve the model, generate our dynamic stochastic projections of real GDP, and plot the data in Figure 4.8.

4.2.5 *Iran – Baseline Permanent Income Estimate*

We fit VAR ($k = 5, p = 2$) from 1982 to 2019 *without* a constant term because of the Iranian data problems early in the 1970s. Tables A4.21–A4.25 report the lag selection statistics and the residual diagnostics of the Iranian data. The Information Criteria predict three lags, but the Wald test suggests two lags, although not for all equations. The number of lags is two, except for the first equation of $lnP_t^o q_t^o$ and probably the human capital equation, where the second lag is insignificant. Therefore, one to two lags are needed. We fit two lags. The null of no serial correlation cannot be rejected. The null hypothesis of no heteroskedasticity cannot be rejected in most cases either, but the joint test value indicates a marginal heteroskedasticity. The residuals are normal. Table A4.25 reports the tests. The residuals are serially uncorrelated, homoskedastic, and normal. These are the best diagnostic results we have so far. Figure 4.9 plots the variance decomposition. The variance decomposition for Iran is very interesting and different from the African countries. About 40 percent of the variance of real GDP is due to oil, and 30 percent is due to labor. Although explaining human capital itself is beyond the scope of this book, oil explains about 60 percent of the variations of human capital (Plot 2.1). It seems that

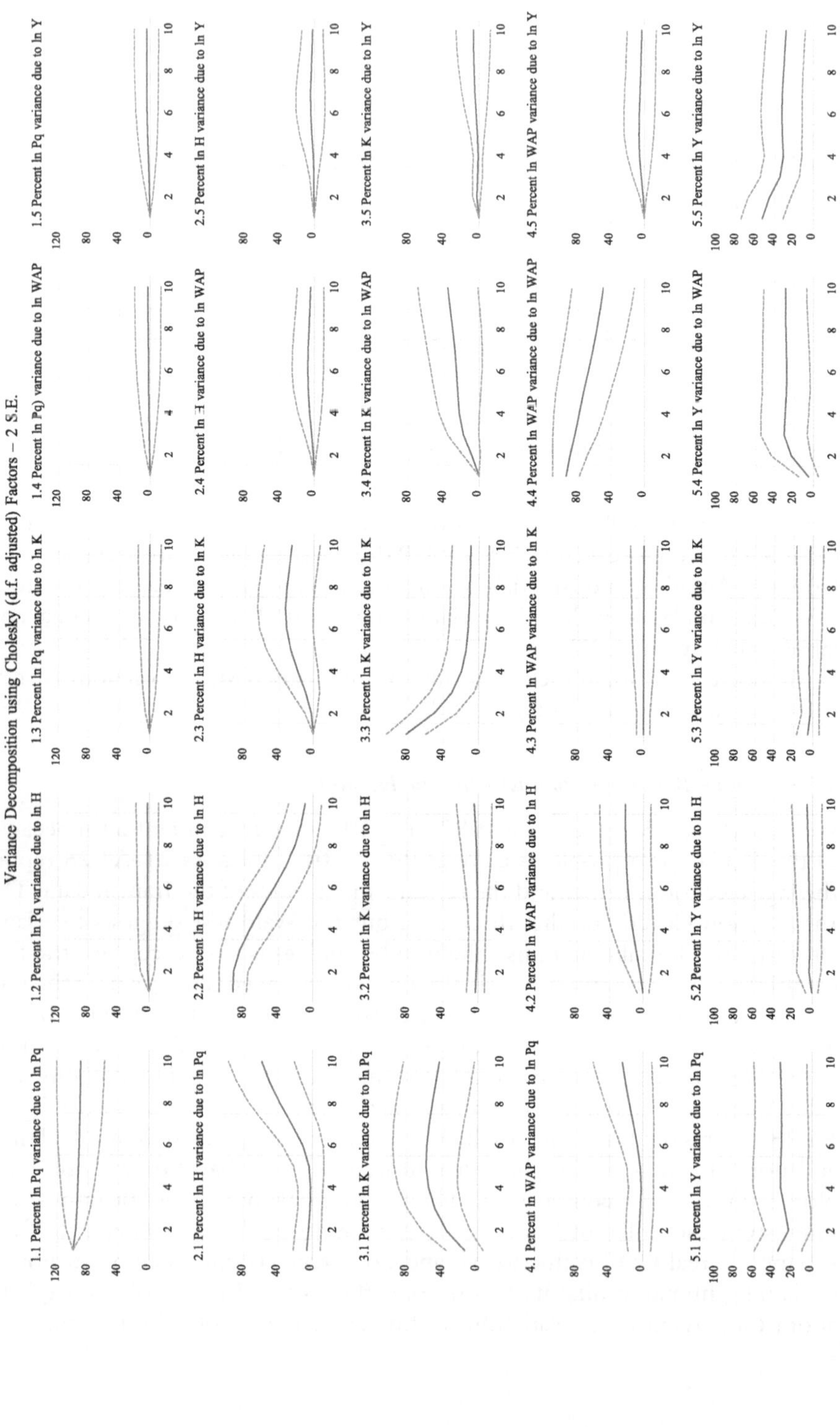

Figure 4.9 Iran's Baseline VAR Variance Decomposition

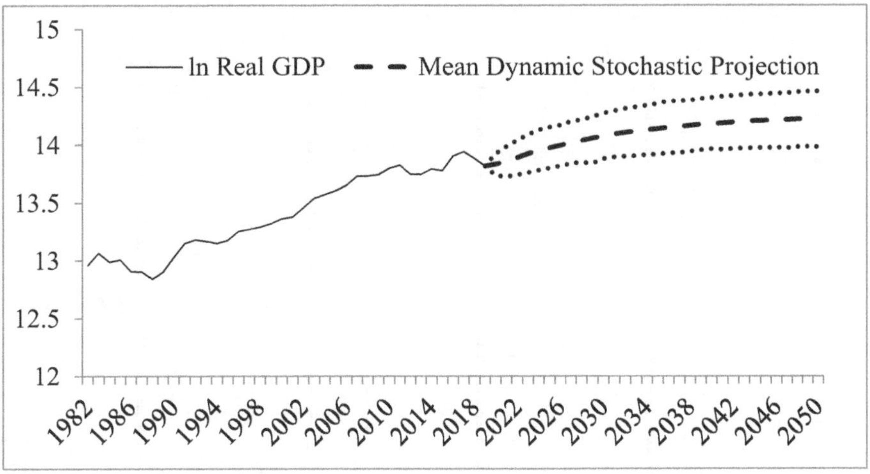

Figure 4.10 Iran's Estimated Baseline Permanent Income

oil played a relatively larger part in the development in Iran than in the previous African countries. About 40 percent of the variance of the stock of capital is due to oil. The variation of the stock of capital due to oil also increases, and then flattens, and eventually declines in a clear hump shape (Plot 3.1). Plot 4.1 also shows that oil explains an increasing amount of the variations of labor. Oil seems to play a more significant role in Iran than in the previous four African OPEC countries. Figure 4.10 plots our estimated permanent income for Iran.

4.2.6 Iraq – Baseline Permanent Income Estimate

We fit a VAR $(k = 5, p = 2)$ for Iraq from 1970 to 2019 with a constant term, and four dummy variables; one dummy variable takes a value of 1 in 1980 and 0 elsewhere to account for the war with Iran; another dummy variable that takes a value of 1 in 1990 and 0 elsewhere to account for the First Gulf War; a third dummy variable takes a value if 1 in 1995 and 0 elsewhere to account for UN sanctions that caused a huge adverse impact; and finally a dummy variable that takes a value of 1 in 2003 and 0 elsewhere to account for the Second Gulf War and the invasion of Iraq, which smashed the economy. We test the number of lags using the same Information Criteria we used earlier and the test for lag exclusions using the Wald statistic by fitting a longer more general lag specification and then eliminating the insignificant ones. Table A4.26 reports the Information Criteria, which indicates that two lags could be chosen, and Table A4.27 reports the Wald lag exclusion test results, where two lags are significant, except for the first and fifth equation (the oil and real GDP), where only one lag is significant. However, one lag is insufficient for dealing with serial correlation in the system, so we will fit the VAR with two

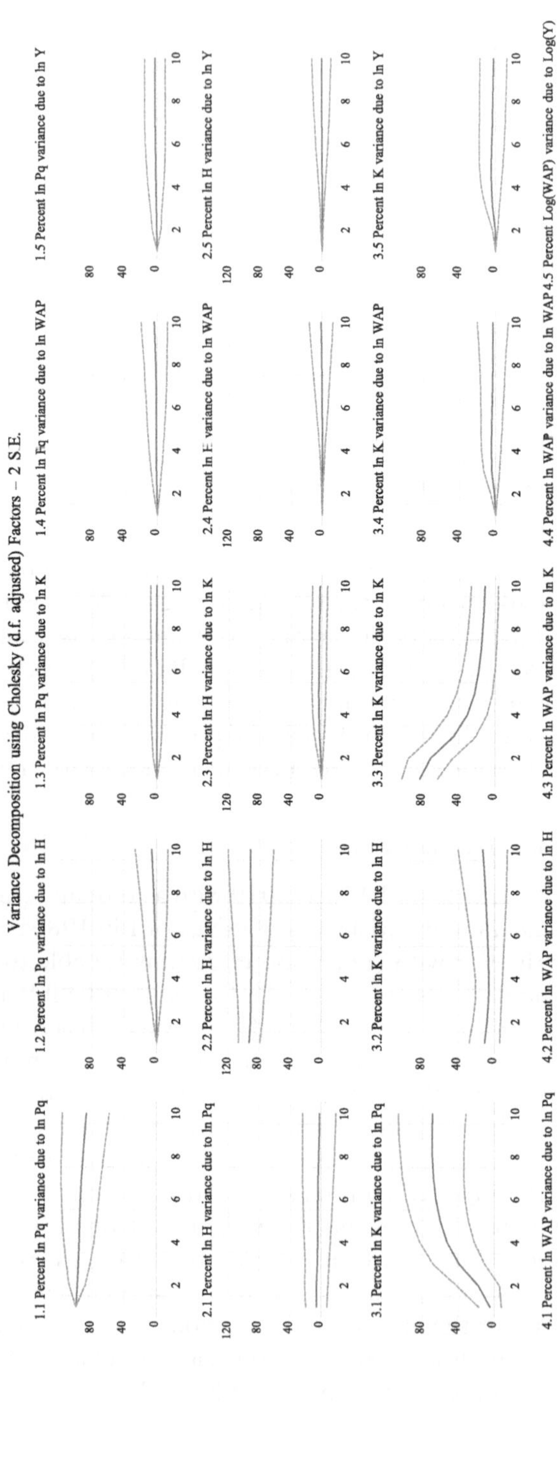

Figure 4.11 Iraq's Baseline VAR Variance Decomposition

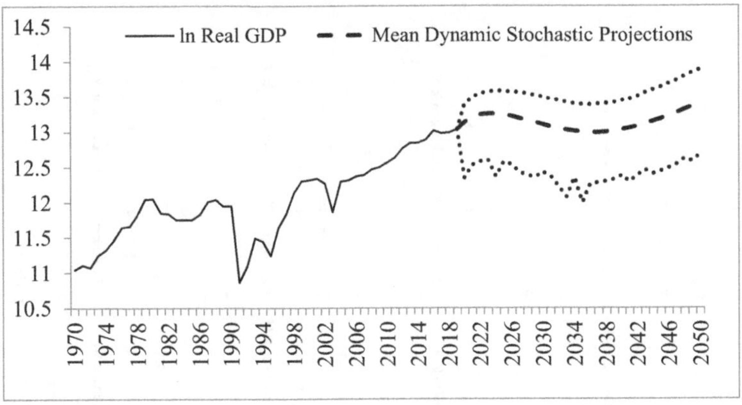

Figure 4.12 Iraq's Estimated Baseline Permanent Income

lags. Table A4.28 reports the LM test's results. The null hypothesis of no serial correlation could not be rejected. The residuals of the VAR $(k = 5, p = 2)$ are serially uncorrelated. And, there is no evidence of heteroskedasticity either, so far so good. The last tests are normality tests of the residuals, which are shown in Table A4.30. There is evidence of Skewness in the residuals of equations (1), (2), and (5) of the VAR; these are the oil, human capital, and real GDP equations. There is evidence of Kurtosis in equations (1), (2), and (4), the working-age population equation. And, the Jarque–Bera test shows evidence of non-normality in the residuals in these equations; however, the residuals of the real GDP equation are marginally non-normal with the test's P-value of 0.40. The standard errors of the variance decomposition are derived using 1000-iteration Monte Carlo. Figure 4.11 plots the variance decomposition for Iraq's VAR. The resulting decomposition strongly suggests a larger role for oil in explaining the variance of real GDP in Iraq. The variance of real GDP, which is due to oil, is 60 percent (Plot 5.1). None of the other variables seem to have anything significant to explain. Iraq is clearly different from all the other previous cases, where oil is a key determinant of real GDP. In addition, oil explains most of the variance of the stock of capital (Plot 3.1). Finally, we plot our estimate of the baseline permanent income for Iraq in Figure 4.12.

4.2.7 Kuwait – Baseline Permanent Income Estimate

We fit a VAR $(k = 5, p = 2)$ from 1980 to 2019 with a constant term and one dummy variable that takes a value of 1 in 1991 to account for the First Gulf War (the Iraqi invasion of Kuwait) and 0 elsewhere. One must keep in mind that the Kuwaiti data for the period 1990–1992 might be estimated by the Penn World Table and not actual. I know from my experience in Kuwait that the official data were missing. We test the number of lags using the same Information Criteria we used earlier and the test for lag exclusions using the Wald statistic by fitting a longer more general lag specification and then eliminating the insignificant ones. Table A4.31 reports the Information Criteria, which indicates that two

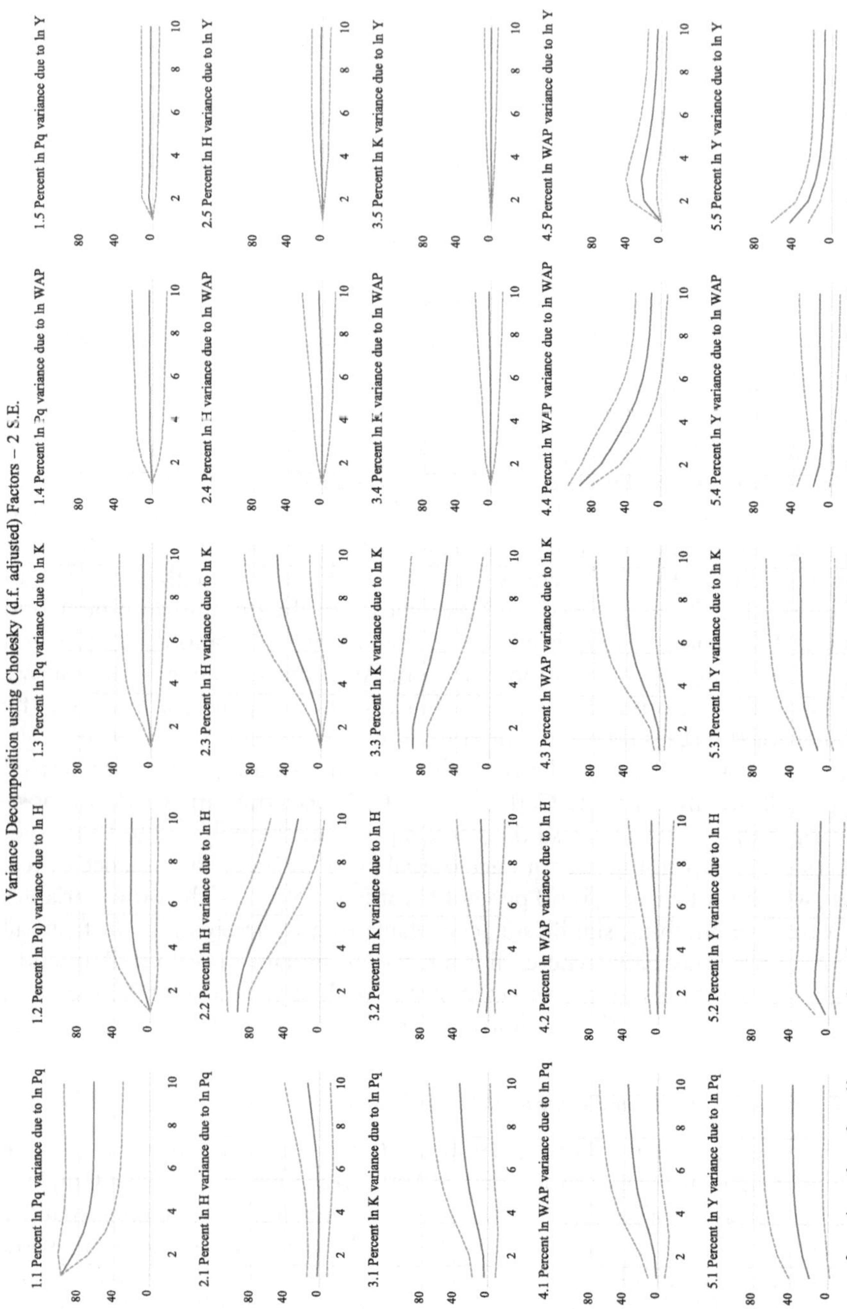

Figure 4.13 Kuwait's Baseline VAR Variance Decomposition

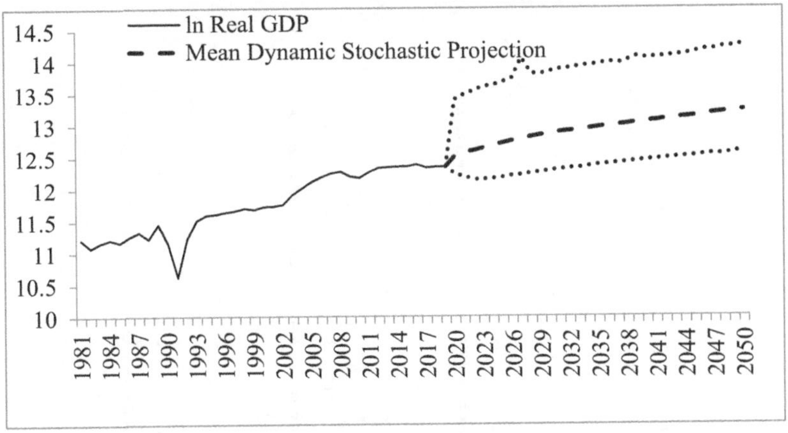

Figure 4.14 Kuwait's Estimated Baseline Permanent Income

lags could be chosen, and Table A4.32 reports the Wald lag exclusion test results. Tables A4.33, A4.34, and A4.35 report the LM statistic, the White statistic, and the statistics for testing the residuals of Kuwait's baseline VAR. The null hypothesis could not be rejected. The residuals are serially uncorrelated. There is no evidence of heteroskedasticity either. These are good results. The last tests are normality tests of the residuals, which are shown in Table A4.35. Joint tests show non-normality of the residuals, and the individual components show that Skewness is due to non-normality in the residuals of equation (4); Kurtosis is due to equation (4) (the working-age population) and equation (5) (the real GDP); and the Jarque-Bera confirms that these two equations are the source of the problem. Equations (1)–(3) have normal residuals, which is a concern. Figure 4.13 plots the variance decomposition of the baseline VAR with the standard errors computed using 1000 Monte Carlo iterations. Figure 4.14 plots the estimated permanent income for Kuwait. Like Angola, Iraq, and Iran, oil plays a significant role in the Kuwaiti economy; the variance of real GDP due to oil is 40 percent. The variations in labor and capital due to the variation in oil are about 40 percent, respectively. Real GDP is primarily explained by oil and the stock of capital. Human capital plays a small role in producing output; however, it explains about 40 percent of the variance of the stock of capital.

4.2.8 Nigeria – Baseline Permanent Income Estimate

Nigeria is the fifth and the last African country in the sample; however, it has relatively better data. We fit a VAR $(k = 5, p = 2)$ from 1985 to 2019 with a constant term. Tables A4.36 and A4.37 report the Information Criteria and lag exclusion tests for the determination of the number of lags. Note that the second lag in equations (1) and (3) is insignificant, but we fit a two-lag VAR to the data. Table A4.38 reports the LM test statistic; Table A4.39 reports the White test statistics; and Table A4.40 reports the normality tests of the residuals. The null of no serial correlation cannot be rejected at the 10 percent level for lags 1 and 2. The null hypothesis of no heteroskedasticity cannot be rejected in most

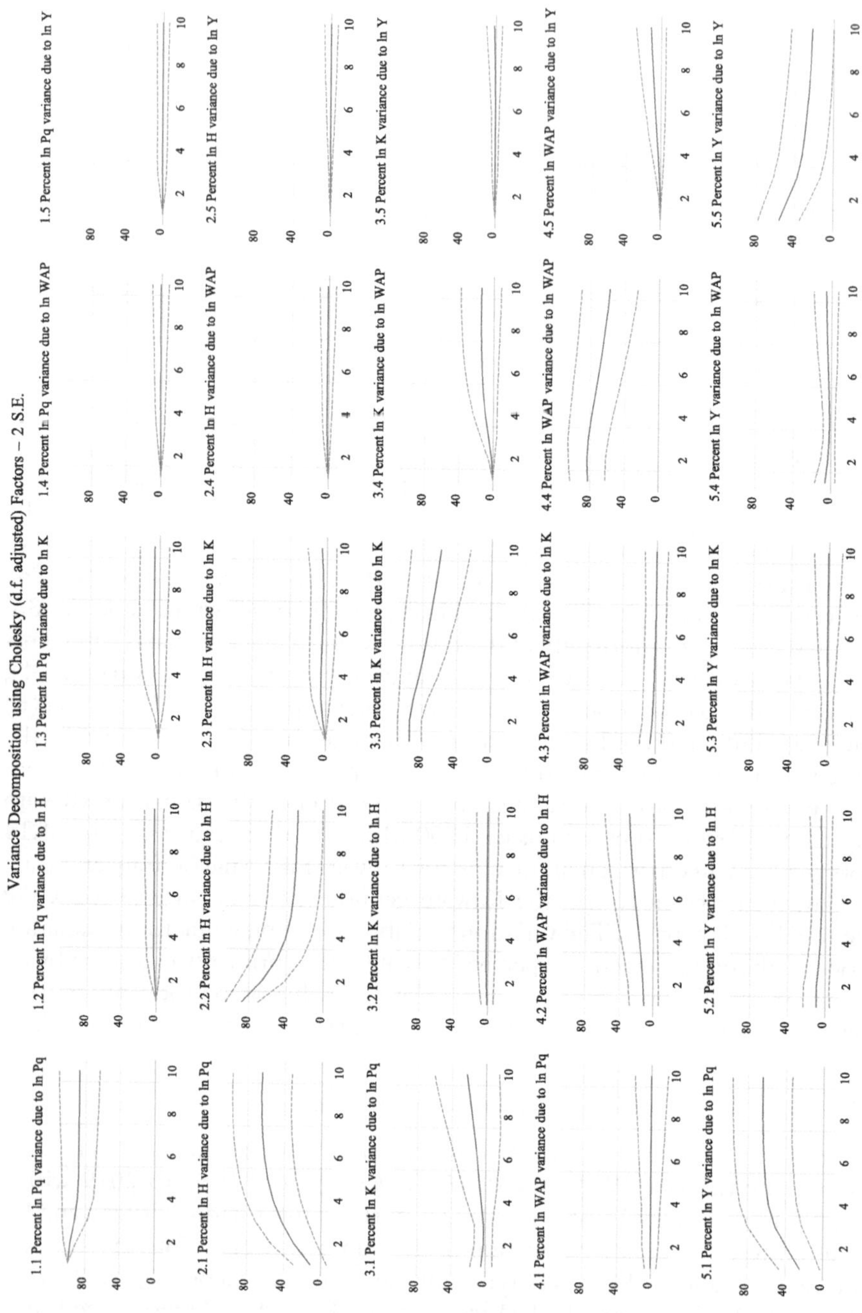

Figure 4.15 Nigeria's Baseline VAR Variance Decomposition

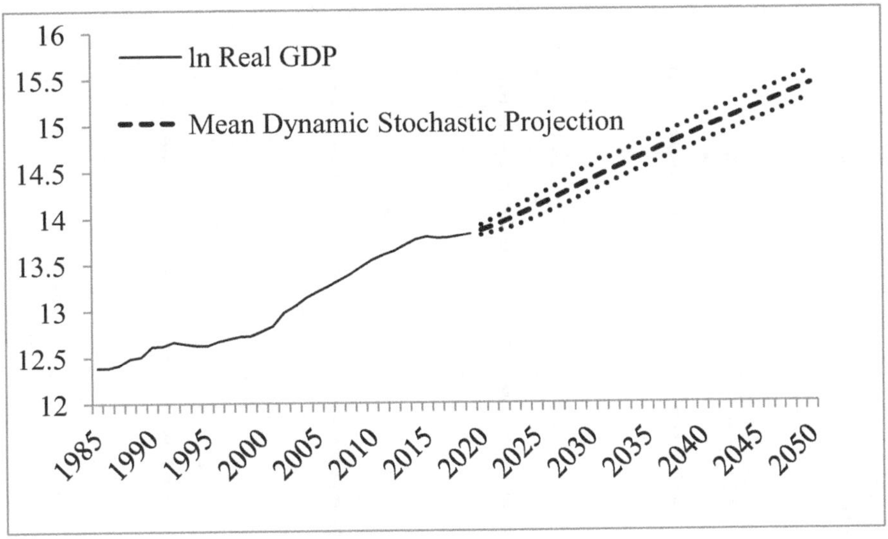

Figure 4.16 Nigeria's Estimated Baseline Permanent Income

cases, and the joint test value indicates no heteroskedasticity at the 10 percent level. The residuals are normal. Table A4.40 reports the tests. Figure 4.15 plots the variance decomposition. Oil explains most of the variation of real GDP, more than 60 percent (Plot 5.1). None of the other factors explain the variance of real GDP. The variance of human capital due to the variance of oil is also high, about 60–70 percent, which is remarkable (Plot 2.1). Nigeria must have invested its oil wealth in building education and human capital. The variance of the stock of capital is increasingly explained by the variance of oil, nearly 40 percent. Figure 4.16 plots the estimated permanent income for Nigeria.

4.2.9 Saudi Arabia – Baseline Permanent Income Estimate

We fit a VAR $(k = 5, p = 2)$ from 1980to 2019 with a constant term and two dummy variables; a dummy variable takes a value of 1 in 1991, the First Gulf War and 0 elsewhere, and another dummy variable takes a value of 1 in 2009 and 0 elsewhere. The 2009 dummy variable is for the Great Recession in the US, which seems to have a significant effect on the Kingdom's economy. Tables A4.41 and A4.42 report the Information Criteria and lag exclusion tests for the determination of the number of lags. Two lags are chosen. The second lag in equation (5) is only marginally significant, but the system needs at least two lags. Table A4.43 reports the LM test statistic; Table A4.44 reports the White test statistics; and Table A4.45 reports the normality tests of the residuals. The null of no serial correlation cannot be rejected. Also, the

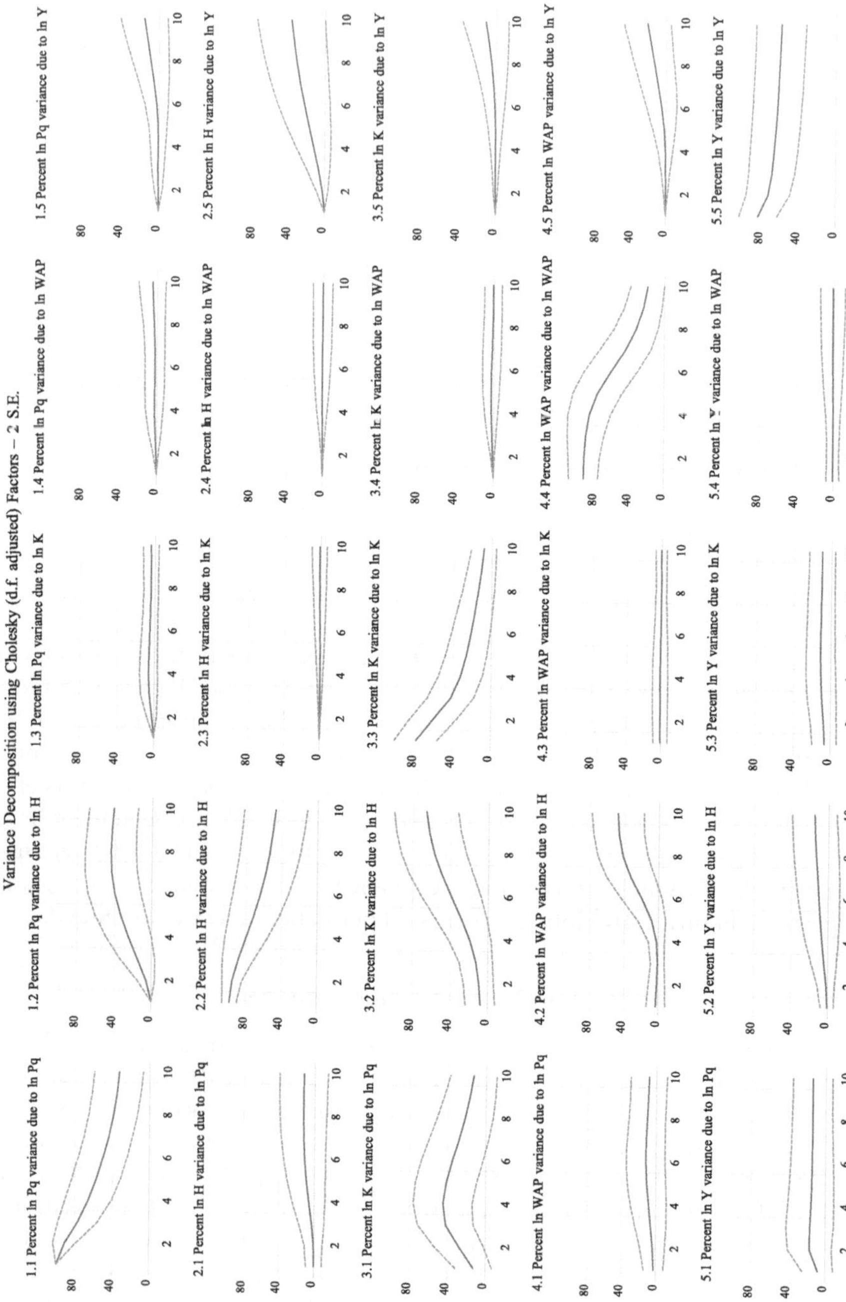

Figure 4.17 Saudi Arabia's Baseline VAR Variance Decomposition

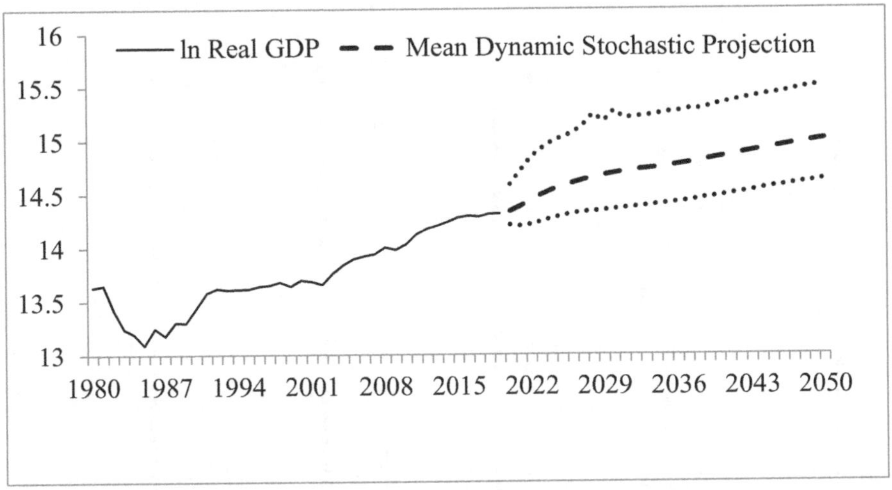

Figure 4.18 Saudi Arabia's Estimated Baseline Permanent Income

null hypothesis of no heteroskedasticity cannot be rejected. The residuals are normal. Table A4.45 reports the tests for Skewness, Kurtosis, and the Jarqu-Bera test. There are no indications of Skewness. There is some Kurtosis in equations (2) and (4), but the real GDP equation has none. The Jarque-Bera test shows some non-normality in the residuals of equation (4) only. Figure 4.17 plots the variance decomposition. Different from all of the previous countries, the variance of real oil production $lnP_t^o q_t^o$ is increasingly explained by human capital, up to 40 percent (Plot 1.2). The variance of human capital due to variation in real GDP is also large, increasing up to 40 percent, which we have not seen in previous countries (Plot 2.5). Oil also explains the stock of capital but it looks like a hump shape, rising to more than 40 percent, and then falling (Plot 3.1). The variance of human capital explains 65 percent of the variance of the stock of capital (Plot 3.2). The variance of working-age population due to human capital exceeds 40 percent (Plot 4.2). Oil, however, does not explain more than 30 percent of real GDP (Plot 5.1). The variance of real GDP due to human capital and the stock of capital is also 30 percent at most respectively. Figure 4.18 plots the estimated permanent income for Saudi Arabia.

4.2.10 UAE – Baseline Permanent Income Estimate

We fit a VAR $(k = 5, p = 2)$ from 1985 to 2019 with a constant term. Tables A4.46 and A4.47 report the Information Criteria and lag exclusion tests for the determination of the number of lags. Two lags seem to be significant except for equations (1) and (5). Table A4.48 reports the LM test statistic;

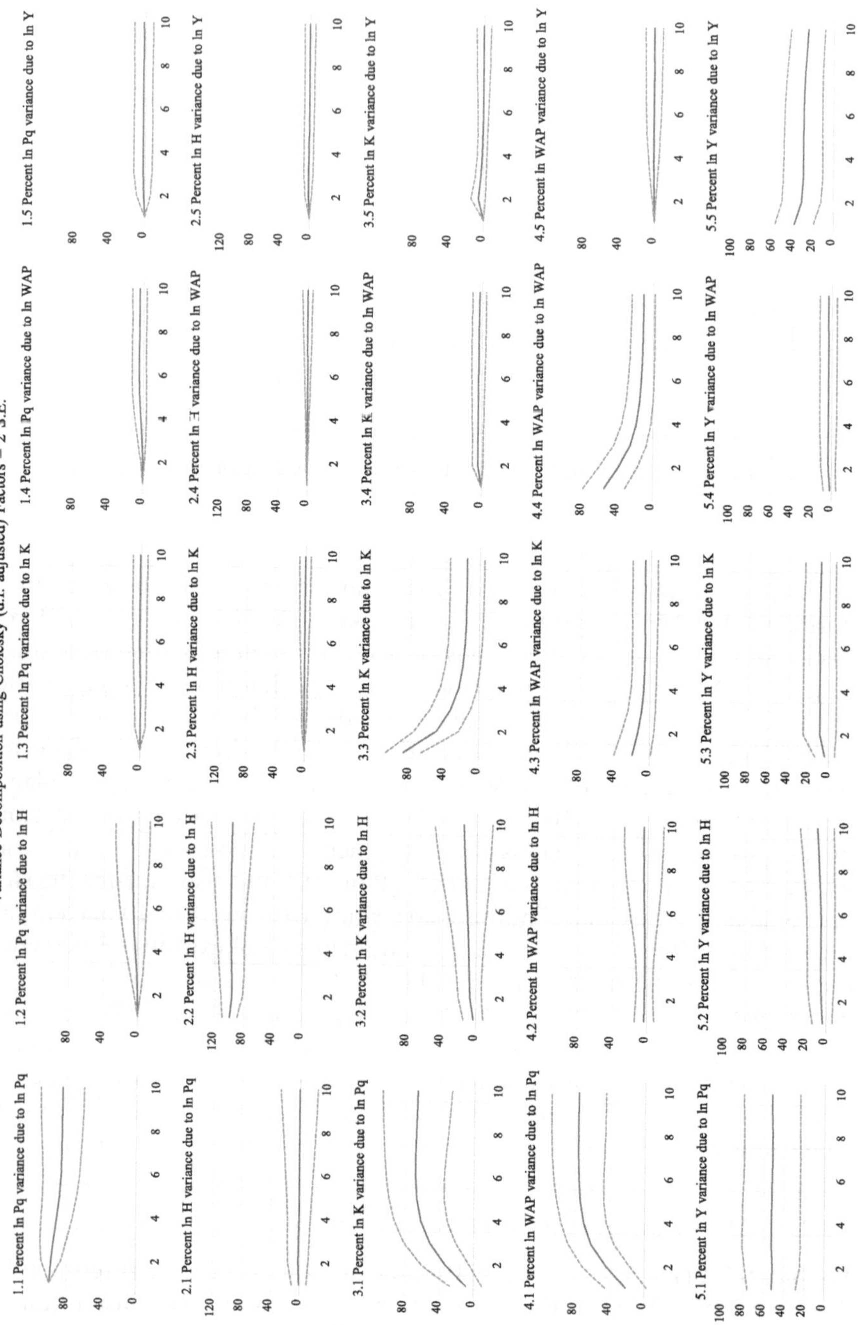

Figure 4.19 UAE's Baseline VAR Variance Decomposition

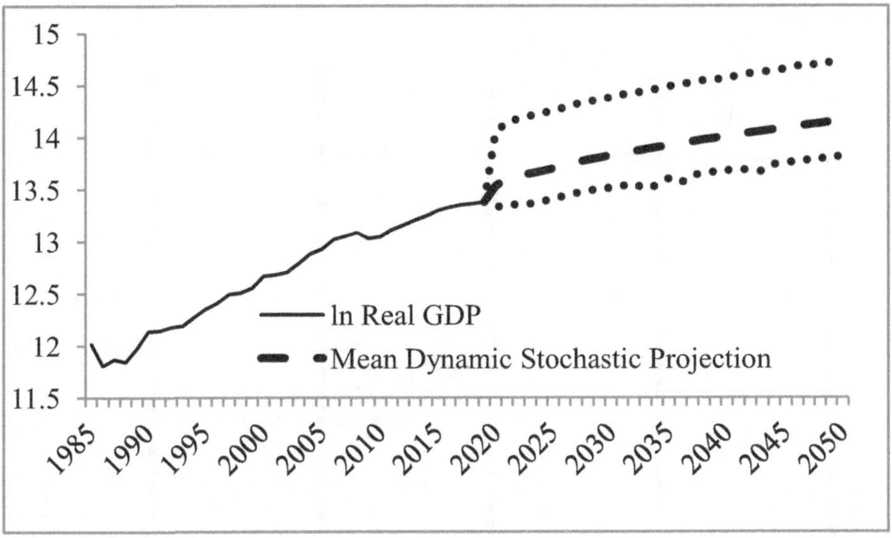

Figure 4.20 UAE's Estimated Baseline Permanent Income

Table A4.49 reports the White test statistics; and Table A4.50 reports the normality tests of the residuals. There is a serial correlation at the first lag, but no serial correlation is present beyond that lag. There is no evidence of heteroskedasticity in the residuals. And, they are normally distributed as shown in Table A4.50. Figure 4.19 plots the variance decomposition. The variance of oil, however, explains about 70 percent of the variations of the stock of capital, about 80 percent of the variations of labor, and 60 percent of the variation of real GDP. No other factor in the VAR explains the variations of real GDP, and 60 percent of the variance of real GDP is explained by oil (Plot 5.1). It is quite obvious that none of the variables in the VAR explain the variance of human capital, and human capital plays no role in explaining any variable in the VAR. Figure 4.20 plots the estimated permanent income for the UAE.

4.2.11 Venezuela – Baseline Permanent Income Estimate

Venezuela's data are problematic as we explained earlier. We fit a VAR $(k = 5, p = 2)$ from 1970 to 2011 with a constant term. The data from 2012 onward are unusable. Tables A4.51 and A4.52 report the Information Criteria and lag exclusion tests for the determination of the number of lags. When we use the exclusion test we still find the second lag to be insignificant in equations (1) and (5), but we fit two lags to the system. Table A4.53 reports the LM test statistic; Table A4.54 reports the White test statistics; and Table A4.55 reports the normality tests of the residuals. There is serial correlation

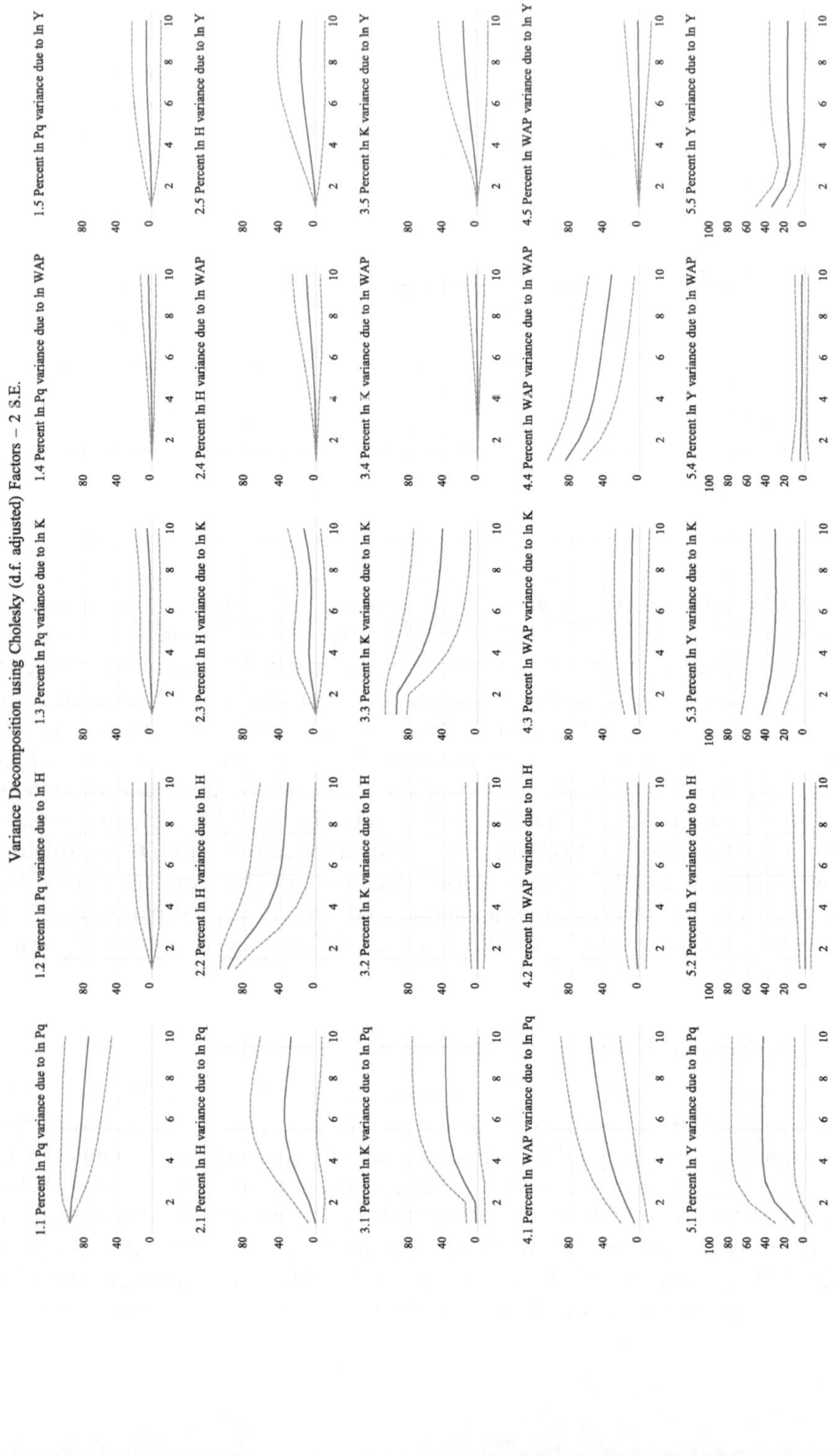

Figure 4.21 Venezuela's Baseline VAR Variance Decomposition

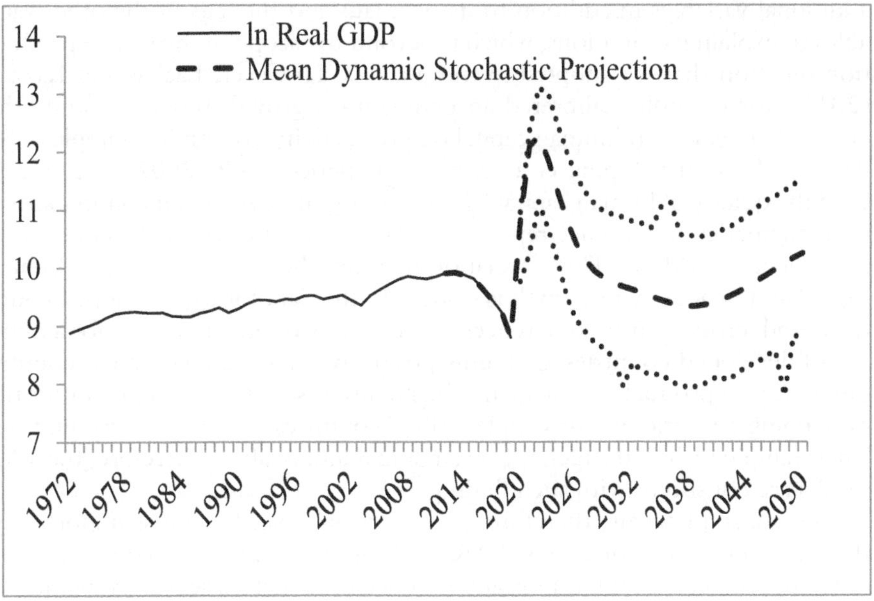

Figure 4.22 Venezuela's Estimated Baseline Permanent Income

at the 1st lag, probably more serial correlation remains at the second lag, which is only marginally significant. There is no evidence of heteroskedasticity in the residuals. And, they are normal as shown in Table A4.55. Figure 4.21 plots the variance decomposition. Very large variations in human capital, the stock of capital, and labor are due to oil (Plots 2.1, 3.1, and 4.1). About 40 percent of the variance of real GDP is due to oil. Figure 4.22 plots our estimate of Venezuela's permanent income. The standard errors are just as volatile as the real GDP projection is because of the sample size and the prevailing trends in Venezuela's economy after 2012. The economy has clearly collapsed in 2012.

4.3 Caveats

The constant terms in all equations of the baseline VARs across countries were statistically significant. The results also indicate that, in many equations, the RHS variables of the baseline VAR equations are statistically insignificant. For example, human capital does not explain real GDP, oil production, and working-age population, or working-age population and the stock of capital do not explain human capital. Therefore, the constant terms in the VARs equations explain more of the variance of the dependent variables and capture the effects of country-specific omitted variables that are not included in each equation. For example, human capital is a complex endogenous variable that requires additional variables in addition to its own lags and the lags of the other variables to explain its variations, which is beyond the scope of the simple production function that we adopted in this analysis. However, Laabas and Razzak (2011), for example, calibrated an endogenous growth model to study the effect of the *quality* of human capital on productivity growth in a sample of 30 developed and developing countries for the period 1980–2007. They measured the quality of human capital by relative cognitive skills and country scores in mathematics and science reported in Trends in International Mathematics and Science (TIMSS). The correlation between the relative quality of human capital and productivity growth is evident in the data for the developed countries. And, cross-country differences in the quality of human capital for a number of developed countries are highly positively associated with cross-country differences in productivity growth. The picture is significantly different for the developing countries in our sample. OPEC countries are developing countries. Their sample included Algeria, Kuwait, and Saudi Arabia. Therefore, the VAR results are consistent with such findings.

The constant terms, therefore, play a crucial role, but most importantly, they influence the projections. VARs without constant terms could result in different projections. It is important to understand that these results are model-specific. The results are specification-sensitive, which is a fact that applies to VARs. Therefore, more models and many more specifications should be used, and for each country differently perhaps, in order to account for robustness. There is always a risk of using one single model in economic analysis. Therefore, 'thick modeling' is necessary for decision-making; in other words, having more than one model to analyze the data. The basic premise of such a decision-making strategy is to spread the risk across models because all model's projections break down at some point in time. In our analysis, we opted to fit the standard model, whereby real GDP is a function of technical progress"and 'actor inputs, to all OPEC countries. These countries, however, are subject to both symmetric and asymmetric shocks. The former are oil price shocks. The asymmetric shocks could dominate and cause the model to fit some countries better or worse than others.

Appendix 4.1 – Residuals Diagnostics of the Baseline VARs

Table A4.1 Algeria's Baseline VAR Lag Length Criteria

Lag	*Log L*	*LR*	*FPE*	*AIC*	*SC*	*HQ*
0	183.3	NA	9.81e-11	−8.8	−8.2	−8.6
1	648.4	734.4	8.79e-21	−32.0	−30.3	−31.4
2	720.5	94.8	8.25e-22	−34.5	−31.7*	−33.5
3	757.9	39.4*	5.60e-22*	−35.1*	−31.3	−33.7*

LR: sequential modified LR test statistic at the 5 percent level;
FPE: final prediction error;
AIC: Akaike Information Criterion;
SC: Schwarz Information Criterion;
HQ: Hannan–Quinn Information Criterion;
The asterisk (*) denotes significant and selected by the criterion.

Table A4.2 Algeria's Baseline VAR Lag Exclusion Test

	lnP_tq_t	lnH_t	lnK_t	$lnWAP_t$	lnY_t	*Joint*
Lag 1	34.2 [0.0000]	79.6 [0.0000]	374.6 [0.0000]	343.9 [0.0000]	59.9 [0.0000]	1057.8 [0.0000]
Lag 2	10.7 [0.0572]	12.9 [0.0237]	91.7 [0.0000]	70.2 [0.0000]	15.8 [0.0075]	241.4 [0.0000]
Degrees of freedom	5	5	5	5	5	25

Wald Chi-squared test statistics for lag exclusion; numbers in square brackets are P-values.

Table A4.3 Algeria LM Test for Serial Correlations in the Residuals of the Baseline VAR

H_0: No Serial Correlation at Lag h

Lag	LRE* Stat	df	P-Value	Rao F-Stat	df	P-Value
1	27.3	25	0.3422	1.1	(25, 60.9)	0.3556
2	41.8	25	0.0187	1.9	(25, 60.9)	0.0213
3	23.3	25	0.5583	0.9	(25, 60.9)	0.5709
			H_0: No Serial Correlation at Lags $1-h$			
Lag	LRE* Stat	df	P-Value	Rao F-Stat	df	P-Value
1	27.3	25	0.3422	1.1	(25, 60.9)	0.3556
2	65.3	50	0.0712	1.4	(50, 53.5)	0.1059
3	99.8	75	0.0290	1.4	(75, 33.0)	0.1369

Asterisk (*): the Edgeworth expansion corrected likelihood ratio statistics.

Table A4.4 Algeria's Test for Heteroskedasticity of the Residuals of the Baseline VAR H_0 : No Heteroskedasticity

Joint Test					
Chi-Sq	*df*	*P-Value*			
318.75	*315*	*0.4305*			
Individual components					
Dependent	R^2	F(21,16)	P-Value	Chi-Sq (21)	P-Value
res1*res1	0.68	1.66	0.1504	26.07	0.2035
res2*res2	0.69	1.73	0.1332	26.38	0.1921
res3*res3	0.65	1.46	0.2220	24.97	0.2485
res4*res4	0.60	1.19	0.3661	23.16	0.3352
res5*res5	0.54	0.90	0.5910	20.63	0.4813
res2*res1	0.79	2.98	0.0148	30.271	0.0866
res3*res1	0.45	0.65	0.8276	17.43	0.6842
res3*res2	0.74	2.28	0.0483	28.49	0.1267
res4*res1	0.60	1.18	0.3708	23.11	0.3381
res4*res2	0.56	0.98	0.5210	21.42	0.4330
res4*res3	0.50	0.76	0.7240	19.00	0.5850
res5*res1	0.61	1.20	0.3548	23.29	0.3284
res5*res2	0.65	1.39	0.2505	24.58	0.2657
res5*res3	0.54	0.90	0.5889	20.66	0.4798
res5*res4	0.53	0.86	0.6248	20.24	0.5059

Table A4.5 Algeria's Test of Normality of the Residuals of the Baseline VAR

Orthogonalization: Cholesky (Lutkepohl)
H_0: Residuals Are Multivariate Normal

Component	Skewness	Chi-Sq	df	P-Value*
1	−0.39	0.99	1	0.3191
2	−0.72	3.28	1	0.0700
3	−0.65	2.75	1	0.0968
4	0.41	1.07	1	0.2989
5	−0.07	0.03	1	0.8528
Joint		8.15	5	0.1483
Component	Kurtosis	Chi-sq	df	P-Value
1	3.19	0.06	1	0.8076
2	4.67	4.45	1	0.0350
3	4.67	4.42	1	0.0356
4	3.51	0.42	1	0.5171
5	2.26	0.85	1	0.3569
Joint		10.2	5	0.0700
Component	Jarque-Bera	df		P-Value
1	1.05	2		0.5910
2	7.73	2		0.0209
3	7.17	2		0.0277
4	1.49	2		0.4727
5	0.88	2		0.6430
Joint	18.33846	10		0.0495

*Approximate P-values do not account for coefficient estimation.

Table A4.6 Angola's Baseline VAR Lag Length Criteria

Lag	*Log L*	*LR*	*FPE*	*AIC*	*SC*	*HQ*
0	163.9	NA	1.60e-10	–8.4	–8.1	–8.3
1	574.3	691.2	2.52e-19	–28.6	–27.3	–28.2
2	659.8	121.4*	1.12e-20	–31.8	–29.5*	–30.9*
3	690.4	35.4	1.01e-20*	–32.1*	–28.6	–30.9

LR: sequential modified LR test statistic at the 5 percent level;
FPE: final prediction error;
AIC: Akaike Information Criterion;
SC: Schwarz Information Criterion;
HQ: Hannan–Quinn Information Criterion;
The asterisk (*) denotes significant and selected by the criterion.

Table A4.7 Angola's Baseline VAR Lag Exclusion Test

	lnP_tq_t	lnH_t	lnK_t	$lnWAP_t$	lnY_t	*Joint*
Lag 1	24.0	198.7	173. 3	697.6	103.9	1218.1
	[0.0002]	[0.0000]	[0.0000]	[0.0000]	[0.0000]	[0.0000]
Lag 2	6.9	44.8	63.7	160.9	28.2	322.7
	[0.2258]	[0.0000]	[0.0000]	[0.0000]	[0.0000]	[0.0000]
Degrees of freedom	5	5	5	5	5	25

Wald Chi-squared test statistics for lag exclusion; numbers in square brackets are P-values.

Table A4.8 Angola LM Test for Serial Correlations in the Residuals of the Baseline VAR H_0: No Serial Correlation at Lag h

Lag	*LRE* Stat*	*df*	*P-Value*	*Rao F-Stat*	*df*	*P-Value*
1	28.3	25	0.2952	1.2	(25, 68.4)	0.3059
2	19.83	25	0.7547	0.7	(25, 68.4)	0.7619
3	26.03	25	0.4059	1.02	(25, 68.4)	0.4171

Asterisk (*): the Edgeworth expansion corrected likelihood ratio statistics.

Table A4.9 Angola's Test for Heteroskedasticity of the Residuals of the Baseline VAR H_0 : No Heteroskedasticity

		Joint Test			
Chi-Sq	*df*	*P-Value*			
308.9	*285*	*0.1581*			
		Individual Components			
Dependent	R^2	F(19,18)	P-Value	Chi-sq(19)	P-Value
res1*res1	0.43	0.71	0.7644	16.32	0.6358
res2*res2	0.67	1.94	0.0830	25.53	0.1437
res3*res3	0.75	2.86	0.0150	28.56	0.0732
res4*res4	0.75	2.78	0.0172	28.36	0.0767

(*Continued*)

Table A4.9 (Continued)

Dependent	R^2	F(19,18)	P-Value	Chi-sq(19)	P-Value
res5*res5	0.68	2.05	0.0675	25.97	0.1308
res2*res1	0.62	1.55	0.1793	23.57	0.2129
res3*res1	0.46	0.82	0.6633	17.65	0.5461
res3*res2	0.71	2.35	0.0383	27.06	0.1031
res4*res1	0.36	0.54	0.9022	13.84	0.7929
res4*res2	0.39	0.63	0.8358	15.19	0.7100
res4*res3	0.27	0.35	0.9846	10.37	0.9431
res5*res1	0.47	0.86	0.6271	18.08	0.5170
res5*res2	0.53	1.09	0.4285	20.34	0.3745
res5*res3	0.61	1.53	0.1859	23.47	0.2173
res5*res4	0.62	1.58	0.1658	23.80	0.2038

Table A4.10 Angola's Test of Normality of the Residuals of the Baseline VAR

Orthogonalization: Cholesky (Lutkepohl) HO: Residuals Are Multivariate Normal

Component	Skewness	Chi-Sq	df	P-Value*
1	−0.49	1.55	1	0.2132
2	1.05	6.97	1	0.0083
3	0.17	0.19	1	0.6617
4	−0.28	0.49	1	0.4823
5	−0.75	3.61	1	0.0574
Joint		12.81	5	0.0252
Component	**Kurtosis**	**Chi-Sq**	**df**	**P-Value**
1	2.36	0.65	1	0.4185
2	7.24	28.49	1	0.0000
3	2.66	0.18	1	0.6663
4	3.45	0.39	1	0.5296
5	5.16	7.41	1	0.0065
Joint		37.14	5	0.0000
Component	**Jarque-Bera**	**df**	**P-Value**	
1	2.20	2	0.3322	
2	35.46	2	0.0000	
3	0.37	2	0.8280	
4	0.88	2	0.6412	
5	11.02	2	0.0040	
Joint	49.96	10	0.0000	

Approximate P-values do not account for coefficient estimation.

Table A4.11 Congo's Baseline VAR Lag Length Criteria

Lag	*Log L*	*LR*	*FPE*	*AIC*	*SC*	*HQ*
0	160.0	NA	9.77e-11	−8.8	−8.6	−8.7
1	498.6	561.0	1.64e-18	−26.7	−25.4	−26.3
2	547.7	67.3	4.55e-19	−28.1	−25.7	−27.3
3	592.4	48.5*	1.90e-19*	−29.2*	−25.7*	−28.0*

LR: sequential modified LR test statistic at the 5 percent level;
FPE: final prediction error;
AIC: Akaike Information Criterion;
SC: Schwarz Information Criterion;
HQ: Hannan–Quinn Information Criterion;
The asterisk (*) denotes significant and selected by the criterion.

Table A4.12 Congo's Baseline VAR Lag Exclusion Test

	lnP_tq_t	lnH_t	lnK_t	$lnWAP_t$	lnY_t	*Joint*
Lag 1	16.7 [0.0051]	82.1 [0.0000]	132.1 [0.0000]	91.6 [0.0000]	66.4 [0.0000]	420.8 [0.0000]
Lag 2	10.2 [0.0700]	19.92 [0.0013]	32.8 [0.0000]	16.9 [0.0047]	15.6 [0.0078]	112.2 [0.0000]
Degrees of freedom	5	5	5	5	5	25

Wald Chi-squared test statistics for lag exclusion; numbers in square brackets are P-values.

Table A4.13 Congo LM Test for Serial Correlations in the Residuals of the Baseline VAR H_0: No Serial Correlation at Lag h

Lag	*LRE* Stat*	*df*	*P-Value*	*Rao F-Stat*	*df*	*P-Value*
1	51.1	25	0.0015	2.5	(25, 57.2)	0.0019
2	43.2	25	0.0133	2.0	(25, 57.2)	0.0156
3	16.4	25	0.9033	0.6	(25, 57.2)	0.9079
4	13.4	25	0.9740	0.50	(25, 57.2)	0.9754

Asterisk (*): the Edgeworth expansion corrected likelihood ratio statistics.

Table A4.14 Congo's Test for Heteroskedasticity of the Residuals of the Baseline VAR H_0 : No Heteroskedasticity

			Joint Test		
Chi-Sq	*df*	*P-Value*			
348.3	*300*	*0.0285*			
			Individual Components		
Dependent	*R²*	*F(20,14)*	*P-Value*	*Chi-Sq (20)*	*P-Value*
res1*res1	0.64	1.24	0.3490	22.33	0.3228
res2*res2	0.89	6.26	0.0005	31.47	0.0492
res3*res3	0.60	1.09	0.4415	21.33	0.3779
res4*res4	0.64	1.27	0.3271	22.57	0.3101
res5*res5	0.75	2.09	0.0796	26.25	0.1577
res2*res1	0.80	2.85	0.0248	28.09	0.1071
res3*res1	0.70	1.67	0.1631	24.68	0.2138
res3*res2	0.75	2.08	0.0819	26.19	0.1595
res4*res1	0.56	0.89	0.5999	19.63	0.4811
res4*res2	0.86	4.40	0.0033	30.19	0.0667
res4*res3	0.73	1.91	0.1086	25.62	0.1786
res5*res1	0.56	0.91	0.5823	19.83	0.4688
res5*res2	0.88	5.10	0.0016	30.78	0.0582
res5*res3	0.62	1.17	0.3856	21.93	0.3443
res5*res4	0.64	1.27	0.3283	22.56	0.3108

Table A4.15 Congo's Test of Normality of the Residuals of the Baseline VAR

Component	*Skewness*	*Chi-Sq*	*df*	*P-Value**
1	–0.80	3.78	1	0.0519
2	–0.97	5.52	1	0.0188
3	1.52	13.36	1	0.0003
4	0.16	0.16	1	0.6863
5	–0.70	2.90	1	0.0883
Joint		25.73	5	0.0001
Component	Kurtosis	Chi-Sq	df	P-Value
1	2.71	0.12	1	0.7268
2	4.82	4.83	1	0.0280
3	7.03	23.74	1	0.0000
4	4.69	4.20	1	0.0404
5	2.91	0.01	1	0.9170
Joint		32.90	5	0.0000
Component	Jarque-Bera	df	P-Value	
1	3.90	2	0.1421	
2	10.35	2	0.0057	
3	37.10	2	0.0000	
4	4.36	2	0.1128	
5	2.91	2	0.2328	
Joint	58.63	10	0.0000	

Approximate P-values do not account for coefficient estimation.

Table A4.16 Gabon's Baseline VAR Lag Length Criteria

Lag	*Log L*	*LR*	*FPE*	*AIC*	*SC*	*HQ*
0	123.7	NA	3.52e-09	–5.3	–5.0	–5.2
1	628.8	875.5	1.92e-18	–26.6	–25.4	–26.1
2	731.4	155.0	6.36e-20	–30.0	–27.8	–29.2
3	801.6	90.5*	9.53e-21*	–32.0*	–28.8*	–30.8*

LR: sequential modified LR test statistic at the 5percent level;
FPE: final prediction error;
AIC: Akaike Information Criterion;
SC: Schwarz Information Criterion;
HQ: Hannan–Quinn Information Criterion;
The asterisk (*) denotes significant and selected by the criterion.

Table A4.17 Gabon's Baseline VAR Lag Exclusion Test

	lnP_tq_t	lnH_t	lnK_t	$lnWAP_t$	lnY_t	*Joint*
Lag 1	57.6 [0.0000]	96.6 [0.0000]	127.5 [0.0000]	1897.2 [0.0000]	35.5 [0.0000]	3329.0 [0.0000]
Lag 2	22.3 [0.0004]	12.6 [0.0275]	27.6 [0.0000]	524.0 [0.0000]	13.7 [0.0172]	929.0 [0.0000]
Degrees of freedom	5	5	5	5	5	25

Wald Chi-squared test statistics for lag exclusion; numbers in square brackets are P-values.

Table A4.18 Gabon LM Test for Serial Correlations in the Residuals of the Baseline VAR H_0: No Serial Correlation at Lag h

Lag	*LRE* Stat*	*df*	*P-Value*	*Rao F-Stat*	*df*	*P-Value*
1	83.3	25	0.0000	4.5	(25, 94.4)	0.0000
2	39.1	25	0.0357	1.7	(25, 94.4)	0.0375
3	25.6	25	0.4278	1.0	(25, 94.4)	0.4341

Asterisk: the Edgeworth expansion corrected likelihood ratio statistics.

Table A4.19 Gabon's Test for Heteroskedasticity of the Residuals of the Baseline VAR H_0 : No Heteroskedasticity

Joint Test

Chi-Sq	*df*	*P-Value*
361.5	*285*	*0.0014*

Individual Components

Dependent	R^2	F(19,25)	P-Value	Chi-Sq (19)	P-Value
res1*res1	0.38	0.83	0.6519	17.48	0.5574
res2*res2	0.76	4.24	0.0005	34.35	0.0167
res3*res3	0.63	2.24	0.0296	28.37	0.0765
res4*res4	0.68	2.84	0.0078	30.75	0.0430
res5*res5	0.72	3.48	0.0020	32.65	0.0264
res2*res1	0.62	2.17	0.0353	28.00	0.0832
res3*res1	0.69	3.02	0.0052	31.35	0.0369
res3*res2	0.80	5.59	0.0000	36.44	0.0093
res4*res1	0.53	1.46	0.1829	23.72	0.2071
res4*res2	0.61	2.11	0.0401	27.74	0.0885
res4*res3	0.59	1.91	0.0645	26.66	0.1128
res5*res1	0.73	3.66	0.0014	33.10	0.0234
res5*res2	0.86	7.94	0.0000	38.60	0.0050
res5*res3	0.72	3.44	0.0022	32.54	0.0271
res5*res4	0.68	2.87	0.0071	30.88	0.0416

Table A4.20 Gabon's Test of Normality of the Residuals of the Baseline VAR

Component	*Skewness*	*Chi-Sq*	*df*	*P-Value**
1	−0.8	5.3	1	0.0215
2	1.5	17.0	1	0.0000
3	0.0	0.0	1	0.7903
4	0.2	0.4	1	0.5432
5	−0.4	1.3	1	0.2522
Joint		24.0	5	0.0002
Component	Kurtosis	Chi-sq	df	P-Value
1	2.7	0.1	1	0.6895
2	5.7	13.5	1	0.0002
3	2.9	0.0	1	0.8942
4	3.0	0.0	1	0.9485
5	3.5	0.5	1	0.4951
Joint		14.1	5	0.0146

(*Continued*)

Table A4.20 (Continued)

Component	*Skewness*	*Chi-Sq*	*df*	*P-Value**
Component	Jarque-Bera	df	P-Value	
1	5.4	2	0.0658	
2	30.5	2	0.0000	
3	0.0	2	0.9568	
4	0.4	2	0.8296	
5	1.7	2	0.4114	
Joint	38.2	10	0.0000	

Approximate P-values do not account for coefficient estimation.

Table A4.21 Iran's Baseline VAR Lag Length Criteria

Lag	*Log L*	*LR*	*FPE*	*AIC*	*SC*	*HQ*
1	560.6	NA	3.97e-19	–28.2	–27.1*	–27.8
2	596.6	53.1	2.34e-19	–28.7	–26.6	–28.0
3	631.5	42.1*	1.64e-19*	–29.3*	–26.0	–28.1*

LR: sequential modified LR test statistic at the 5percent level;
FPE: final prediction error;
AIC: Akaike Information Criterion;
SC: Schwarz Information Criterion;
HQ: Hannan–Quinn Information Criterion;
The asterisk denotes significant and selected by the criterion.

Table A4.22 Iran's Baseline VAR Lag Exclusion Test

	lnP_tq_t	lnH_t	lnK_t	$lnWAP_t$	lnY_t	*Joint*
Lag 1	15.2	51.3	175.9	141.4	42.1	446.4
	[0.0093]	[0.0000]	[0.0000]	[0.0000]	[0.0000]	[0.0000]
Lag 2	2.2	7.5	24. 7	18.8	20.6	76.4
	[0.8192]	[0.1834]	[0.0002]	[0.0021]	[0.0009]	[0.0000]
Degrees of freedom	5	5	5	5	5	25

Wald Chi-squared test statistics for lag exclusion; numbers in square brackets are P-values.

Table A4.23 Iran LM Test for Serial Correlations in the Residuals of the Baseline VAR H_0: No Serial Correlation at Lag h

Lag	*LRE* Stat*	*df*	*P-Value*	*Rao F-Stat*	*df*	*P-Value*
1	36.0	25	0.0706	1.5	(25, 72.1)	0.0754
2	28.9	25	0.2679	1.2	(25, 72.1)	0.2774
3	27.1	25	0.3486	1.1	(25, 72.1)	0.3587

Asterisk: the Edgeworth expansion corrected likelihood ratio statistics.

Table A4.24 Iran's Test for Heteroskedasticity of the Residuals of the Baseline VAR H_0 : No Heteroskedasticity

Joint Test		
Chi-sq	*df*	*P-Value*
344.3	*300*	*0.0397*

Individual Components

Dependent	R^2	F(20,17)	P-Value	Chi-Sq (20)	P-Value
res1*res1	0.44	0.66	0.8087	16.69	0.6725
res2*res2	0.864	5.23	0.0006	32.69	0.0365
res3*res3	0.684	1.87	0.0978	26.14	0.1611
res4*res4	0.574	1.13	0.4006	21.71	0.3561
res5*res5	0.704	2.06	0.0688	26.89	0.1382
res2*res1	0.59	1.22	0.3415	22.40	0.3189
res3*res1	0.59	1.26	0.3156	22.72	0.3028
res3*res2	0.85	4.86	0.0009	32.35	0.0397
res4*res1	0.58	1.18	0.3667	22.10	0.3347
res4*res2	0.38	0.52	0.9144	14.54	0.8022
res4*res3	0.72	2.17	0.0552	27.33	0.1262
res5*res1	0.58	1.17	0.3705	22.06	0.3371
res5*res2	0.63	1.44	0.2226	23.94	0.2449
res5*res3	0.79	3.39	0.0069	30.39	0.0637
res5*res4	0.73	2.32	0.0417	27.84	0.1133

Table A4.25 Iran's Test of Normality of the Residuals of the Baseline VAR

Component	*Skewness*	*Chi-Sq*	*df*	*P-Value**
1	−0.63	2.57	1	0.1086
2	0.07	0.03	1	0.8517
3	−0.25	0.38	1	0.5338
4	−0.85	4.57	1	0.0324
5	0.16	0.17	1	0.6758
Joint		7.75	5	0.1708
Component	Kurtosis	Chi-Sq	df	P-Value
1	2.56	0.30	1	0.5787
2	3.39	0.24	1	0.6243
3	3.12	0.02	1	0.8829
4	4.57	3.92	1	0.0477
5	3.27	0.12	1	0.7286
Joint		4.61	5	0.4651
Component	Jarque-Bera	df	P-Value	
1	2.88	2	0.2366	
2	0.27	2	0.8716	
3	0.40	2	0.8151	
4	8.49	2	0.0143	
5	0.29	2	0.8627	
Joint	12.35	10	0.2618	

Approximate P-values do not account for coefficient estimation.

Table A4.26 Iraq's Baseline VAR Lag Length Criteria

Lag	*Log L*	*LR*	*FPE*	*AIC*	*SC*	*HQ*
0	44.8	NA	2.92e-07	−0.8	0.1	−0.5
1	486.7	691.7	4.03e-15	−18.9	−17.0	−18.2
2	566.6	107.6*	4.05e-16*	−21.4	−18. 4*	−20.2*
3	592.2	28.9	4.76e-16	−21.4	−17.4	−19.9
4	621.1	26.4	5.68e-16	−21.6*	−16.6	−19.7

LR: sequential modified LR test statistic at the 5percent level;
FPE: final prediction error;
AIC: Akaike Information Criterion;
SC: Schwarz Information Criterion;
HQ: Hannan–Quinn Information Criterion;
The asterisk denotes significant and selected by the criterion.

Table A4.27 Iraq's Baseline VAR Lag Exclusion Test

	lnp_t	lnH_t	lnK_t	$lnWAP_t$	lnY_t	*Joint*
Lag 1	13.9	405.1	71.2	475.1	16. 2	1106.3
	[0.0156]	[0.0000]	[0.0000]	[0.0000]	[0.0064]	[0.0000]
Lag 2	1.7	78.7	19.6	108.5	0.6	259.2
	[0.8822]	[0.0000]	[0.0015]	[0.0000]	[0.9891]	[0.0000]
Degrees of freedom	5	5	5	5	5	25

Wald Chi-squared test statistics for lag exclusion; numbers in square brackets are P-values.

Table A4.28 Iraq LM Test for Serial Correlations in the Residuals of the Baseline VAR H_0 : No Serial Correlation at Lag $1-h$

Lag	*LRE* Stat*	*df*	*P-Value*	*Rao F-Stat*	*df*	*P-Value*
1	25.6	25	0.4260	1.0	(25, 90.7)	0.4328
2	31. 5	25	0.1733	1.3	(25, 90.7)	0.1787
3	18.2	25	0.8327	0.7	(25, 90.7)	0.8360

Asterisk: the Edgeworth expansion corrected likelihood ratio statistics.

Table A4.29 Iraq's Test for Heteroskedasticity of the Residuals of the Baseline VAR H_0 : No Heteroskedasticity

		Joint Test			
Chi-Sq	*df*	*P-Value*			
365.0	*360*	*0.4157*			
		Individual Components			
Dependent	R-Squared	F(24,23)	P-Value	Chi-Sq (24)	P-Value
res1*res1	0.67	1.92	0.0610	32.02678	0.1263
res2*res2	0.53	1.05	0.4501	25.15	0.3975

(*Continued*)

Table A4.29 (Continued)

Dependent	R-Squared	F(24,23)	P-Value	Chi-Sq (24)	P-Value
res3*res3	0.74	2.68	0.0103	35.38	0.0629
res4*res4	0.45	0.77	0.7264	21.52	0.6079
res5*res5	0.73	2.62	0.0119	35.16	0.0661
res2*res1	0.58	1.33	0.2478	27.91	0.2638
res3*res1	0.82	4.27	0.0004	39.21	0.0259
res3*res2	0.58	1.34	0.2409	28.01	0.2593
res4*res1	0.49	0.93	0.5671	23.68	0.4800
res4*res2	0.22	0.27	0.9987	10.68	0.9911
res4*res3	0.41	0.67	0.8292	19.80	0.7080
res5*res1	0.72	2.54	0.0142	34.86	0.0704
res5*res2	0.61	1.52	0.1584	29.46	0.2031
res5*res3	0.78	3.50	0.0018	37.69	0.0373
res5*res4	0.71	2.42	0.0188	34.39	0.0780

Table A4.30 Iraq's Test of Normality of the Residuals of the Baseline VAR

Component	*Skewness*	*Chi-Sq*	*df*	*P-Value**
1	-1.5	18.6	1	0.0000
2	1.0	8.5	1	0.0036
3	0.1	0.2	1	0.6379
4	0.0	0.0	1	0.8632
5	−0.8	5.4	1	0.0196
Joint		32.8	5	0.0000
Component	Kurtosis	Chi-Sq	df	P-Value
1	9.3	79.7	1	0.0000
2	6.2	20.5	1	0.0000
3	4.0	2.3	1	0.1258
4	6.1	19. 4	1	0.0000
5	3.8	1.3	1	0.2478
Joint		123.3	5	0.0000
Component	Jarque-Bera	df	P-Value	
1	98.4	2	0.0000	
2	29.0	2	0.0000	
3	2.6	2	0.2773	
4	19.4	2	0.0001	
5	6.7	2	0.0337	
Joint	156.1	10	0.0000	

Approximate P-values do not account for coefficient estimation.

Table A4.31 Kuwait's Baseline VAR Lag Length Criteria

Lag	*Log L*	*LR*	*FPE*	*AIC*	*SC*	*HQ*
0	134.2	NA	1.18e-09	−6.4	−5.9	−6.2
1	400.9	437.7	4.97e-15	−18.7	−17.3*	−18.2
2	446.3	62.87*	1.90e-15*	−19.8*	−17.2	−18.9*
3	467.3	23.77	2.87e-15	−19.6	−15.9	−18.3

LR: sequential modified LR test statistic at the 5percent level;
FPE: final prediction error;
AIC: Akaike Information Criterion;
SC: Schwarz Information Criterion;
HQ: Hannan–Quinn Information Criterion;
The asterisk denotes significant and selected by the criterion.

Table A4.32 Kuwait's Baseline VAR Lag Exclusion Test

	lnP_tq_t	lnH_t	lnK_t	$lnWAP_t$	lnY_t	*Joint*
Lag 1	36.7	87.3	187.4	54.2	62.4	385.7
	[0.0000]	[0.0000]	[0.0000]	[0.0000]	[0.0000]	[0.0000]
Lag 2	12.3	16.7	31.7	30.6	28.8	99.3
	[0.0308]	[0.0051]	[0.0000]	[0.0000]	[0.0000]	[0.0000]
Degrees of freedom	5	5	5	5	5	25

Wald Chi-squared test statistics for lag exclusion; numbers in square brackets are P-values.

Table A4.33 Kuwait LM Test for Serial Correlations in the Residuals of the Baseline VAR H_0 : No Serial Correlation at Lag h

Lag	*LRE* Stat*	*df*	*P-Value*	*Rao F-Stat*	*df*	*P-Value*
1	25.7	25	0.4200	1.0	(25, 68.4)	0.4312
2	25.2	25	0.4501	1.0	(25, 68.4)	0.4611
3	29.6	25	0.2390	1.2	(25, 68.4)	0.2490

Asterisk: the Edgeworth expansion corrected likelihood ratio statistics.

Table A4.34 Kuwait's Test for Heteroskedasticity of the Residuals of the Baseline VAR H_0 : No Heteroskedasticity

		Joint Test			
Chi-Sq	*df*	*P-Value*			
321.8	*315*	*0.3827*			
		Individual Components			
Dependent	R^2	F(21,17)	P-Value	Chi-Sq (21)	P-Value
res1*res1	0.67	1.68	0.1405	26.32	0.1945
res2*res2	0.74	2.38	0.0369	29.11	0.1113
res3*res3	0.63	1.36	0.2601	24.47	0.2706
res4*res4	0.77	2.72	0.0200	30.07	0.0906
res5*res5	0.72	2.12	0.0599	28.24	0.1337
res2*res1	0.62	1.34	0.2696	24.35	0.2764
res3*res1	0.76	2.56	0.0269	29.62	0.0998
res3*res2	0.44	0.66	0.8208	17.47	0.6822
res4*res1	0.68	1.76	0.1200	26.72	0.1803
res4*res2	0.75	2.36	0.0385	29.04	0.1130
res4*res3	0.68	1.74	0.1259	26.60	0.1845
res5*res1	0.74	2.36	0.0385	29.04	0.1130
res5*res2	0.47	0.73	0.7527	18.53	0.6151
res5*res3	0.66	1.59	0.1670	25.85	0.2121
res5*res4	0.49	0.77	0.7168	19.03	0.5833

Table A4.35 Kuwait's Test of Normality of the Residuals of the Baseline VAR

Component	*Skewness*	*Chi-Sq*	*df*	*P-Value**
1	−0.6	2.8	1	0.0908
2	−0.5	1.6	1	0.2084
3	−0.4	0.9	1	0.3296
4	−1.6	17.6	1	0.0000
5	−0.09	0.0	1	0.8104
Joint		23.0	5	0.0003
Component	Kurtosis	Chi-sq	df	P-Value
1	3.4	0.2	1	0.6651
2	3.9	1.3	1	0.2578
3	3.7	0.7	1	0.3961
4	8.9	57.6	1	0.0000
5	5.8	12.8	1	0.0003
Joint		72.6	5	0.0000
Component	Jarque-Bera	Df	P-Value	
1	3.0	2	0.2178	
2	2.8	2	0.2389	
3	1.7	2	0.4337	
4	75.2	2	0.0000	
5	12.8	2	0.0016	
Joint	95.6	10	0.0000	

Approximate P-values do not account for coefficient estimation.

Table A4.36 Nigeria's Baseline VAR Lag Length Criteria

Lag	*Log L*	*LR*	*FPE*	*AIC*	*SC*	*HQ*
0	246.5	NA	6.98e-13	−13.8	−13.6	−13.76
1	596.2	579.5	6.22e-21	−32.3	−31.06	−31.9
2	650.2	74.1*	1.30e-21	−34.0	−31.6*	−33.2*
3	681.5	33. 9	1.17e-21*	−34.4*	−30.86	−33.1

LR: sequential modified LR test statistic at the 5percent level;
FPE: final prediction error;
AIC: Akaike Information Criterion;
SC: Schwarz Information Criterion;
HQ: Hannan–Quinn Information Criterion;
The asterisk denotes significant and selected by the criterion.

Table A4.37 Nigeria's Baseline VAR Lag Exclusion Test

	lnP_tq_t	lnH_t	lnK_t	$lnWAP_t$	lnY_t	*Joint*
Lag 1	32.6 [0.0000]	167.7 [0.0000]	33.0 [0.0000]	275.0 [0.0000]	72.3 [0.0000]	546.8 [0.0000]
Lag 2	9. 7 [0.0842]	63.8 [0.0000]	2.8 [0.7224]	62.9 [0.0000]	16.8 [0.0047]	162.0 [0.0000]
Degrees of freedom	5	5	5	5	5	25

Wald Chi-squared test statistics for lag exclusion; numbers in square brackets are P-values.

Table A4.38 Nigeria LM Test for Serial Correlations in the Residuals of the Baseline VAR H_0 : No Serial Correlation at Lag h

Lag	*LRE* Stat*	*df*	*P-Value*	*Rao F-Stat*	*df*	*P-Value*
1	35.9	25	0.0726	1.6	(25, 57.2)	0.0799
2	37.3	25	0.0542	1.6	(25, 57.2)	0.0603
3	34.8	25	0.0917	1.5	(25, 57.2)	0.1002

Asterisk: the Edgeworth expansion corrected likelihood ratio statistics.

Table A4.39 Nigeria's Test for Heteroskedasticity of the Residuals of the Baseline VAR H_0 : No Heteroskedasticity

Joint Test					
Chi-Sq	*df*	*P-Value*			
319.2	*285*	*0.0798*			
Individual Components					
Dependent	R^2	F(19,15)	P-Value	Chi-Sq (19)	P-Value
res1*res1	0.49	0.78	0.6922	17.48	0.5573
res2*res2	0.92	9.44	0.0000	32.30	0.0289
res3*res3	0.54	0.94	0.5527	19.07	0.4521
res4*res4	0.69	1.74	0.1412	24.06	0.1939
res5*res5	0.72	2.00	0.0878	25.12	0.1566
res2*res1	0.69	1.76	0.1345	24.17	0.1895
res3*res1	0.74	2.29	0.0535	26.05	0.1287
res3*res2	0.53	0.89	0.5943	18.62	0.4816
res4*res1	0.54	0.94	0.5550	19.05	0.4537
res4*res2	0.55	0.95	0.5478	19.13	0.4487
res4*res3	0.36	0.45	0.9481	12.74	0.8517
res5*res1	0.84	4.29	0.0031	29.57	0.0575
res5*res2	0.73	2.16	0.0673	25.64	0.1406
res5*res3	0.50	0.79	0.6844	17.57	0.5509
res5*res4	0.64	1.44	0.2400	22.59410	0.2557

Table A4.40 Nigeria's Test of Normality of the Residuals of the Baseline VAR

Component	*Skewness*	*Chi-Sq*	*df*	*P-Value**
1	−0.67	2.6	1	0.1048
2	0.21	0.26	1	0.6117
3	0.65	2.49	1	0.1143
4	0.12	0.09	1	0.7600
5	−0.09	0.05	1	0.8156
Joint		5.53	5	0.3548
Component	Kurtosis	Chi-Sq	df	P-Value
1	2.91	0.01	1	0.9174
2	5.25	7.42	1	0.0064
3	3.69	0.71	1	0.3989

(*Continued*)

Table A4.40 (Continued)

Component	Kurtosis	Chi-Sq	df	P-Value
4	2.63	0.19	1	0.6598
5	2.28	0.74	1	0.3890
Joint		9.083	5	0.1057

Component	Jarque-Bera	df	P-Value
1	2.64	2	0.2670
2	7.68	2	0.0214
3	3.20	2	0.2014
4	0.29	2	0.8663
5	0.79	2	0.6715
Joint	14.61	10	0.1468

Approximate P-values do not account for coefficient estimation.

Table A4.41 Saudi Arabia's Baseline VAR Lag Length Criteria

Lag	*Log L*	*LR*	*FPE*	*AIC*	*SC*	*HQ*
0	159.3	NA	5.07e-10	−7.2	−6.56	−6.9
1	569.6	656.5	2.23e-18	−26.5	−24.8	−25.9
2	654.9	115.1	1.20e-19	−29.5	−26.78*	−28.5
3	694.3	43.3*	7.34e-20*	−30.2*	−26.48	−28.8*

LR: sequential modified LR test statistic at the 5percent level;
FPE: final prediction error;
AIC: Akaike Information Criterion;
SC: Schwarz Information Criterion;
HQ: Hannan–Quinn Information Criterion;
The asterisk denotes significant and selected by the criterion.

Table A4.42 Saudi Arabia's Baseline VAR Lag Exclusion Test

	lnP_tq_t	lnH_t	lnK_t	$lnWAP_t$	lnY_t	*Joint*
Lag 1	107.5 [0.0000]	386.86 [0.0000]	505.6 [0.0000]	390.9 [0.0000]	50.9 [0.0000]	1346.9 [0.0000]
Lag 2	22.6 [0.0004]	71.7 [0.0000]	44.76 [0.0000]	109.5 [0.0000]	7.7 [0.1704]	288.8 [0.0000]
Degrees of freedom	5	5	5	5	5	25

Wald Chi-squared test statistics for lag exclusion; numbers in square brackets are P-values.

Table A4.43 Saudi Arabia LM Test for Serial Correlations in the Residuals of the Baseline VAR H_0 : No Serial Correlation at Lag h

Lag	*LRE* Stat*	*df*	*P-Value*	*Rao F-Stat*	*df*	*P-Value*
1	26.0	25	0.4071	1.0	(25, 68.4)	0.4183
2	29.5	25	0.2431	1.2	(25, 68.4)	0.2532
3	24.7	25	0.4788	0.9	(25, 68.4)	0.4897

Asterisk: the Edgeworth expansion corrected likelihood ratio statistics.

Table A4.44 Saudi Arabia's Test for Heteroskedasticity of the Residuals of the Baseline VAR H_0 : No Heteroskedasticity

Joint Test					
Chi-Sq	*df*	*P-Value*			
314.4	*330*	*0.7225*			
Individual Components					
Dependent	R^2	F(22,17)	P-Value	Chi-Sq (22)	P-Value
res1*res1	0.44	0.61	0.8579	17.75	0.7207
res2*res2	0.78	2.78	0.0177	31.30	0.0901
res3*res3	0.57	1.02	0.4913	22.75	0.4158
res4*res4	0.75	2.31	0.0409	29.99	0.1187
res5*res5	0.87	5.27	0.0005	34.89	0.0398
res2*res1	0.41	0.55	0.9064	16.63	0.7833
res3*res1	0.49	0.76	0.7284	19.86	0.5913
res3*res2	0.75	2.37	0.0366	30.18	0.1141
res4*res1	0.20	0.19	0.9997	8.12	0.9968
res4*res2	0.32	0.36	0.9872	12.70	0.9411
res4*res3	0.38	0.48	0.9455	15.37	0.8456
res5*res1	0.59	1.15	0.3893	23.92	0.3513
res5*res2	0.88	5.64	0.0003	35.18	0.0371
res5*res3	0.82	3.62	0.0045	32.96	0.0624
res5*res4	0.47	0.69	0.7928	18.91	0.6507

Table A4.45 Saudi Arabia's Test of Normality of the Residuals of the Baseline VAR

Component	*Skewness*	*Chi-Sq*	*df*	*P-Value**
1	−0.53	1.90	1	0.1677
2	−0.30	0.60	1	0.4352
3	−0.20	0.27	1	0.5976
4	0.46	1.41	1	0.2350
5	0.09	0.06	1	0.8051
Joint		4.26	5	0.5124
Component	Kurtosis	Chi-Sq	df	P-Value
1	2.69	0.15	1	0.6978
2	4.73	5.01	1	0.0251
3	2.49	0.42	1	0.5138
4	4.99	6.63	1	0.0100
5	2.67	0.17	1	0.6763
Joint		12.39	5	0.0297
Component	Jarque-Bera	df	P-Value	
1	2.05	2	0.3581	
2	5.62	2	0.0600	
3	0.70	2	0.7029	
4	8.04	2	0.0179	
5	0.23	2	0.8891	
Joint	16.66	10	0.0822	

Approximate P-values do not account for coefficient estimation.

Table A4.46 UAE's Baseline VAR Lag Length Criteria

Lag	*Log L*	*LR*	*FPE*	*AIC*	*SC*	*HQ*
0	106.6	NA	2.06e-09	–5.8	–5.6	–5.7
1	432.1	539.3	7.33e-17	–22.9	–21.6	–22.5
2	507.5	103.3*	4.53e-18*	–25.8	–23.4*	–25.0*
3	533.1	27.8	5.63e-18	–25. 9*	–22.3	–24.6

LR: sequential modified LR test statistic at the 5percent level;
FPE: final prediction error;
AIC: Akaike Information Criterion;
SC: Schwarz Information Criterion;
HQ: Hannan–Quinn Information Criterion;
The asterisk denotes significant and selected by the criterion.

Table A4.47 UAE's Baseline VAR Lag Exclusion Test

	lnP_tq_t	lnH_t	lnK_t	$lnWAP_t$	lnY_t	*Joint*
Lag 1	16.6	386.6	148.2	504.7	18.7	1094.4
	[0.0053]	[0.0000]	[0.0000]	[0.0000]	[0.0021]	[0.0000]
Lag 2	4.5	89.9	23.2	124.6	2.9	290.7
	[0.4727]	[0.0000]	[0.0003]	[0.0000]	[0.7165]	[0.0000]
Degrees of freedom	5	5	5	5	5	25

Wald Chi-squared test statistics for lag exclusion; numbers in square brackets are P-values.

Table A4.48 UAE LM Test for Serial Correlations in the Residuals of the Baseline VAR H_0 : No Serial Correlation at Lag *h*

Lag	*LRE* Stat*	*df*	*P-Value*	*Rao F-Stat*	*df*	*P-Value*
1	40.9	25	0.0231	1.8	(25, 57.2)	0.0264
2	28.3	25	0.2952	1.1	(25, 57.2)	0.3097
3	23.6	25	0.5385	0.9	(25, 57.2)	0.5527

The Edgeworth expansion corrected likelihood ratio statistics.

Table A4.49 UAE's Test for Heteroskedasticity of the Residuals of the Baseline VAR H_0 : No Heteroskedasticity

		Joint Test			
Chi-Sq	*df*	*P-Value*			
326.0	*300*	*0.1442*			
		Individual Components:			
Dependent	R^2	F(20,14)	P-Value	Chi-Sq (20)	P-Value
res1*res1	0.59	1.00	0.5066	20.64	0.4185
res2*res2	0.63	1.23	0.3568	22.24	0.3274
res3*res3	0.68	1.44	0.2461	23.54	0.2632
res4*res4	0.59	0.97	0.5331	20.36	0.4356

(*Continued*)

Table A4.49 (Continued)

Dependent	R^2	F(20,14)	P-Value	Chi-Sq (20)	P-Value
res5*res5	0.79	2.69	0.0313	27.77	0.1148
res2*res1	0.52	0.76	0.7198	18.21	0.5732
res3*res1	0.57	0.95	0.5546	20.13	0.4499
res3*res2	0.56	0.90	0.5870	19.77	0.4720
res4*res1	0.59	1.05	0.4747	20.98	0.3983
res4*res2	0.54	0.82	0.6684	18.85	0.5317
res4*res3	0.43	0.52	0.9091	14.98	0.7775
res5*res1	0.69	1.63	0.1768	24.47	0.2222
res5*res2	0.69	1.62	0.1783	24.45	0.2230
res5*res3	0.47	0.63	0.8321	16.57	0.6804
res5*res4	0.55	0.87	0.6179	19.43	0.4939

Table A4.50 UAE's Test of Normality of the Residuals of the Baseline VAR

Component	*Skewness*	*Chi-Sq*	*df*	*P-Value**
1	−0.81	3.87	1	0.0491
2	−0.63	2.34	1	0.1260
3	0.29	0.49	1	0.4837
4	0.13	0.09	1	0.7538
5	0.16	0.16	1	0.6895
Joint		6.96	5	0.2235
Component	Kurtosis	Chi-Sq	df	P-Value
1	2.76	0.08	1	0.7756
2	3.97	1.38	1	0.2395
3	2.69	0.13	1	0.7156
4	3.49	0.35	1	0.5538
5	2.20	0.92	1	0.3373
Joint		2.86	5	0.7202
Component	Jarque-Bera	df	P-Value	
1	3.95	2	0.1385	
2	3.72	2	0.1553	
3	0.62	2	0.7322	
4	0.45	2	0.7989	
5	1.08	2	0.5827	
Joint	9.83	10	0.4554	

Approximate P-values do not account for coefficient estimation.

Table A4.51 Venezuela's Baseline VAR Lag Length Criteria

Lag	*Log L*	*LR*	*FPE*	*AIC*	*SC*	*HQ*
0	144.0	NA	5.51e-10	−7.1	−6.9	−7.0
1	589.8	754.3	2.37e-19	−28.7	−27.4	−28.2
2	687.1	139.7	6.21e-21	−32.4	−30.0	−31.6
3	746.8	70.4*	1.26e-21*	−34.2*	−30.8*	−32.9*

LR: sequential modified LR test statistic at the 5percent level;
FPE: final prediction error;
AIC: Akaike Information Criterion;
SC: Schwarz Information Criterion;
HQ: Hannan–Quinn Information Criterion;
The asterisk denotes significant and selected by the criterion.

Table A4.52 Venezuela's Baseline VAR Lag Exclusion Test

	lnP_tq_t	lnH_t	lnK_t	$lnWAP_t$	lnY_t	*Joint*
Lag 1	16.9	289.7	229. 5	2635.0	43.6	3816.9
	[0.0047]	[0.0000]	[0.0000]	[0.0000]	[0.0000]	[0.0000]
Lag 2	3.7	71.4	40.9	698.9	7.2	969.0
	[0.5962]	[0.0000]	[0.0000]	[0.0000]	[0.2061]	[0.0000]
Degrees of freedom	5	5	5	5	5	25

Wald Chi-squared test statistics for lag exclusion; numbers in square brackets are P-values.

Table A4.53 Venezuela LM Test for Serial Correlations in the Residuals of the Baseline VAR H_0 : No Serial Correlation at Lag h

Lag	*LRE* Stat*	*df*	*P-Value*	*Rao F-Stat*	*df*	*P-Value*
1	71.5	25	0.0000	3.8	(25, 75.8)	0.0000
2	37.0	25	0.0575	1.6	(25, 75.8)	0.0613
3	25.6	25	0.4292	1.0	(25, 75.8)	0.4385

Asterisk: the Edgeworth expansion corrected likelihood ratio statistics.

Table A4.54 Venezuela's Test for Heteroskedasticity of the Residuals of the Baseline VAR H_0 : No Heteroskedasticity

		Joint Test			
Chi-Sq	*df*	*P-Value*			
309.3	*285*	*0.1540*			
		Individual Components			
Dependent	R^2	F(19,20)	P-Value	Chi-Sq (19)	P-Value
res1*res1	0.51	1.11	0.4051	20.57	0.3610
res2*res2	0.77	3.62	0.0031	30.98	0.0405
res3*res3	0.42	0.77	0.7124	16.91	0.5956
res4*res4	0.37	0.64	0.8307	15.15	0.7130
res5*res5	0.49	1.03	0.4728	19.78	0.4078
res2*res1	0.52	1.14	0.3882	20.77	0.3495
res3*res1	0.81	4.52	0.0008	32.45	0.0278
res3*res2	0.59	1.53	0.1756	23.71	0.2074
res4*res1	0.58	1.49	0.1924	23.43	0.2189
res4*res2	0.72	2.70	0.0162	28.79	0.0693
res4*res3	0.51	1.12	0.4024	20.60	0.3592
res5*res1	0.59	1.53	0.1749	23.72	0.2069
res5*res2	0.44	0.85	0.6369	17.87	0.5313
res5*res3	0.52	1.14	0.3854	20.80	0.3476
res5*res4	0.43	0.79	0.6877	17.23	0.5738

Table A4.55 Venezuela's Test of Normality of the Residuals of the Baseline VAR

Component	*Skewness*	*Chi-Sq*	*df*	*P-Value**
1	0.09	0.06	1	0.7969
2	−0.07	0.03	1	0.8552
3	0.33	0.73	1	0.3925
4	0.58	2.25	1	0.1328
5	−0.67	2.98	1	0.0841
Joint		6.07	5	0.2991
Component	Kurtosis	Chi-Sq	df	P-Value
1	3.40	0.27	1	0.6009
2	4.96	6.39	1	0.0114
3	3.06	0.00	1	0.9336
4	3.01	0.00	1	0.9872
5	3.08	0.01	1	0.9159
Joint		6.68	5	0.2449
Component	Jarque-Bera	df	P-Value	
1	0.34	2	0.8437	
2	6.43	2	0.0402	
3	0.74	2	0.6914	
4	2.26	2	0.3232	
5	2.99	2	0.2237	
Joint	12.76119	10	0.2373	

Approximate P-values do not account for coefficient estimation.

Appendix 4.2 – Baseline Dynamic Stochastic Projections

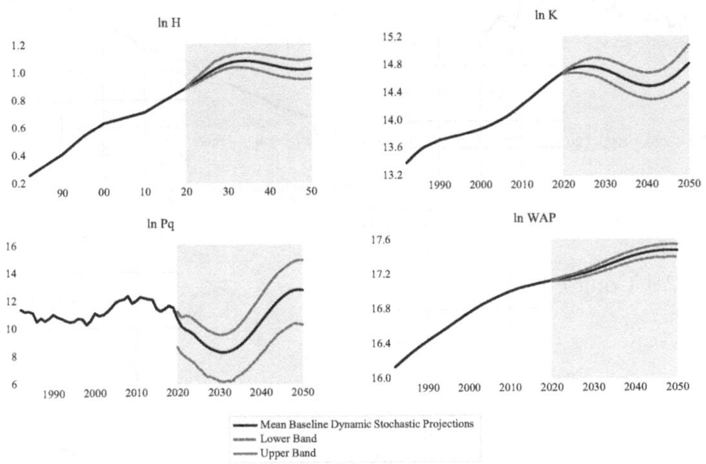

Figure A4.2.1 Algeria

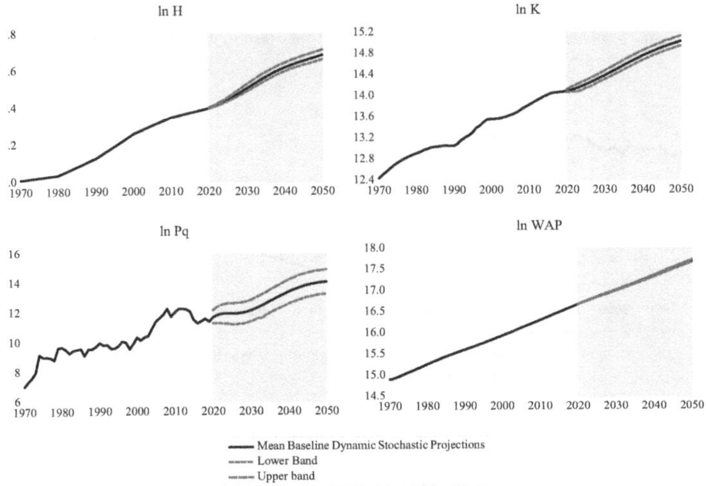

Figure A4.2.2 Angola

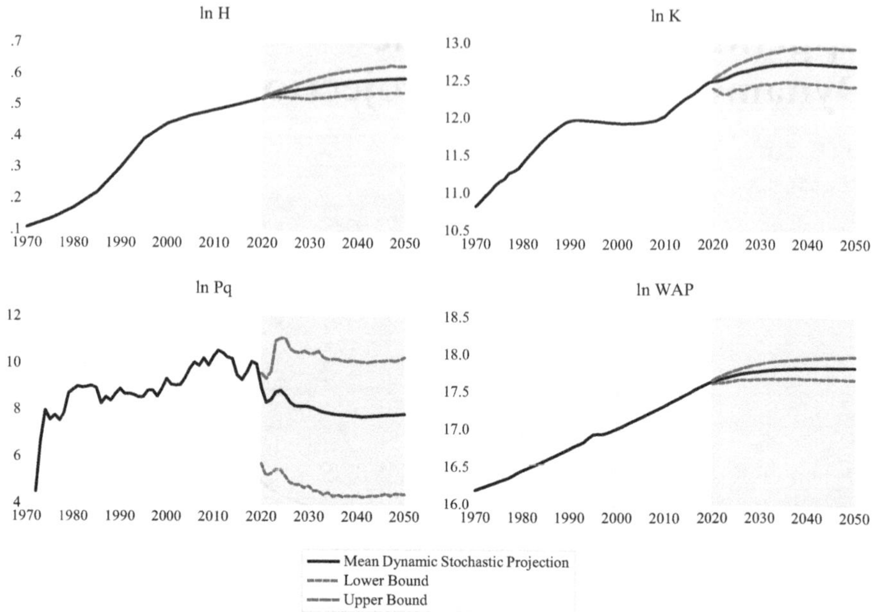

Figure A4.2.3 Congo, DR

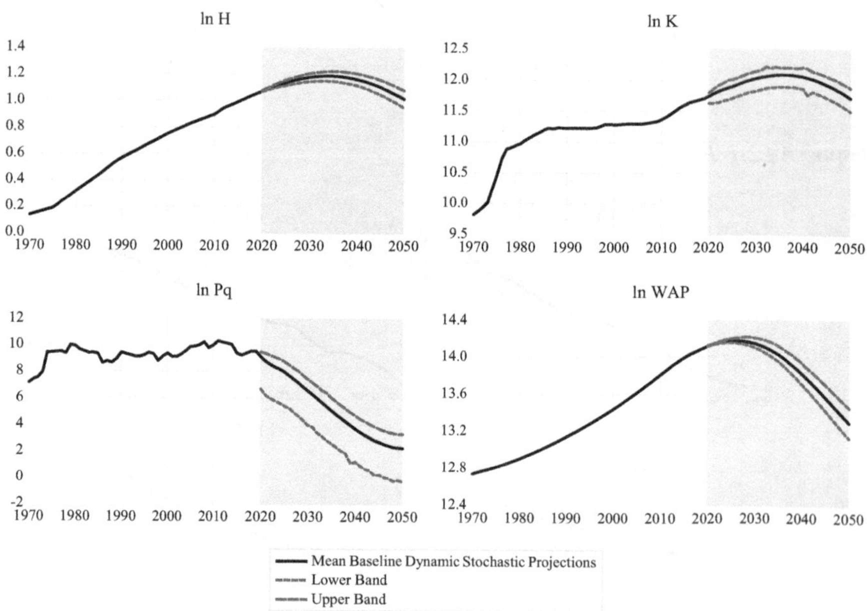

Figure A4.2.4 Gabon

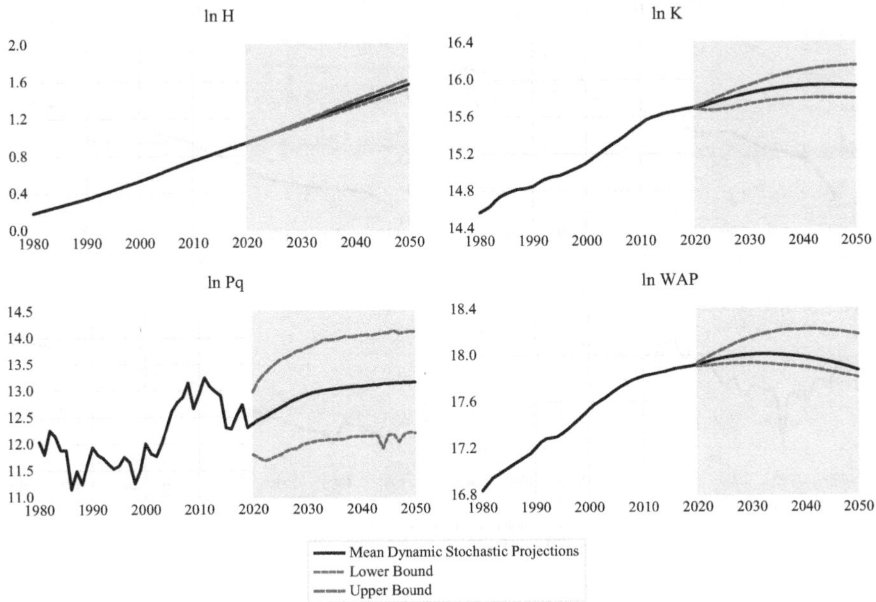

Figure A4.2.5 Iran

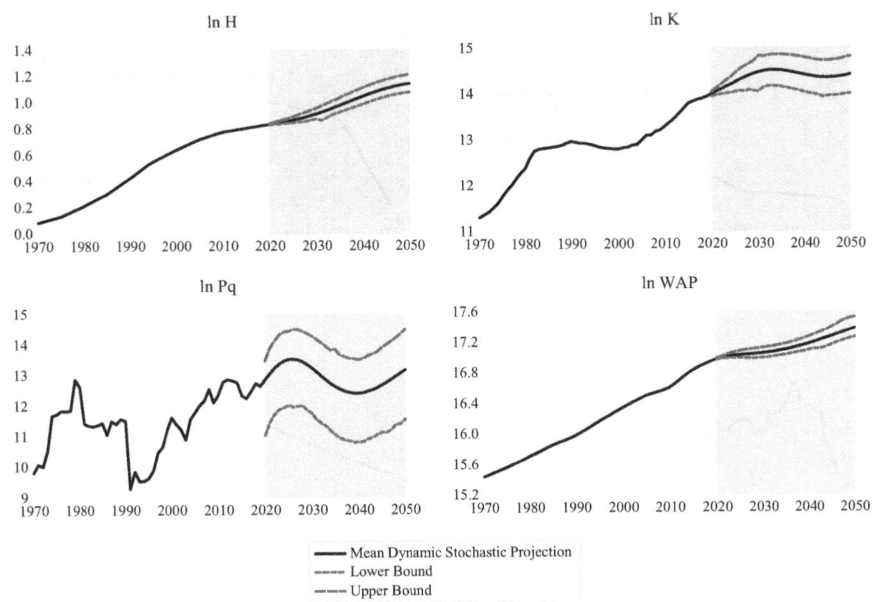

Figure A4.2.6 Iraq

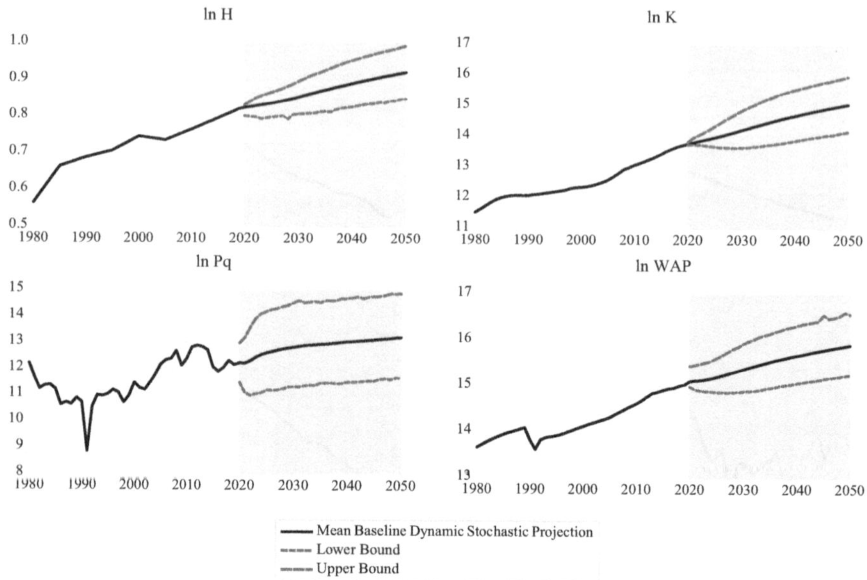

Figure A4.2.7 Kuwait

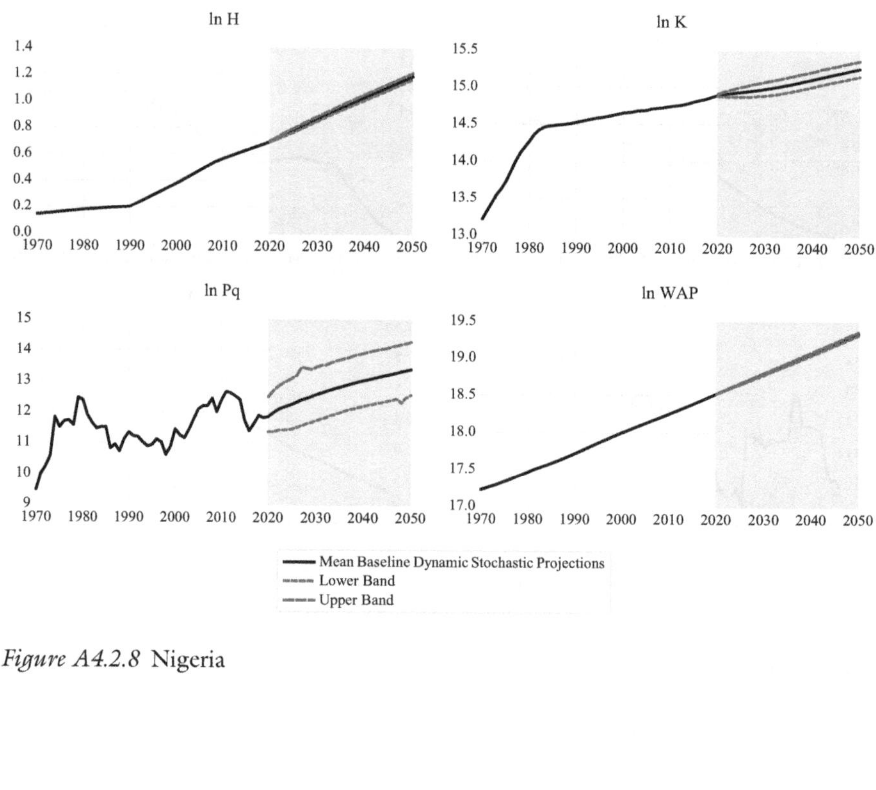

Figure A4.2.8 Nigeria

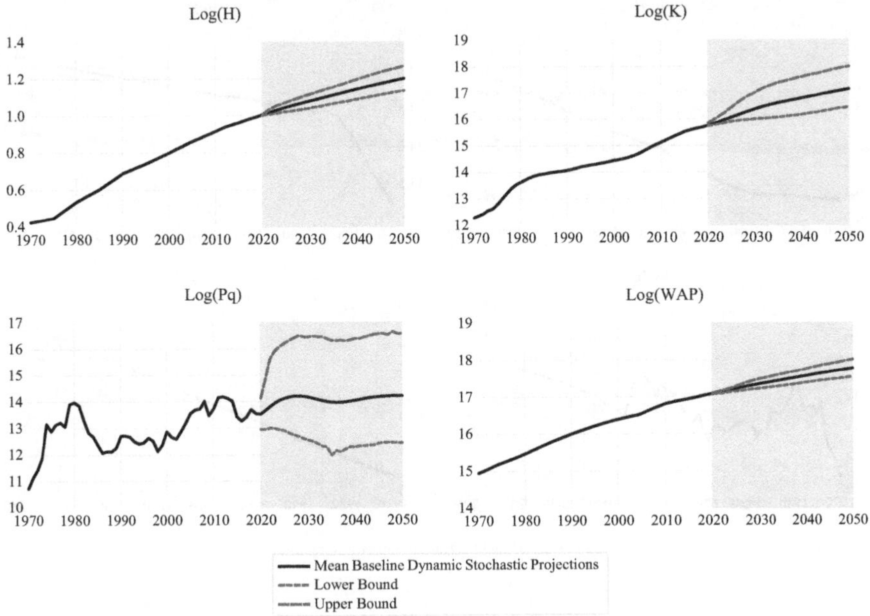

Figure A4.2.9 Saudi Arabia

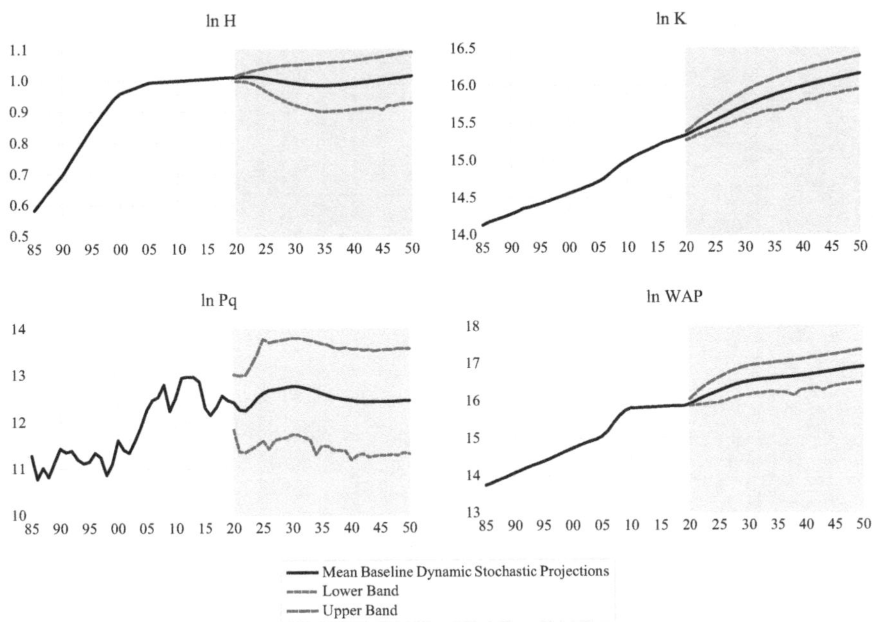

Figure A4.2.10 UAE

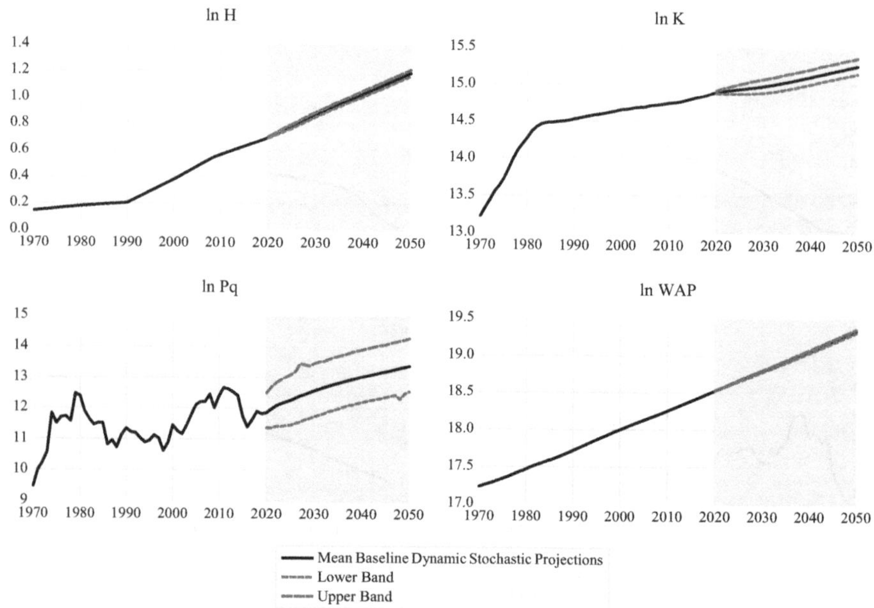

Figure A4.2.11 Venezuela

5 Counterfactual Design and Empirical Stress Tests

Abstract

We conduct counterfactual experiments to stress-test OPEC economies. Scenario (1) examines the impact of excessive oil production cuts to maintain oil prices, mimicking current situation, while Scenario (2) assumes competitive behavior, with OPEC nations adjusting production to market prices. Assumptions about production cuts are based on oil production's responsiveness to global consumption changes. Results show (1) significant permanent income reduction compared to Scenario 2, indicating a welfare loss due to decreased current consumption, aligning with the Permanent Income Hypothesis. These experiments shed light on the economic consequences of OPEC's actions and underline the importance of market-driven strategies for permanent income and welfare.

5.1 Counterfactuals

Now we are ready to carry out the stress test, which is our main objective. We use two counterfactual experiments to estimate *permanent incomes* and then compute the deviation of these counterfactual permanent incomes from the baseline estimate of permanent incomes that we reported in the previous chapter. The first is the deviation of permanent income under the current state-owned oil industry, i.e., the monopolist's permanent income from the baseline. The second is the deviation of permanent income of a hypothetical competitive oil industry from the baseline.

We use the same VAR we used in the previous chapter to estimate *permanent income* under two sets of assumptions about the price and the quantity of oil produced under the two scenarios of a state-owned oil monopoly and a competitive oil industry. As before, *permanent income* is our dynamic stochastic projection of real GDP over the period 2020–2050. All the variables in the VAR remain the same, except $lnP_t q_t$, which we replace with two new measures under the two counterfactual scenarios. Recall that in Chapter2 we laid the microeconomic theory, which resulted in the monopolist equilibriums $P_1^m q_1^m$ and $P_1^m q_2^m$, where $q_2^m < q_1^m$, and the competitive producer's $P_1^c q_1^c$ and $P_2^c q_2^c$, where $P_2^c < p_1^c$, $q_2^c < q_1^c$, and $q_2^m < q_2^c$. The first scenario maintains that the oil industries in the OPEC countries are state-owned, i.e., state monopolies.

DOI: 10.4324/9781003488125-5

Currently, OPEC countries' oil industries cut oil production in order to peg the price of oil to satisfy a certain breakeven price. We make an assumption about this breakeven price and estimate the amount of oil cut by OPEC by country. In the second scenario, we estimate *permanent income* under the assumption that the oil industries in the OPEC countries are competitive; they cut oil production in-line with Net Zero when the demand for oil falls, and take the prevailing lower market prices instead of a higher breakeven price. Under the state-owned oil industry scenario, the VAR is given by

$$lnPqm_t; lnH_t; lnK_t; ln\,WAP_t; lnY_t, \tag{5.1}$$

where m denotes the monopolist. And under the competitive oil industry scenario, the VAR is

$$lnPqc_t; lnH_t; lnK_t; ln\,WAP_t; lnY_t, \tag{5.2}$$

where c denotes the competitive producer.

5.2 Constructing $lnPqm_t$ and $lnPqc_t$

We make a number of assumptions about the price and the quantity of oil cut to design the two counterfactual time series, i.e., Pqm_t and Pqc_t.

Assumption 1: We will assume that OPEC's oil production responds to *actual* global oil consumption. Global oil consumption is highly associated with global emission. We will show that global oil consumption and global carbon emissions are cointegrated, i.e., they share a long-run common trend. Figure 5.1 plots the two variables. Table 5.1 reports the test of the null hypothesis that global oil consumption C_t^o and emission E_t are not cointegrated using the Engle–Granger (1987) test, which is rejected by the data.

Assumption 2: The Net Zero plan required emission cuts by 45 percent by 2030. Because global emission and global oil consumption are cointegrated, we assume that global oil consumption will also be reduced in the long run by 45 percent, by 2030. However, the Net Zero plan does not explain how these reductions are achieved *annually*.[1] Because we are estimating a VAR with time series data, our task is to construct a hypothetical time series Pqm_t and Pqc_t ; thus, we need to make assumptions about q_t. We construct a hypothetical time series for the quantity of oil production under the first scenario. For the purpose of estimation and simplicity, we assume that there are *equal annual constant cuts* in q_t, i.e., the quantity is reduced by the same amount every year until it is 45 percent lower in 2030 than it was in 2016. Since OPEC ratified the Agreement

1 Different countries have different policies such as taxing oil production and consumption, subsidizing alternative energy productions and consumption, regulations, and all of the above. There could be cases of carbon credit and carbon offset markets that might reduce emission, albeit the evidence is yet to be provided.

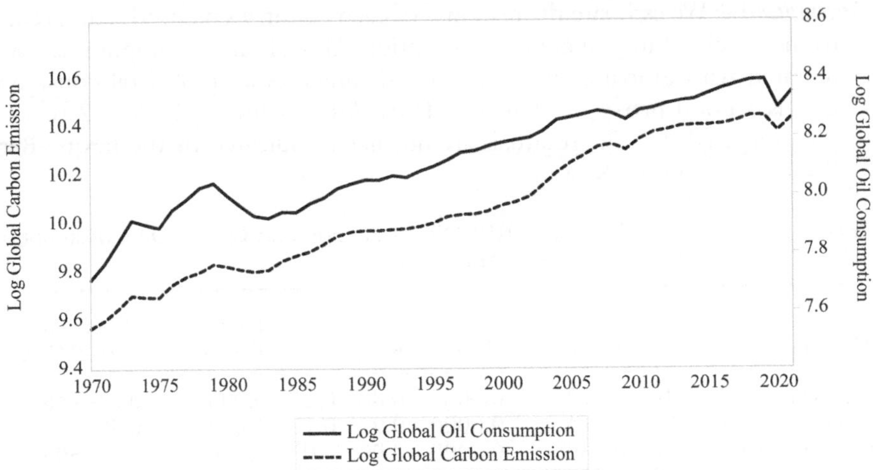

Figure 5.1 Global Oil Consumption and Global Emission Share a Common Trend

Table 5.1 Global Oil Consumption and Global Emission Are Cointegrated

Dependent	*τ -Statistic*	*P-Value*	*z-Statistic*	*P-Value*
lnC_t^o	–3.09	0.1080	–23.6	0.0118
$\ln E_t$	–2.90	0.1522	–21.4	0.0215

Null hypothesis: series are not cointegrated. Cointegration eq. deterministic constant.

	lnC_t^o	$\ln E_t$
ρ	–0.231258	–0.205941
ρSE	0.074777	0.070806
Residual variance	0.000232	0.000478
Long-run residual variance	0.001003	0.002159
Number of lags	2	2
Number of observations	49	49
Number of stochastic trends**	2	2

**Number of stochastic trends in asymptotic distribution.

in 2016 and said that it is fully engaged and supportive of the Net Zero Paris Agreement (OPEC 2017), oil production in 2030 is supposed to be 45 percent lower than oil production in 2016, i.e., q_{2030} is $0.45 \times q_{2016}$.

Assumption 3: The *annual equal* amount of reduction of oil production required by the Net Zero UN plan is $(q_{2016} - q_{2030})$ /15 years. Given the *actual* oil production in 2016, we calculate qUN_t, which is the annual oil production reduction required to meet the Net Zero. However, when the price of oil declines below the breakeven price, OPEC cuts oil by more than qUN_t. OPEC cuts oil production by more than the reduction stipulated by Net Zero.

Assumption 4: We estimate the response of each country's oil production (cuts) to the (decline) in global oil consumption. Global oil consumption is cointegrated with global emission as shown earlier. And, global oil consumption is a good proxy for demand. Thus, $lnq_t = \delta lnC_t^o$.[2] Table 5.2 reports the estimated δ.[3] The residuals are normal as indicated by the Jarque-Bera P-values, except for Kuwait.

Table 5.2 Dynamic OLS (1970–2019) Oil Production and Global Oil Consumption Are Cointegrated $lnq_t = \delta lnC_t^o + \varepsilon_t$

Variable	δ	*Std. Error*	*P-Value*	R^2	σ	*Long Run* σ	ε_t *Jarque–Bera P-Value*
Algeria i	1.48	0.222	0.0000	0.88	0.07	0.008	0.614445
Angola ii	7.29	0.474	0.0000	0.97	0.12	0.017	0.997743
Congo, DR iii	2.72	0.039	0.0000	0.99	0.03	0.000	0.805509
Gabon iv	6.50	0.300	0.0000	0.98	0.03	0.000	0.364148
Iran v	1.15	0.005	0.0000	0.86	0.10	0.035	0.926928
Iraq vi	1.28	0.027	0.0000	0.65	0.38	0.069	0.677096
Kuwait vii	1.18	0.006	0.0000	0.59	0.32	0.219	0.007884*
Nigeria viii	4.72	2.144	0.0365	0.70	0.08	0.018	0.660580
Saudi Arabia ix	1.20	0.007	0.0000	0.92	0.08	0.005	0.285354
UAE x	2.19	0.278	0.0000	0.94	0.07	0.009	0.618881
Venezuela xi	1.10	0.004	0.0000	0.96	0.04	0.001	0.737329

q_t is the oil production in millions of barrels/day and C_t^o is the global oil consumption in millions of barrels/day. σ is the standard error of the regression. The asterisk denotes statistically significant.

(i) Regression includes a constant. Automatic leads/lags specification 9/9 based on AIC, max = 10, long-run variance estimate (pre-whitening with lag = 2 from AIC with max lags = 3, Bartlett kernel, Newey-West automatic bandwidth 2.3209, NW automatic lag length = 3).

2 The parameter δ could be approximately equal the ratio of the price elasticity of the demand to the price elasticity of the supply. Let the oil supply (oil production) be given by $lnP_t^s = alnq_t^s$, where P_t^s is the price of oil is, q_t^s is the quantity of oil production, s denotes the supply, and a is the elasticity. The demand of oil be given by $lnP_t^d = blnq_t^d$, where P_t^d is the price of oil, q_t^d is the quantity of oil demanded, d denotes the demand, and b is the elasticity. We assume that the state-owned oil company in OPEC wants to peg the price of oil to a certain breakeven price, P_t^*, such that $lnP_t^s = lnP_t^d = lnP_t^*$. Equating demand and supply gives, $alnq_t^s = blnq_t^d$; therefore, $lnq_t^s = \frac{b}{a}lnq_t^d$. Global oil consumption C_t^o is a proxy for demand, therefore, $lnq_t^s = \delta lnC_t^o$, where δ is the ratio $\frac{b}{a}$. If $b > a$, which is highly probable, δ could be >1. We test this empirically.

3 First, we test the null hypothesis that oil production q_t and global oil consumption C_t^o are not cointegrated. This is a bi-variate system; therefore, the Engle and Granger (1987) test is the way to test the null. They suggested six tests, among them the ADF test for unit root in the residuals from the OLS regression of one variable on the other, also whether the OLS regression in log-levels has a high R^2 and a low Durbin-Watson statistics, i.e., the regression is spurious. The ADF rejects the null of a unit root in the residuals. Other tests such as the Phillips-Perron (1988) test of unit root in the residuals could be used and would give similar results. A better test is the error-correction test, whereby the coefficient of the lagged residuals from the first OLS regression of the log of oil production on the log of global oil consumption in the OLS regression of the log difference of oil production on log-difference global oil consumption is *highly* statistically significant. These tests produce a very large output, so we do not report the results of these tests. Instead, we report the dynamic OLS regressions. See Saikkonen (1992), Phillips and Loretan (1991), and Stock and Watson (1993), where cointegration is assumed to hold in the data. Dynamic OLS is a very efficient estimator. It accounts for endogeneity and serial correlation in the residuals because it fits more leads/lags, provided that we do not commit over-fitting.

(ii) Regression includes a constant. Automatic leads/lags specification 10/10 based on AIC, max = 10, long-run variance estimate (pre-whitening with lag = 0 from AIC with max lags = 3, Bartlett kernel, Newey-West automatic bandwidth 3.1620, NW automatic lag length = 3).

(iii) Regression includes a constant. Automatic leads/lags specification 10/10 based on AIC, max = 10, long-run variance estimate (pre-whitening with lag = 3 from AIC with max lags = 3, Bartlett kernel, Newey-West automatic bandwidth 3.1215, NW automatic lag length = 3).

(iv) Regression includes a constant. Automatic leads/lags specification 10/10 based on AIC, max = 10, long-run variance estimate (pre-whitening with lag = 3 from AIC with max lags = 3, Bartlett kernel, Newey-West automatic bandwidth 11.7169, NW automatic lag length = 3).

(v) Automatic leads/lags specification 1/8 based on AIC, max = 10, long-run variance estimate (pre-whitening with lag = 3 from AIC with max lags = 3, Bartlett kernel, Newey-West automatic bandwidth 2.9295, NW automatic lag length = 3).

(vi) Automatic leads/lags specification 10/10 based on AIC, max = 10, long-run variance estimate (pre-whitening with lag = 0 from AIC with max lags = 3, Bartlett kernel, Newey-West automatic bandwidth 2.7467, NW automatic lag length = 3).

(vii) Regression includes a dummy variable for the First Gulf War in 1991. Automatic leads/lags specification 10/10 based on AIC, max = 10, long-run variance estimate (pre-whitening with lag = 3 from AIC with max lags = 3, Bartlett kernel, Newey-West automatic bandwidth 3.4400, NW automatic lag length = 3).

(viii) Regression includes a constant and trend. Automatic leads/lags specification 0/7 based on AIC, max = 8, long-run variance estimate (pre-whitening with lag = 3 from AIC with max lags = 3, Bartlett kernel, Newey-West automatic bandwidth 3.3935, NW automatic lag length = 3).

(ix) Automatic leads/lags specification 10/8 based on AIC, max = 10, long-run variance estimate (pre-whitening with lag = 0 from AIC with max lags = 3, Bartlett kernel, Newey-West automatic bandwidth 3.2938, NW automatic lag length = 3).

(x) Automatic leads/lags specification 10/10 based on AIC, max = 10, long-run variance estimate (pre-whitening with lag = 0 from AIC with max lags = 3, Bartlett kernel, Newey-West automatic bandwidth 2.3059, NW automatic lag length = 3).

(xi) Automatic leads/lags specification 10/10 based on AIC, max = 10, long-run variance estimate (pre-whitening with lag = 0 from AIC with max lags = 3, Bartlett kernel, Newey-West automatic bandwidth 6.1711, NW automatic lag length = 3).

The estimated δ is >1. We use the estimated values of δ to compute $q_t^m = \delta.qUN_t$; therefore, the monopolist cuts oil production by more than the reductions stipulated by the Net Zero. Tables 5.3a, 5.3b, 5.3c . . . .5.3k report our calculated counterfactual times series Pqm_t and Pqc_t, which we will use to estimate the VAR under both the monopolist and the competitive oil producer scenarios.

Assumption 5: OPEC breakeven oil price, P_t^m, is fixed at $80 US dollars/barrel over the simulation period. We explained earlier in the book that this assumed fiscal breakeven oil price is taken to approximate the average breakeven price of oil of Algeria, Iran, Iraq, Kuwait, Saudi Arabia and the UAE from 2000 to 2023. The data are reported by the IMF annually along with projections. The data for the other members of OPEC are not reported. We assume $80 USD, which is much higher than market price for our sample. The IMF projection of the average breakeven price of oil for 2024 exceeds $90 USD.

Assumption 6: OPEC oil price under the competitive industry scenario is the actual market price over the simulation period.

Each table (Tables 5.3a–5.3k) includes 11 columns, which will make it clear how the counterfactual time series are constructed:

Column 1 is the year when the oil cuts began. In 2016, OPEC countries ratified the Net Zero UN Paris Agreement and publicly announced that they would adhere to it.

Column 2 is q_t, the ***actual*** oil production in thousands of barrels/day.

Column 3 with the header X is the constant amount of oil reduction in thousands of barrels/day that we assumed to be stipulated by the UN, which is 45 percent by 2030. We computed $X = (q_{2016} - q_{2030})/15$, where $q_{2030} = 0.45q_{2016}$. For example, if oil production in 2016 is 1 million barrels a day, then it should be producing 450,000 barrels in 2030.

Column 4 is Column 2 less Column 3, which is $qUN_t = q_t - X$, which is the oil reduction stipulated by the UN. For example, (1,000,000–450,000)/15 years (from 2016 to 2030) is 36,667 barrels annually.

Column 5 is the state-owned oil monopolist cut. The monopolist cuts oil production in excess of the reduction in oil production stipulated by the UN. Production responds to the decline in global oil consumption is >1; $Xm = \delta.X$, and $\delta > 1$ as estimated and reported in Table 5.2.

Column 6 is, therefore, the quantity of oil cut by the monopolist, $q_t^m = qUN_t - Xm$, Column 4 less column 5.

Column 7 is the assumed breakeven real price of oil in US dollars per barrel for OPEC.

Column 8 is the real value of oil production, Pqm_t, which is the product of the quantity of oil in Column 6, q_t^m and the breakeven price in Column 7; this is the time series that we will use in estimating the next VAR instead of Pq_t that we used in the baseline VAR.

Column 9 is the actual real price of oil.

Column 10 is the quantity of oil produced by the counterfactual competitive oil industry. We assumed that the competitive oil industry cuts oil production by the same amount stipulated by Net Zero.

Column 11 is Pqc_t, the product of the actual real price of oil P_t and the quantity of oil produced by the competitive producer q_t^c, which we will use to estimate the VAR for the counterfactual competitive oil producer.

Table 5.3a Algeria – Counterfactual Time Series 2016–2019

Year	q_t	X	qUN_t	Xm	q_t^m	P_t^m	Pqm_t	P_t	q_t^c	Pqc_t
2016	1,577	58.8	1,519.2	86.6	1,433.6	80	114,687.9	46.6	1,519.2	70,778.4
2017	1,540	58.8	1,482.2	86.6	1,396.6	80	111,727.9	56.5	1,482.2	83,772.6
2018	1,511	58.8	1,453.2	86.6	1,367.6	80	109,407.9	72.6	1,453.2	105,500.6
2019	1,487	58.8	1,429.2	86.6	1,343.6	80	107,487.9	64.2	1,429.2	91,767.6

Table 5.3b Angola – Counterfactual Time Series 2016–2019

Year	q_t	X	qUN_t	Xm	q_t^m	P_t^m	Pqm_t	P_t	q_t^c	Pqc_t
2016	1,745	64	1,681	467	1,214	80	97,106	46.6	1,681	78,311
2017	1,671	64	1,607	467	1,140	80	91,228	56.5	1,607	90,849
2018	1,519	64	1,455	467	988	80	79,057	72.6	1,455	105,651
2019	1,420	64	1,356	467	889	80	71,098	64.2	1,356	87,053

Table 5.3c Congo, DR – Counterfactual Time Series 2016–2019

Year	q_t	X	qUN_t	Xm	q_t^m	P_t^m	Pqm_t	P_t	q_t^c	Pqc_t
2016	232	9	223	23	200	80	16,028	46.6	223	10,413
2017	270	9	261	23	238	80	19,068	56.5	261	14,780
2018	330	9	321	23	298	80	23,868	72.6	321	23,340
2019	336	9	327	23	304	80	24,348	64.2	327	21,028

Table 5.3d Gabon – Counterfactual Time Series 2016–2019

Year	q_t	X	qUN_t	Xm	q_t^m	P_t^m	Pqm_t	P_t	q_t^c	Pqc_t
2016	221	8	213	53	160	80	12,818	46.6	213	9,919
2017	210	8	202	53	149	80	11,938	56.5	202	11,411
2018	193	8	185	53	132	80	10,578	72.6	185	13,423
2019	218	8	210	53	157	80	12,578	64.2	210	13,477

Table 5.3e Iran – Counterfactual Time Series 2016–2019

Year	q_t	X	qUN_t	Xm	q_t^m	P_t^m	Pqm_t	P_t	q_t^c	Pqc_t
2016	4,578	168	4,410	193	4,217	80	337,368	46.6	4,410	205,468
2017	4,854	168	4,242	193	4,049	80	323,939	56.5	4,686	264,861
2018	4,608	168	4,074	193	3,881	80	310,510	72.6	4,440	322,354
2019	3,399	168	3,907	193	3,714	80	297,082	64.2	3,231	207,471

Table 5.3f Iraq – Counterfactual Time Series 2016–2019

Year	q_t	X	qUN_t	Xm	q_t^m	P_t^m	Pqm_t	P_t	q_t^c	Pqc_t
2016	4,423	162	4,261	211	4,050	80	323,999	46.6	4,261	198,512
2017	4,538	162	4,376	211	4,165	80	333,199	56.5	4,376	247,322
2018	4,632	162	4,470	211	4,259	80	340,719	72.6	4,470	324,509
2019	4,779	162	4,617	211	4,406	80	352,479	64.2	4,617	296,446

Table 5.3g Kuwait – Counterfactual Time Series 2016–2019

Year	q_t	X	qUN_t	Xm	q_t^m	P_t^m	Pqm_t	P_t	q_t^c	Pqc_t
2016	3,150	116	3,035	129	2,905	80	232,411	46.6	3,035	141,377
2017	3,009	116	2,894	129	2,764	80	221,131	56.5	2,894	163,541
2018	3,050	116	2,935	129	2,805	80	224,411	72.6	2,935	213,045
2019	2,976	116	2,861	129	2,731	80	218,491	64.2	2,861	183,673

Table 5.3h Nigeria – Counterfactual Time Series 2016–2019

Year	q_t	X	qUN_t	Xm	q_t^m	P_t^m	Pqm_t	P_t	q_t^c	Pqc_t
2016	1,898	70	1,828	328	1,500	80	119,994	46.6	1,828	85,185
2017	1,968	70	1,898	328	1,570	80	125,594	56.5	1,898	107,298
2018	2,005	70	1,935	328	1,607	80	128,554	72.6	1,935	140,511
2019	2,101	70	2,031	328	1,703	80	136,234	64.2	2,031	130,437

Table 5.3i Saudi Arabia – Counterfactual Time Series 2016–2019

Year	q_t	X	qUN_t	Xm	q_t^m	P_t^m	Pqm_t	P_t	q_t^c	Pqc_t
2016	12,406	455	11,951	546	11,405	80	912,420	46.6	11,951	556,802
2017	11,892	455	11,437	546	10,891	80	871,300	56.5	11,437	646,426
2018	12,261	455	11,806	546	11,260	80	900,820	72.6	11,806	857,124
2019	11,832	455	11,377	546	10,831	80	866,500	64.2	11,377	730,524

Table 5.3j UAE – Counterfactual Time Series 2016–2019

Year	q_t	X	qUN_t	Xm	q_t^m	P_t^m	Pqm_t	P_t	q_t^c	Pqc_t
2016	4,038	148	3,890	326	3,564	80	285,137	46.6	3,890	181,232
2017	3,910	148	3,762	326	3,436	80	274,897	56.5	3,762	212,625
2018	3,912	148	3,764	326	3,438	80	275,057	72.6	3,764	273,262
2019	3,999	148	3,851	326	3,525	80	282,017	64.2	3,851	247,269

Table 5.3k Venezuela – Counterfactual Time Series 2016–2019

Year	q_t	X	qUN_t	Xm	q_t^m	P_t^m	Pqm_t	P_t	q_t^c	Pqc_t
2016	2,566	99	2,467	109	2,358	80.0	188,623	46.6	2,467	114,931
2017	2,220	99	2,121	109	2,012	80.0	160,943	56.5	2,121	119,871
2018	1,631	99	1,532	109	1,423	80.0	113,823	72.6	1,532	111,213
2019	1,022	99	923	109	814	80.0	65,103	64.2	923	59,256

Numbers are rounded.

Footnote for all the aforementioned tables: q_t is the actual oil production; X is a constant annual reduction in production consistent with the 45 percent reduction stipulated by Net Zero by

2030; thus, qUN_t is the actual production less the constant amount of reduction in production; the monopolist cuts oil production by Xm, which is more than X; $Xm = \delta \times X$, and $\delta > 1$; q_t^m is the monopolist's cut which is $qUN_t - Xm$; P_t^m is the assumed breakeven price of oil of the monopolist which is \$80 US dollars/barrel; hence, Pqm_t is the breakeven price $P_t^m \times q_t^m$. The actual market price of oil is P_t; the quantity of oil cut by the competitive oil industry is the same as the reduction amount recommended by the UN; and Pqc_t is the market price × the quantity q_t^c.

Saudi Arabia, Iraq, the UAE, Kuwait, and Iran cut oil production in relatively larger quantities to peg the price.

Reuters published this table in April 2023.[4] We do not know how these excess cuts are calculated by either OPEC or Reuters. According to Reuters, Saudi Arabia cuts oil by 500,000 barrels/day; the UAE cuts by 144,000 barrels/day; Iraq by 211,000 barrels/day; Kuwait by 128,000 barrels/day; Algeria by 48,000 barrels/day; and Gabon by 8000 barrels/day. Our calculations for these countries are nearly identical; see Column 4 in all the earlier tables, except perhaps for Gabon. Also note that Venezuela is a special sample case as explained earlier in the book. The Venezuelan economy and production collapsed in 2012 under the US sanctions.

Figures 5.2–5.12 plot Pq_t, Pqm_t, and Pqc_t. The data before 2016 are identical because the changes occurred in 2016 after the ratification of the Net Zero Paris Agreement. Permanent income under the two counterfactuals will be the mean dynamic stochastic projection of real GDP from 2020 to 2050. These are shown in shaded areas.

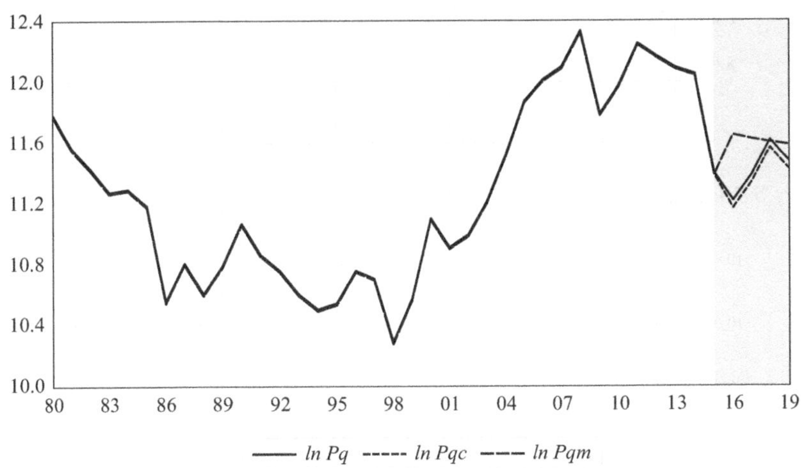

Figure 5.2 Algeria – Counterfactual Time Series

4 www.reuters.com/business/energy/sarabia-other-opec-producers-announce-voluntary-oil-output-cuts-2023-04-02/ We do not copy the image here, but the reader could download it and check the numbers.

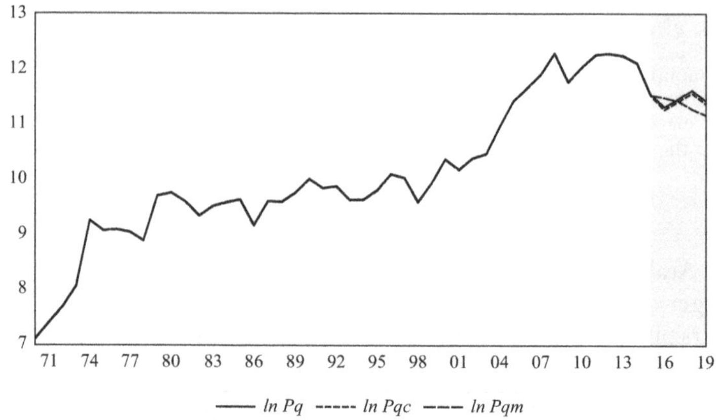

Figure 5.3 Angola – Counterfactual Time Series

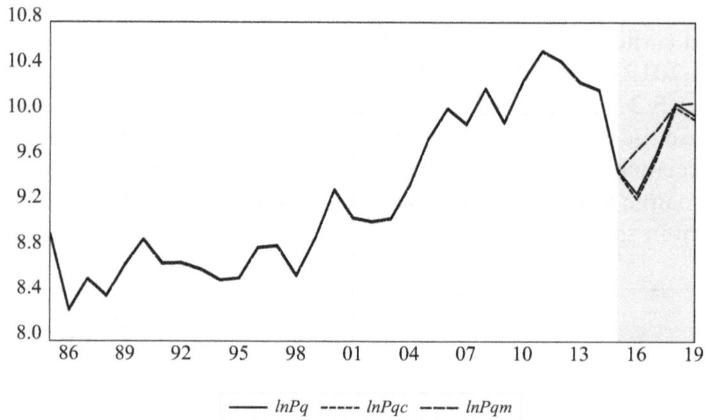

Figure 5.4 Congo, DR – Counterfactual Time Series

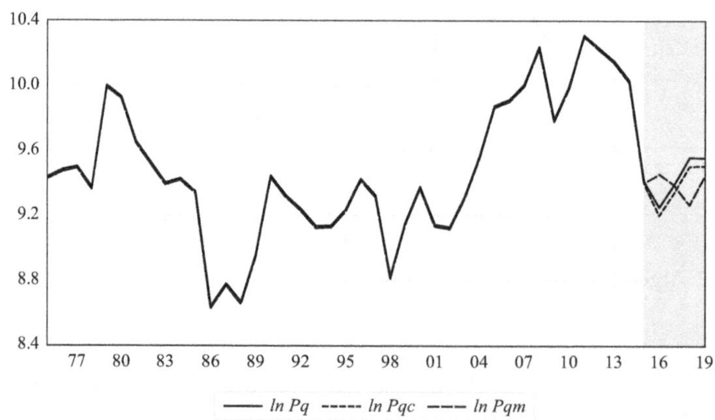

Figure 5.5 Gabon – Counterfactual Time Series

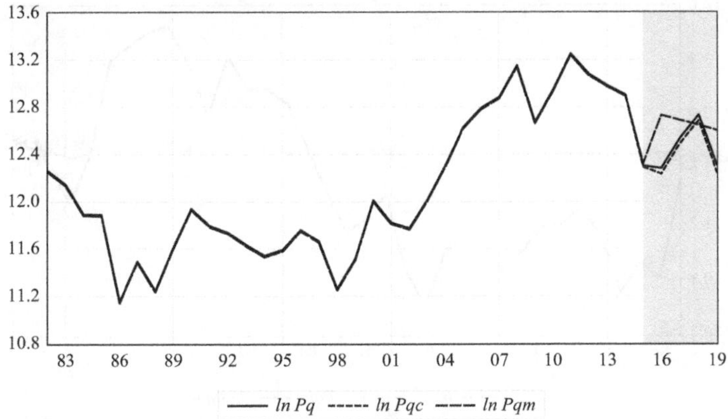

Figure 5.6 Iran – Counterfactual Time Series

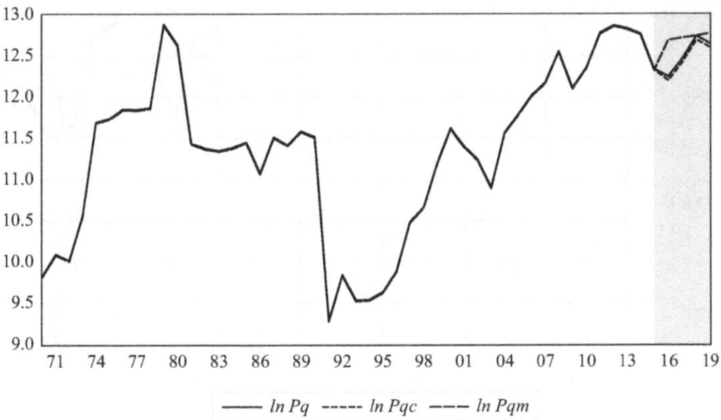

Figure 5.7 Iraq – Counterfactual Time Series

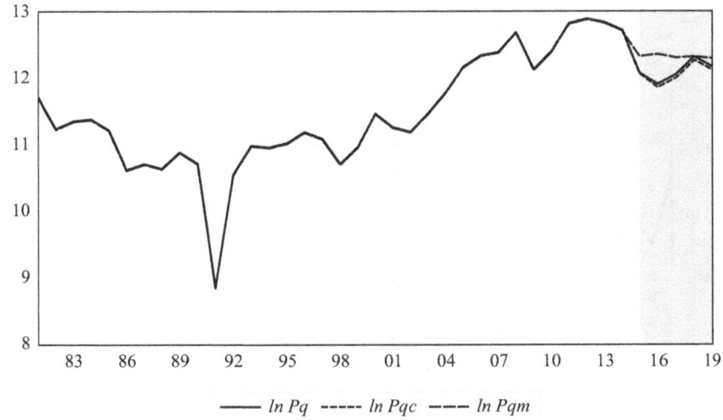

Figure 5.8 Kuwait – Counterfactual Time Series

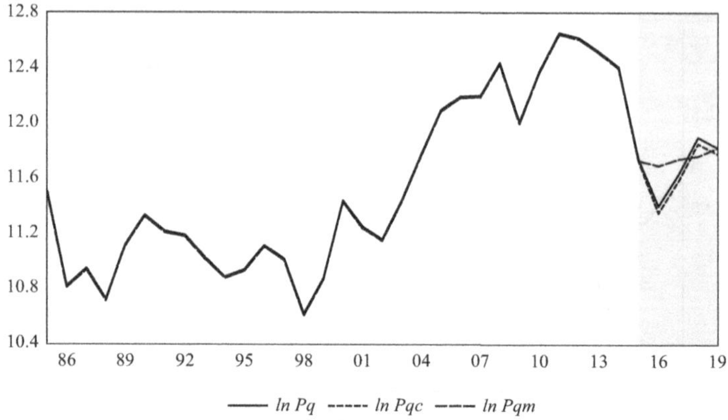

Figure 5.9 Nigeria – Counterfactual Time Series

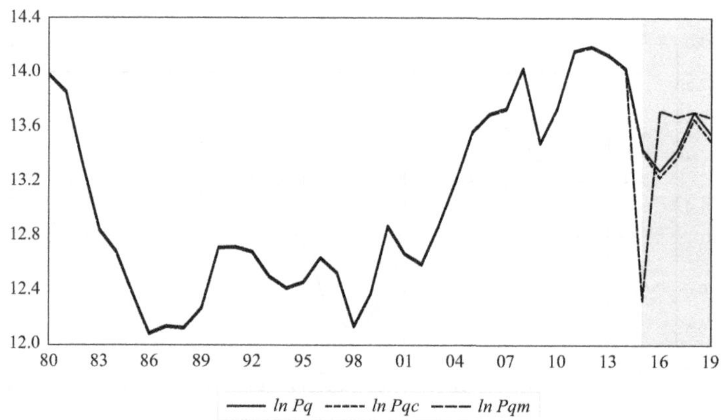

Figure 5.10 Saudi Arabia – Counterfactual Time Series

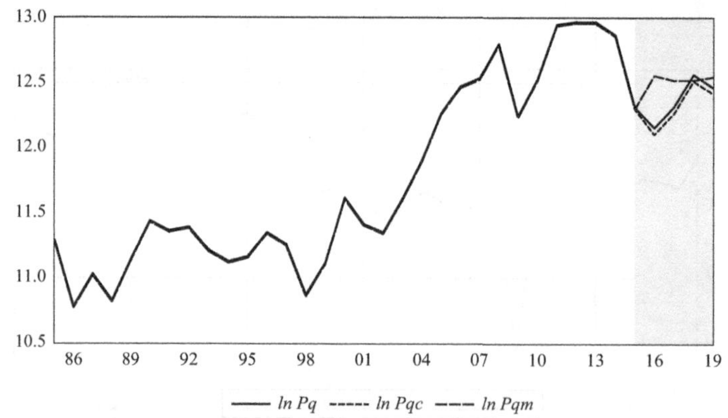

Figure 5.11 UAE – Counterfactual Time Series

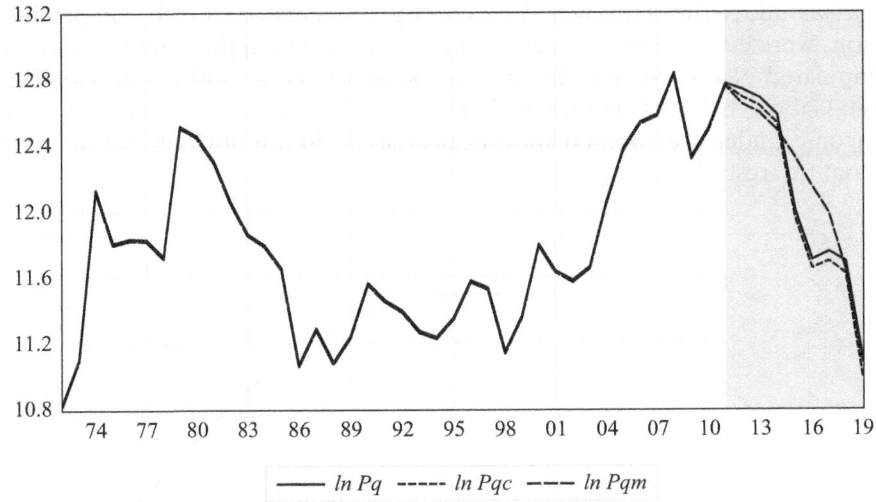

Figure 5.12 Venezuela – Counterfactual Time Series

5.3 Stress Tests

Now we re-estimate the VARs, equations (5.1) and (5.2), with the constructed counterfactual time series $lnPqm_t$ and $lnPqc_t$, which are plotted earlier. We maintain the same lag structure as before and generate dynamic stochastic projections for real GDP, lnY_t. Figures 5.13–5.23 plot the deviations of lnY_t dynamic stochastic projections 2020–2050 of the state-owned oil producer scenario from the baseline and the competitive oil producer scenario from the baseline. The outcome of the OPEC countries' model of state oil industries is inferior to that of a competitive industry model. The reduction of oil production in excess of the amount stipulated by Net Zero to peg the price of oil at $80 US dollars/barrel results in a significant decline in *permanent income*. OPEC's real GDP is highly negatively affected by the reduction in oil production, which is consistent with the stylized facts that OPEC's real output is mainly oil production. The OPEC countries benefit in terms of rising oil revenues, but in real terms, they lose real expected output.

Note that Algeria is a gas producer, not a major oil producer. Nonetheless, it loses a significant amount of *permanent income* under the monopolist state-owned oil model if it reacts by cutting oil production in excess of the amount stipulated by Net Zero. The deviation of *permanent income* of the monopolist state-owned oil scenario from baseline in Iraq is different from the rest of OPEC in two aspects. First, it is more volatile. This might be due to fitting more dummy variables to account for the *ex-post* spikes and dips in the data. Second, it increases above the deviation of the competitive industry scenario then it dips fast. So, in the long run, it is still a big loss. The rest of the OPEC countries show significant continuous losses in *permanent income* under the state-owned oil monopoly scenario, whereby oil productions were cut in excess of the amounts of reduction in the production of oil stipulated Net Zero, and the price of oil is pegged at $80 US dollars/barrel. Gabon, the GCC countries, Nigeria, and Venezuela gains in permanent income under the competitive producer scenario are obvious and different from the rest of OPEC.

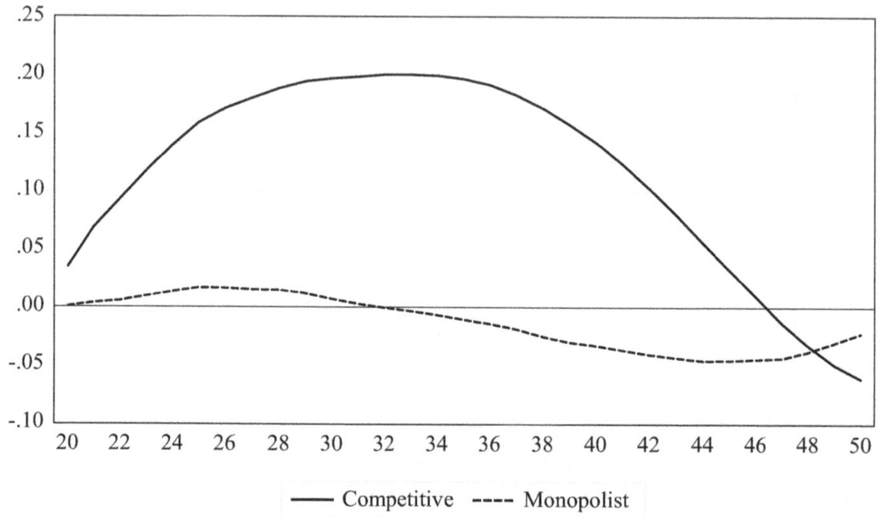

Figure 5.13 Algeria – Permanent Income Deviations from Baseline

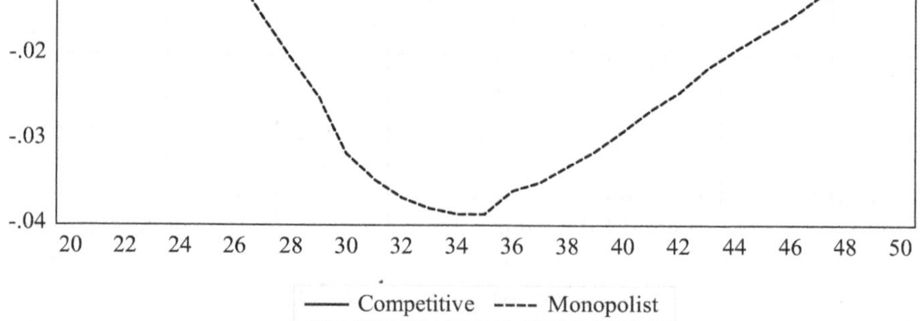

Figure 5.14 Angola – Permanent Income Deviations from Baseline

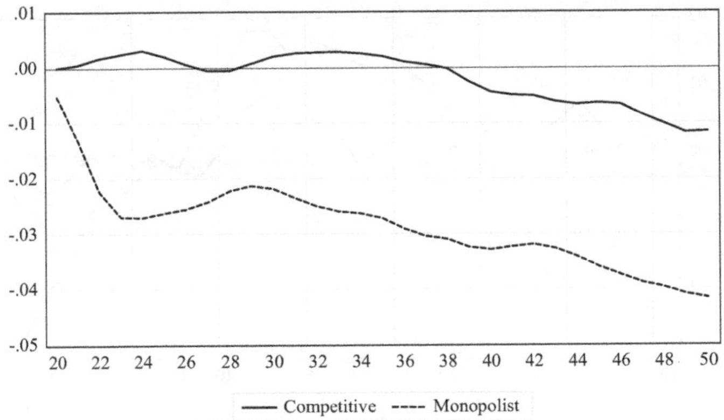

Figure 5.15 Congo, DR – Permanent Income Deviations from Baseline

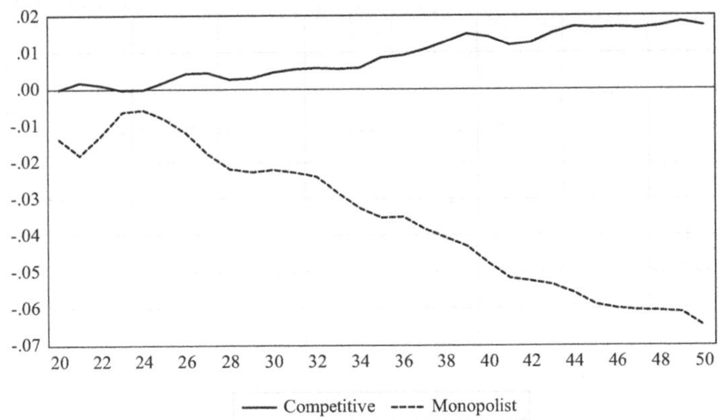

Figure 5.16 Gabon – Permanent Income Deviations from Baseline

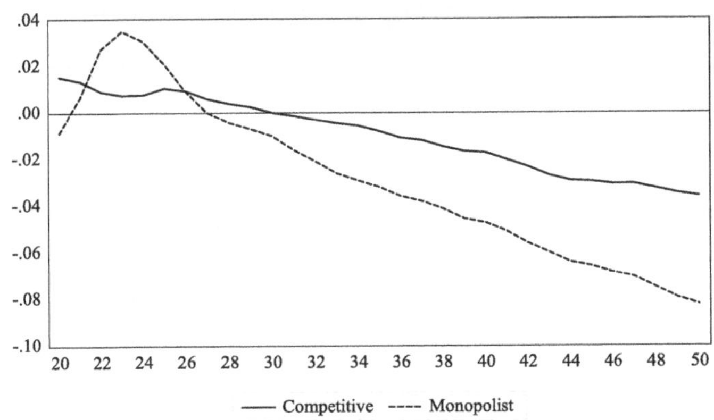

Figure 5.17 Iran – Permanent Income Deviations from Baseline

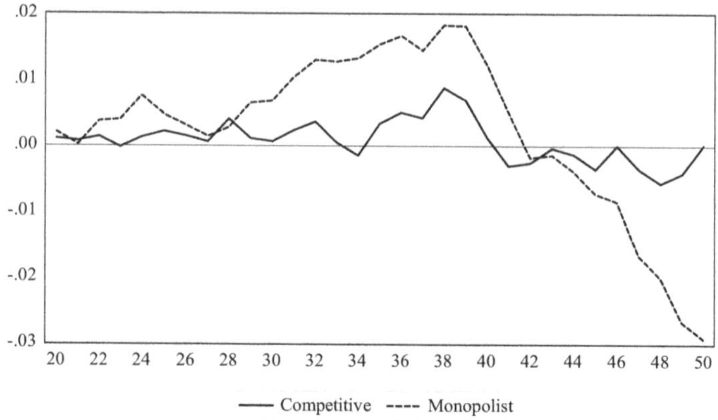

Figure 5.18 Iraq – Permanent Income Deviations from Baseline

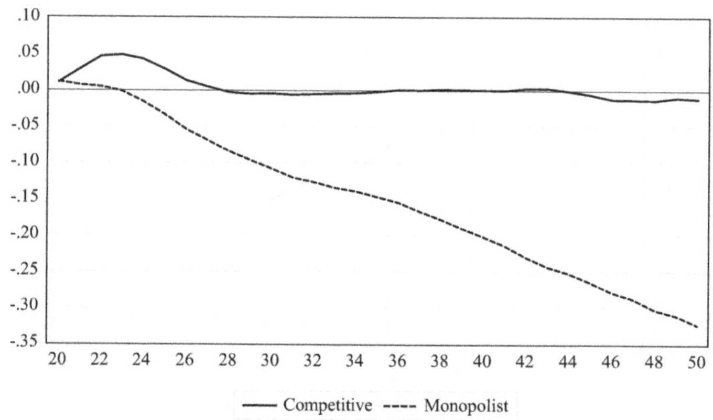

Figure 5.19 Kuwait – Permanent Income Deviations from Baseline

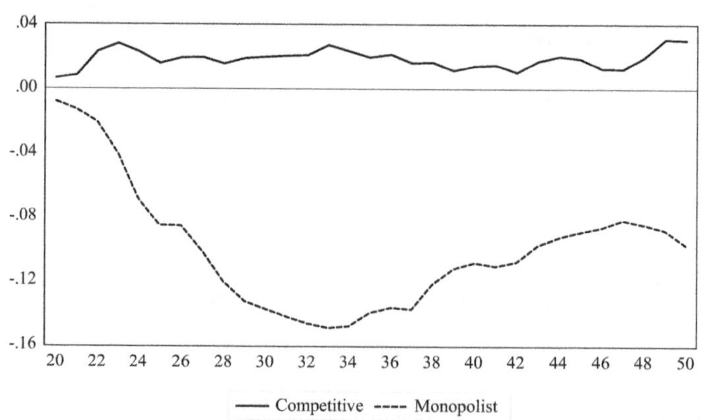

Figure 5.20 Nigeria – Permanent Income Deviations from Baseline

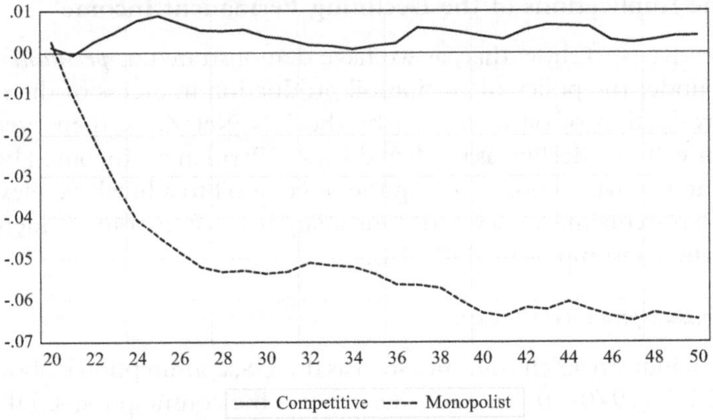

Figure 5.21 Saudi Arabia – Permanent Income Deviations from Baseline

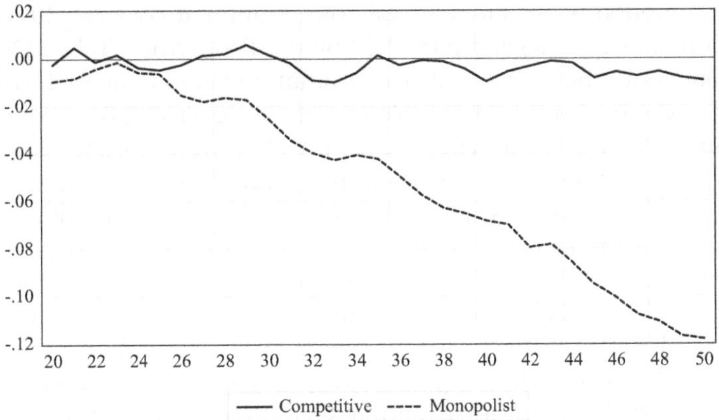

Figure 5.22 UAE – Permanent Income Deviations from Baseline

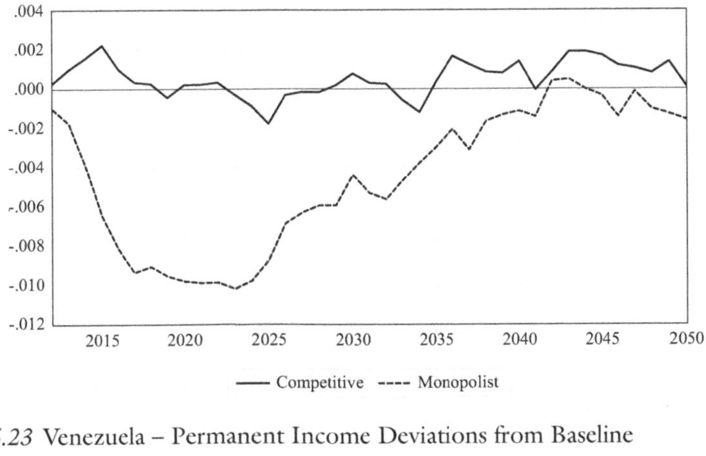

Figure 5.23 Venezuela – Permanent Income Deviations from Baseline

5.4 The Implications of the Declining Permanent Income

The objective is to show that, as we have demonstrated, if *permanent income* declines under the policy of cutting oil production in excess of the reduction in the production of oil mandated by the UN Net Zero, then *current* consumption will also decline as predicted by the Permanent Income Hypothesis. Such an aggressive oil policy to peg the price of oil to a breakeven level would be a welfare-reducing policy too. Our analysis involves some evidence based on, first the consumption–GDP ratio.

5.4.1 Consumption–GDP Ratio

In Western industrial rich countries such as the US, consumption is about 83 percent of GDP (1970–2019). Table 5.4 reports the consumption–GDP ratios of the OPEC countries. Some of the OPEC countries have relatively low consumption–GDP ratios. In particular, Iraq, Kuwait, Saudi Arabia, the UAE, and Gabon have relatively lower consumption than others in OPEC and relative to OECD too. Consumption is measured as real consumption at constant 2017 national prices (in mil. 2017US$) and published by the Penn World Table. One should be cautious about these low levels of consumption because the Arab countries in OPEC do not use monthly household income surveys to measure consumption. We are unsure whether the same is true in Gabon. Iraq, Kuwait, Saudi Arabia, and the UAE compute consumption as the *residual* from the National Income Identity $C = Y - I - G - X$, where C, Y, I, G, and X are the consumption, output, investment, government expenditures, and net exports, respectively. The output on this expenditure side is less than or equal to the output on the production side. This probably explains why consumption levels are relatively low in Iraq, Kuwait, Saudi Arabia, and the UAE. It is likely that consumption is measured the same way in African countries, e.g., Gabon. Conversely, Venezuela's consumption level is peculiarly high; the consumption–GDP ratio is >1. Earlier, we explained that the Venezuelan data are anomalous, especially after 2011. Nonetheless, even when restricting the sample to 2011, the consumption–GDP ratio is >1.

Table 5.4 OPEC's Average Consumption–GDP Ratios 1970–2019

Country	*Average Consumption–GDP Ratio*
Algeria	0.69
Angola	0.77
Congo, DR	0.87
Gabon	0.49
Iran	0.66
Iraq	0.55
Kuwait	0.58
Nigeria	0.90
Saudi Arabia	0.48
UAE	0.43
Venezuela*	1.08

Asterisk: the ratio is 1.01 if the sample is restricted to 1970–2011.
Data Source: Penn World Table 10.01.

5.4.2 *The Marginal Propensity to Consume*

Consumption is a function of *permanent income*. The theory predicts *current* consumption increases with permanent income (expected income), not current income, even though current consumption could be sensitive to *current* real income. Current income changes with age. Younger and retired people have less income than middle-aged people. Therefore, appropriate macroeconomic analysis requires an estimate of average or expected income, i.e., permanent income. We estimated *permanent income* as the mean dynamic stochastic projection of real GDP using the VAR described earlier, which has different sample spans. We plot log real consumption; log real GDP, and log *permanent income* in Figures 5.24–5.34 and the consumption–GDP and consumption–permanent income ratios.

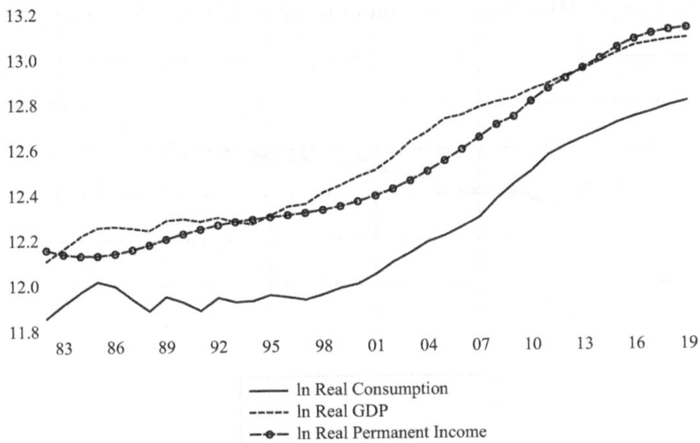

Figure 5.24 Algeria – Real Consumption, Real GDP, and Real Permanent Income Trend Up

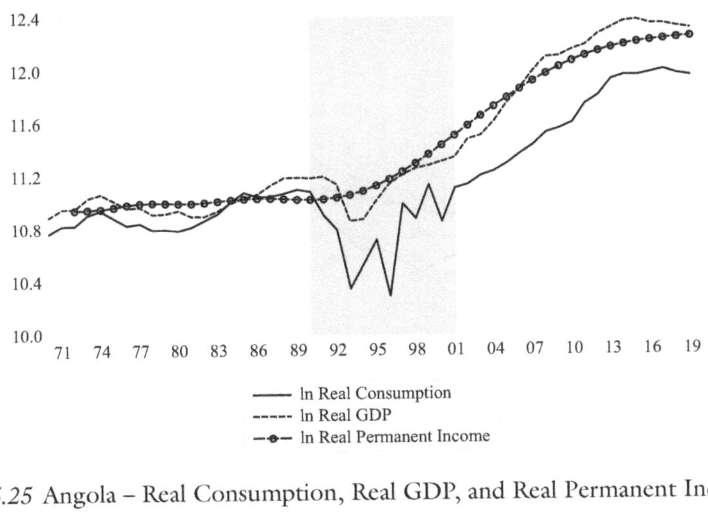

Figure 5.25 Angola – Real Consumption, Real GDP, and Real Permanent Income

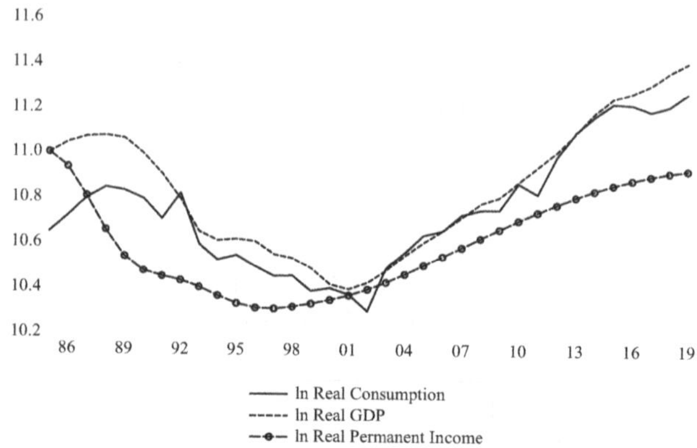

Figure 5.26 Congo, DR – Real Consumption, Real GDP, and Real Permanent Income

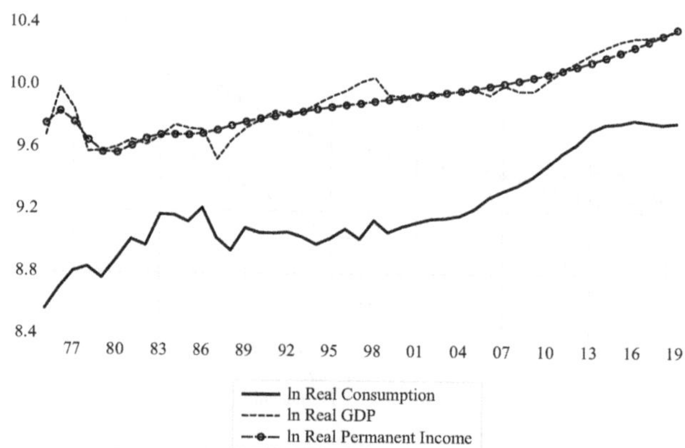

Figure 5.27 Gabon – Real Consumption, Real GDP, and Real Permanent Income

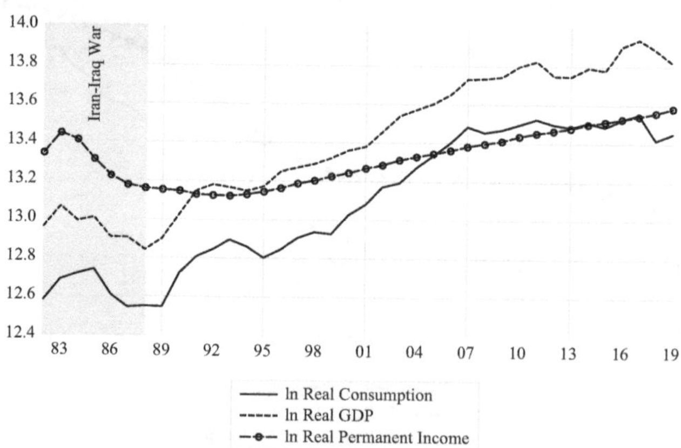

Figure 5.28 Iran – Real Consumption, Real GDP, and Real Permanent Income

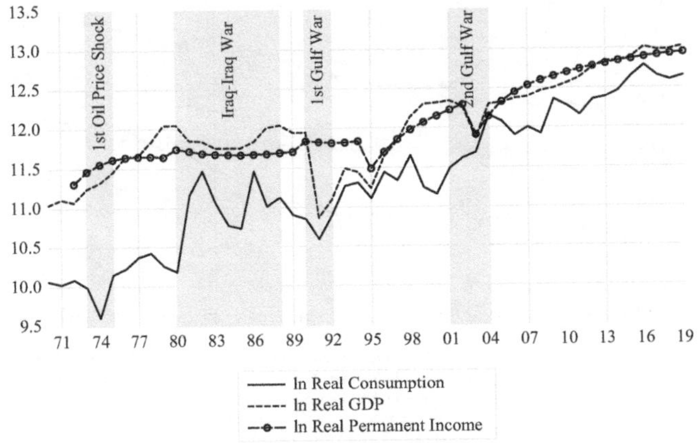

Figure 5.29 Iraq – Real Consumption, Real GDP, and Real Permanent Income

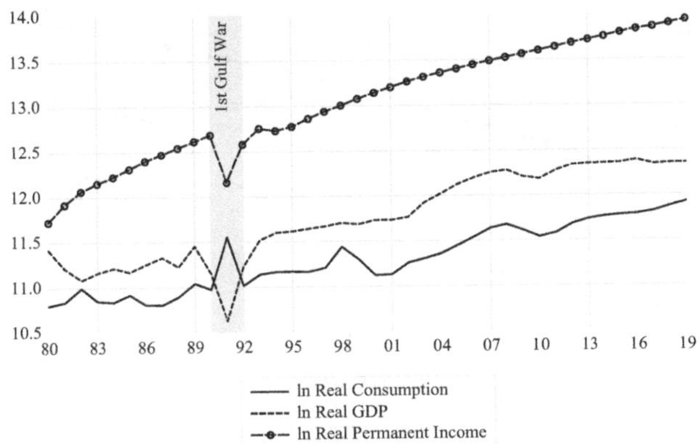

Figure 5.30 Kuwait – Real Consumption, Real GDP, and Real Permanent Income: Smooth Trends Except for the War Period

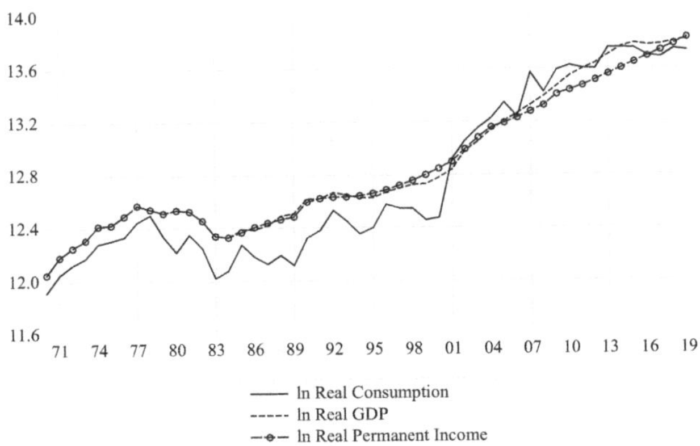

Figure 5.31 Nigeria – Real Consumption, Real GDP, and Real Permanent Income

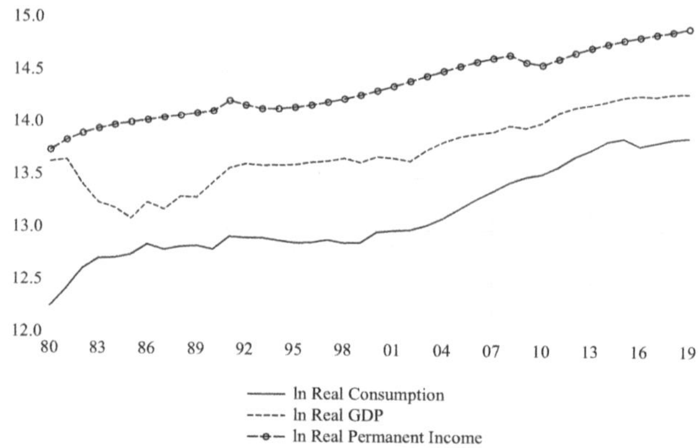

Figure 5.32 Saudi Arabia – Real Consumption, Real GDP, and Real Permanent Income

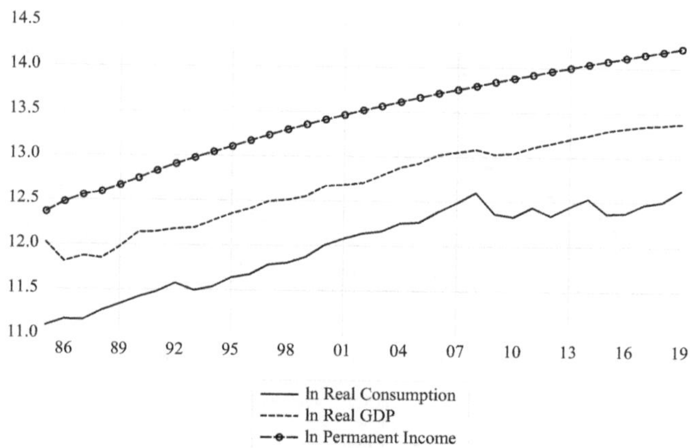

Figure 5.33 UAE – Real Consumption, Real GDP, and Real Permanent Income

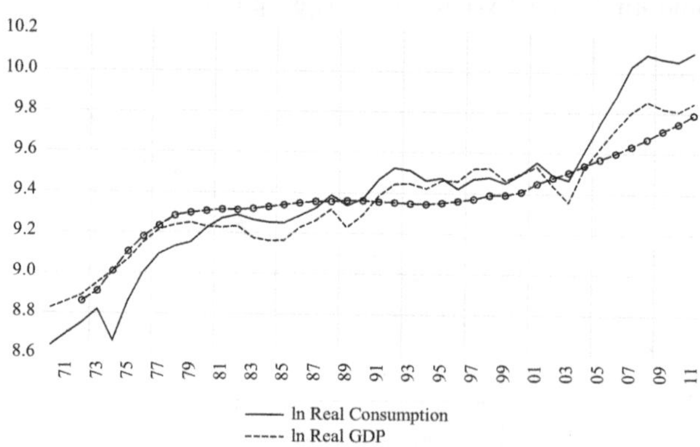

Figure 5.34 Venezuela – Real Consumption, Real GDP, and Real Permanent Income

Algeria's real consumption is lower than both current and *permanent income* albeit they have similar trends. The same is true for Angola with the exception of the high volatility in consumption between 1990 and 2001; consumption is more correlated with current income. Current income dipped during the same period. Consumption is also more correlated with current income in the Congo. For Gabon, consumption has the same trend as current and *permanent income*, but falls significantly below. Consumption is significantly below income from 1983 but from 2004 onward, consumption is highly correlated with *permanent income*. Iraq is similar to Algeria and the African countries, where consumption is significantly lower than both measures of income, more volatile than predicted by economic theory and more correlated to current income. Kuwait's consumption is also significantly smaller than *permanent income*, associated more with current income, and the correlation is inconsistent with the theory during the First Gulf War, which I think is a measurement error. Nigeria, Saudi Arabia, and the UAE have similar patterns, whereby consumption is significantly below income. Venezuela's consumption is more correlated with current income. So the three variables share similar trends in all countries, but on average, consumption is much lower than income. That does not necessarily mean OPEC countries are net savers, and it is more likely implies that consumption is measured with error.

We examine the nature of the trend in consumption before we estimate the marginal propensity to consume. We use a number of commonly used unit root tests, the ADF test (Said and Dickey 1984), the Phillips and Perron (1988), Elliott, Rothenberg, and Stock (1996), Ng and Perron (2001) two test statistics Z_α and Z_t, Bhargava (1986), and finally the ADF with breakpoint, the Kwiatkowski et al. (1992) KPSS test. We use a number of regression specifications: without a constant and trend, with a constant and trend, with a constant only, and with trend only; Dickey and Fuller showed that these specifications have different distributions. We also use a number of Information Criteria to pick up the lag length automatically, such as the AIC, SIC, Hannan–Quinn, and their modified versions. We do not report the results because the output is very large; however, the tests overwhelmingly fail to reject the unit root in lnC_t at the 5 and 10 percent levels. It has been established in the literature that these tests vary in power, but generally, they all have low powers. Note that we cannot compare the powers of these tests that have different null hypotheses. Unlike the other tests whose null hypothesis is 'unit root,' the KPSS's null hypothesis is I(0). Real consumption and permanent income are highly correlated and the *stochastic* trend is a big part of this correlation. Figure 5.35 plots the 95 percent Chi-squared Confidence Ellipse (Johnson and Wichern 1992, 189).

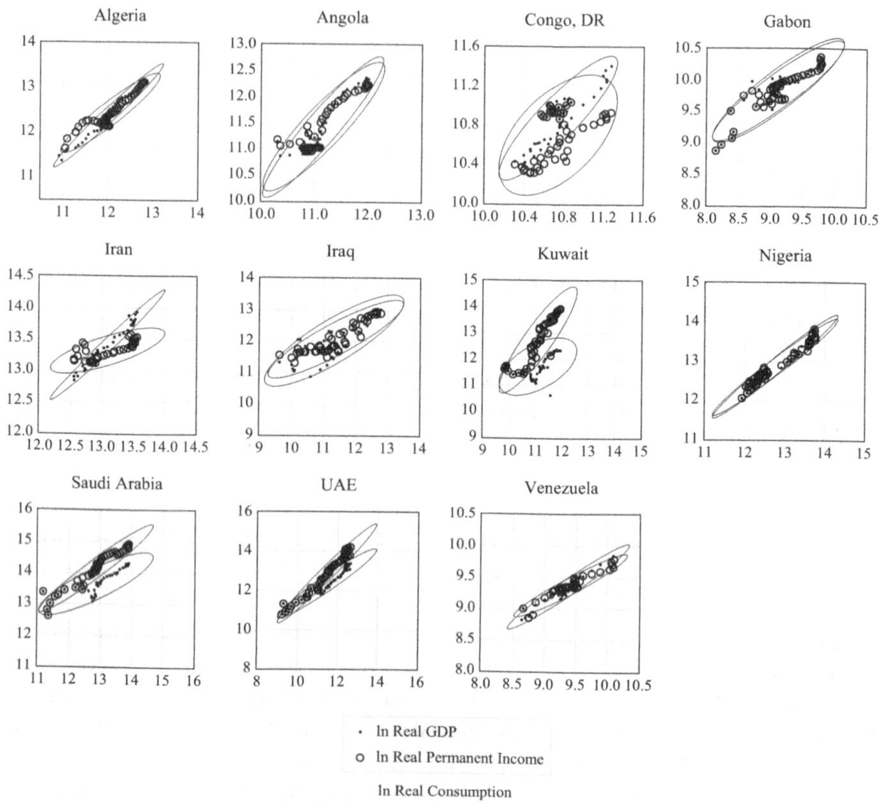

Figure 5.35 95 Percent Chi-Squared Confidence Ellipse

There is a difference between current real GDP and *permanent income*, significant in some cases such as Congo, Iran, Kuwait, Saudi Arabia, and the UAE. For permanent income – consumption, which is the *Permanent Income Hypothesis*, the correlation is positive and statistically significant, except for the Congo, DR, which is less significant albeit positive. As we have unit root in both lnY_t^p and lnC_t, we proceed to test for cointegration. If these two time series are cointegrated then an OLS regression or a DOLS regression of consumption on *permanent income* would be appropriate methods to estimate the marginal propensity to consume, and that should capture the correlation in Figure 5.35.

Testing the null hypothesis that lnC_t and *permanent income* lnY_t^p are not cointegrated, which is a bi-variate case, could be accomplished by using the Engle and Granger (1987) and the Phillips and Ouliaris (1990) test or any other test. Engle and Granger (1987) recommended six tests. Table 5.5 reports the statistics. The first test is that the OLS regression in the levels is spurious, which R^2 is very high and the Durbin–Watson statistic DW is low. The second test involves testing the residuals from the first regression for unit root using the ADF test for unit root (or any other test). Rejections of the unit root using the commonly known low-power tests such as the ADF are

Table 5.5 The Engle–Granger Test for Consumption and Permanent Income

OLS						*DOLS*
Country	$lnC_t = \beta lnY_t^p + e_t$			$ADFe_t$	$\Delta lnC_t = \alpha \Delta ln Y_t^p + \rho e_{t-1} + v_t$	$lnC_t = \gamma lnY_t^p + \varepsilon_t$
		First Test		*Second Test*	*Third Test*	*MPC*
	β	R^2	DW	τ_ρ	$t_{\rho-1}$	γ
Algeria	0.97 (1) (0.0000)	0.97	0.29	(0.0242)	(0.0282) (2)	0.94 (3) (0.0000)
Angola	1.0 (4) (0.0000)	0.78	0.59	(0.0604)	(0.0807) (5)	0.87 (6) (0.0000)
Congo, DR	1.0 (7) (0.0000)	0.66	0.31	(0.0009)	(0.0014) (8)	1.0 (9) (0.0000)
Gabon	0.92 (10) (0.0000)	0.69	0.18	(0.0329)	(0.0153) (11)	1.0 (12) (0.0000)
Iran	0.98 (13) (0.0000)	0.57	0.09	(0.0125)	(0.0519) (14)	0.97 (15) (0.0000)
Iraq	0.94 (16) (0.0000)	0.69	0.41	(0.0167)	(0.0263) (17)	0.92 (18) (0.0000)
Kuwait	0.49 (19) (0.0000)	0.78	1.53	(0.0000)	(0.0000) (20)	0.23 (21) (0.0000)
Nigeria	0.99 (22) (0.0000)	0.92	0.40	(0.0201)	(0.0000) (23)	0.99 (24) (0.0000)
S. Arabia	0.91(25) (0.0000)	0.85	0.09	(0.1013)	(0.2718) (26)	0.92 (27) (0.0000)
UAE	0.85 (28) (0.0000)	0.95	0.63	(0.0145)	(0.0233) (29)	0.89 (30) (0.0000)
Venezuela	1.0 (31) (0.0000)	0.76	0.16	(0.2167)	(0.3634) (32)	1.0 (33) (0.0000)

Source: P-values are in parentheses.
The ADF test's regressions do not include constants and time trend.
The OLS and DOLS regressions are Heteroskedasticity and Autocorrelation Consistent (HAC) standard errors and covariance, pre-whitening with max lags from AIC, Bartlett kernels, and Newey-West with automatic selections of bandwidth and lags. Not all regressions include constant terms.

(1) The sample is 1982–2019. Bandwidth = 3.7199; auto lag length = 3;
(2) Bandwidth = 3.7548 auto lag length = 3;
(3) Lead/lag (0/9). Bandwidth 4.7995;
(4) The sample is 1970–2019. Bandwidth = 4.1874; auto lag length = 3;
(5) Bandwidth = 6.1653; auto lag length = 3;
(6) Lead/lag (2/0). Bandwidth 4.1048;
(7) The sample is 1985–2019. Bandwidth = 4.7665; auto lag length = 3;
(8) Bandwidth = 3.1961; auto lag length = 3;
(9) Lead/lag (10/9). Bandwidth 36.8754;
(10) The sample is 1975–2019. Bandwidth = 6.4133; auto lag length = 3;
(11) Bandwidth = 4.4278; auto lag length = 3;
(12) Lead/lag (1/9). Bandwidth 4.5198;
(13) The sample is 1982–2019. Bandwidth = 4.2585; auto lag length = 3;
(14) Bandwidth = 7.3002; auto lag length = 3;
(15) Lead/lag (1/3). Bandwidth 6.0185;
(16) The sample is 1970–2019. Bandwidth = 8.9625; auto lag length = 3;
(17) Bandwidth = 5.0152; auto lag length = 3;
(18) Lead/lag (4/0). Bandwidth 5.7258;

(19) The sample is 1980–2019. Bandwidth =1.4002; auto lag length = 3;
(20) Bandwidth = 3.2234; auto lag length = 3;
(21) Lead/lag (9/9). Bandwidth = 5.5004;
(22) The sample is 1970–2019. Bandwidth = 3.0234; auto lag length = 3;
(23) Bandwidth =12.2088; auto lag length = 3;
(24) Lead/lag (9/8). Bandwidth =1.7638;
(25) The sample is 1980–2019. Bandwidth =4.9598; auto lag length = 3;
(26) Bandwidth = 1.5204; auto lag length = 3;
(27) Lead/lag (10/1). Bandwidth = 4.9648;
(28) The sample is 1985–2019. Bandwidth = 4.0742; auto lag length = 3;
(29) Bandwidth = 6.3057; auto lag length = 3;
(30) Lead/lag (5/9). Bandwidth = 4.8111;
(31) The sample is 1970–2011. Bandwidth = 3.7829; auto lag length =4;
(32) Bandwidth = 3.4552; auto lag length = 3;
(33) Lead/lag (9/9). Bandwidth = 35.7125.

quite a strong test for cointegration. And finally, the most powerful test is an OLS error correction model (ECM), where the lagged residuals are ***highly*** statistically significant. We do not know the distribution of this test, but t value must be large (the P-value must be close to zero). The last column is the Dynamic OLS estimate for the ***marginal propensity to consume.*** These tests suggest that the natural log of real consumption and the natural log of real permanent income, lnC_t and lnY_t^p, for Algeria are most probably cointegrated, i.e", the'share a common trend in the long run – the high R^2 and low DW statistics of the OLS level regression of lnC_t on lnY_t^p, the ADF unit root test of the residuals of that regression, and the ECM regression indicate cointegration. The marginal propensity to consume is 0.94, which means that the Algerians spend 94 cents from every dollar of ***permanent income.*** So, when ***permanent income*** is projected to decline under current oil cut policies, i.e., in excess of the oil cut required by the Zero-carbon 2050 UN plan, consumption will fall too; hence, a significant decline in welfare should be expected in the future. We obtained the same results for all OPEC countries, except for Congo, DR, Gabon, and Venezuela, where the marginal propensity to consume is 1.0. However, because the Venezuelan data are short span (1970–2011), consumption and permanent income are not cointegrated. This renders the OLS and DOLS regression in the levels inappropriate to estimate the marginal propensity to consume. The error correction equation is more appropriate; the estimated α is 0.92. Saudi Arabia's ADF test of the residuals has a slightly higher P-value, which is significant at the 10 percent level.

Algeria, Congo, Gabon, Iran, Iraq, Nigeria, and Saudi Arabia estimated marginal propensities to consume are between 0.90 and 1, i.e., extraordinarily high. Kuwait has a very low marginal propensity to consume, 0.23. Angola and the UAE estimates are slightly less than 0.90. Kuwait is probably the only country, which is not expected to suffer welfare loss if its permanent income declines as a result of oil cuts in excess of the Net Zero stipulated oil cut and if its consumption is measured properly; if it is, then Kuwait is the thriftiest country in OPEC. One must interpret the estimated marginal propensities to consume for OPEC with extra caution because of the measurement errors in the variables of the regressions.

The estimated permanent incomes under the state-owned oil industry assumption, whereby the state cuts oil production excessively when faced with a negative demand shock in order to maintain a higher price of oil (the break-even price), result in a significant reduction in current consumption; hence, the policy implies a welfare loss.

6 OPEC's Options Are Limited and Challenging

Abstract

Amidst global Net Zero commitments, oil-dependent OPEC nations grapple with maximizing revenues while adhering to environmental goals. Their entrenched oil dependency limits options, with government spending heavily reliant on oil income. Despite declarations, reconciling environmental and economic interests proves challenging. Scenarios test OPEC's response to declining global oil consumption under Net Zero. Balancing reduced production for higher prices with GDP impacts poses dilemmas. Diversification efforts remain stagnant despite rhetoric. Proposed reforms aim to decentralize control and transferring oil wealth directly to citizens might face formidable obstacles. The chapter underscores the complexities hindering change within OPEC, stressing the need for transformative reforms in the OPEC economies.

The data show that the OPEC economies are non-industrial and oil-dependent. Oil production (measured in real US dollars) shares a long-run common trend with, and is highly responsive to, global oil consumption in every OPEC country. Real GDP also shares a long-run common trend and a common cycle with oil production. Government expenditures are highly dependent on oil revenues. Generally, oil is a state-owned monopoly and centrally managed by the OPEC governments. OPEC countries, especially the rich GCC such as Saudi Arabia, Kuwait, and the UAE in addition to Iraq and Iran have a high breakeven oil price. This is the estimated price required to maximize oil revenues and satisfy government expenditures in US dollars. Oil prices are volatile because they behave like asset prices, which are subject to volatile persistent shocks. Maintaining constantly high breakeven prices is, therefore, difficult. The most recent IMF projections indicate even higher fiscal breakeven oil prices. Influencing the price of oil by OPEC has been clearly demonstrated lately, although with the support of Russia, which is a non-OPEC, i.e., OPEC+. They did so by continuous sizable cuts in oil supply.

The Net Zero main publicly stated objective is to reduce global emission by 45 percent in 2030 and zero by 2050. OPEC publicly announced that it would adhere to this goal. OPEC also publicly declared that it is most concerned about environmental issues. So, given this global commitment to Net Zero, the question is how would OPEC fully adhere to the Net Zero plan and at the same

DOI: 10.4324/9781003488125-6

time maximize oil revenues and pursue economic development plans depending on oil as the main source of income? It seems somehow contradictory.

OPEC oil industries are state-owned monopolies in the sense that the government decides the levels of production among many other things. They cut oil production *by more than the reductions in oil production required by Net Zero*, if needed, to prevent the breakeven price of oil from falling below their desired price. OPEC+ has cut oil production several times since the COVID pandemic, in 2022 and 2023, and by large amounts up to 500,000 barrels/day by Saudi Arabia, and 300,000 barrels/day by Iraq. These cuts pushed the price of oil to more than 80 US dollars/barrel in 2023. Clearly, OPEC would be content with such a price, if maintained. The problem is that it could not possibly be maintained with more frequent production cuts. We have seen the price of oil to fall below $80 US dollars in early 2024 even though OPEC+ cut oil production more.

Net Zero reduces global demand and global oil consumption, which puts a downward pressure on the price of oil, reduces export revenues, and real GDP in oil-producing countries. The IEA's recent report in 2023 suggests that demand will continue to fall. Then we would expect OPEC to continue to cut oil production to peg the price of oil, but reducing oil production also reduces real GDP by more, i.e., reduces expected (permanent) income because oil production is a big chunk of total output (measured in real US dollars). The decline in *permanent income* reduces *current* consumption (the *Permanent Income Hypothesis*) significantly because the estimated marginal propensity to consume out of permanent income is very high. It seems obvious that adhering to the Net Zero Agreement while at the same time depending on oil as the main source of income are conflicting goals. This is what we call the OPEC's dilemma.

OPEC countries have been talking publicly about diversifying income for decades; nothing serious happened so far to show up in the data. Oil remained a major source of foreign currency. OPEC economies will suffer without oil. Sharp, sudden, and persistent negative oil price shocks, e.g., in 2014, sent a few oil-producing countries to the capital markets borrowing at very high interest rates. Therefore, income diversification is not really a gimmick or a slogan in stump speeches and five-year development plan reports, but rather necessary for OPEC's future. They know that, but they have been unable to do it; export data show that oil is the main export. There are efforts to build transportation networks such as railways, airports, and ports in OPEC countries, which serve international trade regionally, and internationally. Meanwhile, it is all about oil. Oil alters the incentives. Essentially, it does not give the incentive to industrialize faster, increase work effort, increase the productivity of the non-oil sectors, and produce research and new ideas for growth. Oil is a tranquilizer especially when the price is high.

OPEC's dilemma could be resolved, temporarily, however, if the Net Zero Agreement collapses, which is a trivial resolution that does not seem likely at the moment because of the great global popular and governmental support for Net Zero. One could not foresee the future of oil because the world is going through a period of great political instability, migrations, and cultural change. So what are the other policy options for OPEC?

Stress tests to measure the response of the OPEC economies to a severe adverse shock to global oil consumption show that future real GDP dynamic stochastic projection from 2020 to 2050, i.e., *permanent income*, falls significantly and steadily under the current government oil monopoly model. Conversely, no decline in *permanent income* is shown under the scenario of a hypothetical competitive oil industry, which cuts oil production by less (i.e., as much as required to achieve the Net Zero objective, no more) and most importantly, takes up lower market prices. OPEC countries could use different models, assumptions, and methods to do more stress tests to further assist policymakers.

There is no other viable and easy option for the OPEC governments under Net Zero, except restructuring the oil industry away from total government control by creating a competitive oil industry as I argued in Razzak (2022) explained using Iraq as a case study, or they could stop cutting oil production in excess of the reductions required by Net Zero to prop-up higher oil prices. The latter is easier than the former. However, with governments unable or unwilling to reduce expenditures, OPEC oil dependence will keep OPEC governments doing what they have been doing.

Adopting a *competitive* economic model is the better option, but it is disruptive, however. It requires significant changes in the political and the economic institutions. To deal with the expected permanent decline in the global demand for oil and the expected fall in *trend* oil prices, government revenues, and the fall in permanent income, we argue for a complete and immediate change in the political and economic institutions. Here is the point, oil is the property of the people; therefore, the people must own it, not the government. Hence, significant political and economic institutional changes must take place.

In Razzak (2022) I argued that from an economic standpoint, *people's ownership* of the factors of production is associated with political and economic freedom and democracy. See, for example, Hayek (1944), Friedman (1962), Pipes (2000), and O'Driscoll and Hoskibs (2003). Sound economic development requires market institutions and most importantly private property rights. Even the Chinese Communist Party has realized that the government cannot dictate market prices.

There is reliable empirical evidence on the significance of private ownership on GDP growth. For example, historians North and Thomas (1973), and Rosenberg and Birdzell (1986) presented evidence that private property played a major role in enriching the West. Barro (1991) used proxies for the quality of private property to test the effect on GDP growth. Kormendi and MeGuire (1985) used measures of political freedom and civil liberties to proxy the quality of property rights and reported a positive association with GDP growth. Heitger (2002) illustrates the same point.[1]

Ross (2001) examines the effect of oil on democracy empirically. He examined a panel of 113 countries over the period from 1970 to 1997. Testing

1 It might be worth mentioning that the solution of the neoclassical growth model, Ramsey (1928), Cass (1965), and Koopmans (1965) under the social planner is the same as under the private market.

several hypotheses (the rent state, the repression effect, and the modernization effect) revealed that oil adversely affects democracy and more so in poorer countries. Elbadawi and Makdisi (2011) provide evidence that oil is one of the main reasons for the lack of democracy in Arab countries. Rotunda (2004), Birdsall and Subramanian (2004), Wolf (2005), and Razzak (2006, 2022) proposed the privatization of oil for Iraq. It means immediate transfers of the oil wealth to the people *per se* would enhance democracy. It seems that democracy is hard to implement in oil-rich countries because of the entrenched interests of powerful groups of people in the *status quo*. Mokyr (1990) provides stories of people who are threatened by innovations. A well-known example is Luddites, which was a movement in the US that felt its interests were threatened by the industrialization of cotton and wool and took violent actions to destroy the new machines.

Today, we have heated arguments about AI and whether it represents an existential threat to humans. It is the very same case of people who perceive new technologies as a threat to their own, e.g., wages will decline, jobs will be lost, and so on. For OPEC, powerful merchants in the GCC, who have been the backbone of these economies and the exclusive importers of finished goods from abroad, strongly object to industrialization in the GCC because they fear they will lose. There are many; e.g., merchants, rich families, small bourgeoisie, people on benefits, government employees in millions, and others who believe that they would lose the rent from oil if oil wealth is no longer under government control. Contrary to these beliefs, all people would benefit if wealth, whether oil or all assets under the control of the government, is transferred to the people directly. Surely, this strong aversion to private ownership of oil is not limited to OPEC governments; the governments of the Western democratic industrial countries have benefited from the political and economic arrangements in the former colonies and protectorates and would benefit from the status quo in OPEC contrary to what they preach against monopoly and for free market democracy.

We are witnessing military coups in Africa, infightings, and civil unrest in addition to foreign interventions. Wars in the Middle East take different forms, foreign military interventions, terrorism, and autocratic control. The only relatively stable countries are the oil-rich Saudi Arabia and the UAE, but they are small in population and strongly autocratic. We do not expect a significant change as the one we witnessed in the ex-Eastern European communist countries after 1991 to take place in most OPEC countries, but people should think about change along such directions.

In most market-oriented democracies, the people own the resources and the factors of production. All the Eastern European countries (e.g., Russia, Poland, Hungary, the Czech Republic, etc.), which became democracies after the fall of the USSR, changed their economies rather quickly. The fragile democracies in Iraq, Iran, Indonesia, Nigeria, Gabon, Angola, and Algeria, for example, could do the same if the political climate and culture change. They could learn from the mistakes of others. Methods could be different depending on the objectives and the economic and political conditions. The Russian and the Czech Republic, for example, privatization processes were different from Poland, Hungary, or even the UK. The distribution of the oil wealth is different in Alaska from Norway.

Today, most Iraqis, for example, agree that since the establishment of 'democracy' in 2003, (1) economic development has not occurred; (2) oil wealth has been squandered; and as a result, the Iraqi people have been impoverished. Ending the economic hegemony and control of the state on oil wealth is the only solution to free the economy and the people now and to uphold democratic institutions. Except for Saudi Arabia, Kuwait, and the UAE, the majority of people in OPEC countries are poor; although some might argue that there are poverty pockets in Saudi Arabia, we do not have data to support such an argument. The poverty data are patchy, i.e., not available regularly, but everything is relative and they may bear some information to score the point. The African oil-producing countries, although seemingly more *democratic* than the GCC, are relatively poorer. Why are these countries poor? Why is there significant inequality? Maybe there are growth and distribution problems, except for Iraq in 2012 and Venezuela in 2006, none has economic growth and all of them have inequality and distribution problems. The data suggest that a corrupt government does not allow markets to function as they are supposed to, to generate growth, and does not share the oil wealth with the people equally or equitably.

The most natural way of life is that the citizens own their natural resources, mainly oil. Oil shares must be distributed to all the citizens *equally*. It is essential that shares are tradable in a free market immediately so ordinary people can benefit from buying and selling these oil shares; thus, oil wealth could generate oil income. One expects that some people who need cash would sell their shares to other buyers who want to buy the asset at an agreeable price for the share. Allowing the free exchange of shares guarantees the establishment of a functional market.[2] When the people own their oil, no one can steal it anymore.

After the breakup of the Soviet Union and the Warsaw Pact, the Russian new government handed shares in state-owned companies to the people directly. In the Czech Republic, people were given vouchers (each included 1,000 investment points), and then they bid on shares in a large number of state-owned companies. The bid-offer process converted these points into share prices. The Czech Republic's objective of the privatization was to establish a free market economy. In the UK, state-owned companies were sold directly to the public. However, OPEC could learn from others' experiences. The mistakes that occurred in those experiences must be avoided by appropriate regulations. Table 6.1 reports statistics that show poverty and inequality in OPEC, especially in African countries.

Regulations are necessary to protect people; however, the current political structure is not a reliable one for regulating the process of transferring wealth from the government to the people because they are implicated in squandering the oil wealth in Africa, Iraq, and Venezuela in particular. There is no obvious way to deal with regulations in the case of distributing oil shares to the citizens. One possibility is to establish an *independent* court, to manage

2 We would argue that the ownership of government-controlled assets, not only oil, in general and government-controlled lands should also be transferred to people *a la* the Homestead Act in the US (1862), and many other countries (e.g., Anderson 2011).

Table 6.1 The African Nations in OPEC Are Relatively Poorer

	Algeria (2011)	*Angola* (2018)	*Congo, DR* (2012)	*Gabon* (2017)	*Iran* (2019)	*Iraq* (2012)	*Nigeria* (2018)	*Venezuela* (2006)
Poverty gap at $3.65 a day (2017 PPP) (percent)	0.80	24.5	52.3	2.5	1.4	0.40	25.1	6.8
Poverty headcount ratio at $3.65 a day (2017 PPP) (percent of population)	4.0	52.9	87.7	8.1	6.0	2.4	63.5	15.5
Gini index	27.6	51.3	42.1	38	40.9	29.5	35.1	NA
Poverty gap at $2.15 a day (2017 PPP) (percent)	0.20	11.9	32.6	0.60	0.20	0	9.0	3.9
Poverty headcount ratio at $2.15 a day (2017 PPP) (percent of population)	0.50	31.1	69.7	2.5	1	0.10	30.9	7.1
Income held by the lowest 20 percent	9.4	3.8	5.5	6	6	8.8	7.1	
Proportion of people living below 50 percent of median income (percent)	6.3	22.8	16.4	15.7	15.4	7.6	13.2	19.9
Real GDP per Capita Growth (percent)	0.96	–4.6	3.5	–9.0	–3.7	8.9	–0.59	8.1

Data Source: World Bank. The Gini index measures the extent to which the distribution of income (or, in some cases, consumption expenditure) among individuals or households within an economy. Zero means no inequality. The higher the number, the higher inequality is. The use of consumption instead of current income is sensible because what matters for inequality is permanent income, not current income because the latter changes with age. The Permanent Income Hypothesis says that consumption is a function of permanent income.

the process of ownerships, sales, transfer, and inheritance of the oil shares, to safeguard the integrity of the process. It is necessary to protect the rights of women, the elderly, and the sick shareholders from exploitation.[3]

Eventually, the citizen shareholders will have to establish private oil companies with a sound governance system to manage their own wealth. Private ownership will enhance democratic practices and contribute to the building of market institutions such as the banking system, the tax system to replace oil revenues with more sensible tax revenues, the share market, and so on that are required to achieve efficiency in the distribution of wealth. Iraq, for example, has an old functioning tax system with expertise and rules. Remember that even a significant large communist country like China has adopted market-oriented structures, which has already benefited the Chinese people. The incentive structure will be set properly, which will help allocate resources efficiently. Reforms of such magnitude and depth would take time to work, but it would work at the end of the day. New Zealand, an old Western democracy, which enjoyed political and judicial stability for centuries, took a long time to realize the fruits of its market-oriented policy and institutional reforms of 1984 (e.g., Evans et al. 1996).

Transferring the oil wealth to the people will make people better off by providing them with the financial means and the right incentives to make their own investments and businesses. As a result, we envisage some rearrangements of public sector employment would be needed. Government employees who receive a share in oil either voluntarily exit from the public sector to pursue private businesses are laid off or reassigned, albeit with different negotiated contracts whereby real wages are consistent with labor productivity. This will reduce the swelling of the inefficient public sector and decrease waste and public spending significantly.

When the citizens begin to receive dividends from oil shares they will become more interested in the performance of the oil industry as a whole regardless of the regions because when any one regional company makes profits all people will benefit. Sharing oil wealth and the independence of the oil business will unify the country, as the people will recognize that they own and share their country.

Finally, for the Muslim OPEC countries, people's ownership of oil is more consistent with Islam because it encourages investments in assets rather than receiving interest income so buyers and sellers share the gains and losses. The citizen shareholders will benefit when their oil company, or any regional company, does well and the share price increases. However, if the government elects to pursue the old policies and keeps control over oil, it will become nothing more than an authoritarian government, and economic development will stall. This has been happening already.

That said, OPEC countries, despite the trappings of constitutional governments, are unlikely to make the political and economic institutional changes we discussed earlier. We do not expect current governments to distribute oil wealth

3 High-expected rate of regulations makes corruption more possible. Private individuals who bribe government officials increase in order to have their contracts honored. Iraq is one of the worst countries in the world in terms of freedom from repudiation of contracts. Iraq also scored high on almost all corruption indices (Easterly 2002).

to people. The US recognizes only four OPEC countries as democracies, Angola, Indonesia, Iraq, and Nigeria although these countries lack the proper functional democratic institutions. We have shown earlier that OPEC countries are rentier economies, some are absolute autocracies, and thus there is no incentive for the governments to relinquish their powers to collect oil revenues and spend them freely and without accountability. Furthermore, those who collect oil rent, the powerful merchants who have government's exclusive import licenses, contractors, and most importantly the vast majority of people who pay little for oil, gas, and petrol subsidized prices, among many other groups have no incentive to give up on the current system. There is no doubt that OPEC countries have some people with entrenched interests in the *status quo*. In addition, in some OPEC countries such as Venezuela, Iraq, Iran, and Algeria, there are also people who are socialists at heart and believe that only the government can manage oil resources and distribute services. Ideologically motivated socialists do not accept the idea of giving ownership of the oil wealth to the ordinary people. The majority of people are oblivious to the dangers the future of the Net Zero Agreement holds.

Moreover, rampant corruption in OPEC countries makes economic growth and political reforms difficult.[4] The African members of OPEC face military *coups d'état* relatively more frequently; Gabon is the latest one that happened as we write this chapter and who knows what is coming next. The *Corruption Perception Index* published by Transparency International in 2022, whether we take it seriously or not, does not look good.[5] Table 6.2 reports the statistics. A score of 100 denotes the least corrupt nation. Most OPEC countries are far away from 100 and more toward zero, i.e., toward corruption. What determines corruption is beyond the scope of this book. The point is that we have an issue that would cause a serious challenge to changing the *modus operandi* of the oil industries in OPEC.

Table 6.2 Most of the OPEC Countries Are Corrupt in 2022

Country	*Index*	*Rank*
Algeria	33	116
Angola	33	116
Congo, DR	20	166
Gabon	29	136
Iran	25	147
Indonesia	34	110
Iraq	23	157
Kuwait	42	77
Nigeria	24	150
Saudi Arabia	51	54
UAE	67	27
Venezuela	14	177

Data Source: Transparency International 31 January, 2023.

4 There is evidence about the negative correlation between corruption and economic growth, for example, see Chafuen and Guzman (1996).

5 www.transparency.org/en/cpi/2022?gclid=EAIaIQobChMI4cup1um_gwMVPqRmAh0_HgxBEAAYASAAEgJnGfD_BwE&gad_source=1

The OPEC governments may no longer be able to keep the same size, employment, rent, social welfare payments, and other expenditures. Some governments have recognized that long before but were unable to make changes. Kuwait, among other rich oil producers, has always struggled with swelling public employment. The Kuwaiti constitution requires that the government provides jobs to every citizen who wants a job. These sorts of expenditures would not be tenable if the government loses its total control over oil revenues. The Iraqi government's White Paper (2020) points to economic and demographic pressures on the government's finances. The trend in public sector's employment reached more than 3 million in 2020, 30 percent of the total labor force. The wage bill is approximately 15 percent of GDP and rising. In real terms, public sector salaries and pensions increased by 350 percent between 2006 and 2020. The payroll payments expenditures increased by more than 360 percent, and pensions expenditures increased by more than 30 percent. The population grew 53 percent from 2004 to 2020. The young population (under 30 years) makes up 66 percent, which puts a strong pressure on public spending. The population is expected to grow by 25 percent by 2030; the population under 30 years is expected to grow by 17 percent. The government has to, but it cannot, create 5 million jobs, all in the public sector, between 2020 and 2030.

The Conference Board productivity growth data for the OPEC countries, albeit questionable, showed that productivity growth has been either zero or negative for years (see Chapter 1). It is unclear how OPEC governments view economic and productivity growth. It is unclear because when the price of oil is above 80 dollars/barrel, the government spends more and that is all that matters for them. Human capital is the most important explanatory variable in growth models. It affects the transitional output growth path; yet in the case of OPEC, it has no explanatory power although most of the OPEC countries invested heavily in human capital. Laabas and Razzak (2011), for example, as we explained in Chapter 4, found no significant effect of quality-adjusted human capital on productivity growth in developing countries. For OPEC, most of the variations in real GDP are due to oil production. Oil production will decline with a future decline in the demand for oil and then cease in the long run, then what? What would drive economic growth in the future?

In particular, Iraq, among all others in OPEC, has a better chance of building a democracy after it suffered a dictatorship after another for decades. The political elite, however, will strongly oppose the idea of creating a competitive private oil industry owned by the citizens to save Iraq as a democratic country in the 21st century because they have entrenched interests in the status quo. Educated Iraqis who have grown under military socialist dictatorship could also oppose the idea because they have learned nothing better than social welfare benefits. They like to have a free education and health benefits provided by the government, i.e., public hospitals and public schools, regardless of quality of course, a secure public job, and a fully funded retirement pension. This is the only game played in Iraq historically and despite the disastrous outcomes, many people hesitate to play another game. There is one big hope, however, that the new generations of Iraqis, which did not grow up under dictatorships and are more outward and forward-looking, may be able to force the change. Meanwhile, the clock seems to be ticking for the end of fossil fuel in the world.

References

Anderson, H. 2011. "That Settles It: The Debate and Consequences of the Homestead Act of 1862." *The History Teacher* 45(1): 117–37.

Anderson, R., J. Danielsson, C. Baba, U. S. Das, H. Kang, and M. A. Segoviano. 2018. *Macroprudential Tests and Policies: Searching for Robust and Implementable Frameworks*. Washington, DC: IMF.

Barro, R. 1991. "Economic Growth in a Cross-Section of Countries." *Quarterly Journal of Economics* 106: 407–43.

Bhargava, A. 1986. "On the Theory of Testing for Unit Roots in Observed Time Series." *Review of Economic Studies* 53: 369–84.

Birdsall, Nancy, and Arvind Subramanian. 2004. *Saving Iraq from Its Oil Foreign Affairs*. Vol. 83, No. 4, 77–89. New York: Council on Foreign Relations, USA.

Buchanan, J. (1969). *Cost and Choice*. Chicago, ILChicago: Markham Publishing, USA.

Buchanan, J. (1975). *The Limits of Liberty*. Chicago, IL: University of Chicago Press, Chicago, IL.

Buchanan, J. (1977). *Freedom in Constitutional Contract*. College Station: Texas A&M University Press, USA.

Buchanan, J. (1986). *Liberty, Market and the State: Political Economy in the 1980s*. Brighton, UK: Harvester Press, UK.

Buchanan, J. (1988). "The Constitution of Economic Policy." *In Public Choice and Constitutional Economics*, edited by J. Gwartney, J. and R. Wagner, R. London: JAI Press.

Buchanan, J. (1991). *The Economics and Ethics of Constitutional Order*. Ann Arbor: University of Michigan Press, USA.

Claes, Dag Harald, and Giuliano Garavini, eds. 2020. *Handbook of OPEC and the Global Energy Order: Past, Present and Future Challenges*. New York, NY: Routledge, Taylor and Francis.

Cass, David. 1965. "Optimum Growth in An Aggregative Model of Capital Accumulation." *Review of Economic Studies* 32: 233–40.

Chafuen, A., and E. Guzman. 1996. "Bureaucratic Corruption in Africa: The Futility of Cleanups." *Cato Journal* 16 (1).

Cheung, Y. W., and Kon S. Lai. 1993. "Finite-Sample Sizes of Johansen's Likelihood Ration Tests for Conintegration." *Oxford Bulletin of Economics and Statistics* 55 (3): 313–28.

Christiano, Lawrence J., and M. Eichenbaum. 1990. "Unit Roots in Real GNP: Do We Know, and Do We Care?." *Carnegie-Rochester Conference Series on Public Policy* 32 (Spring): 7–62.

Christiano, Lawrence J., and M. Eichenbaum. 1992. "Current Real Business Cycle Theories and Aggregate Labor Market Fluctuations." *American Economic Review* 82 (June): 430–50.

Cihak, M. 2007. *Introduction to Applied Stress Testing*. Washington, DC: IMF.

Cochrane, J. 1991. *Comments, NBER Macroeconomics Annual Committee on the Global Financial System – CGFS. 2005. Stress Testing at Major Financial Institutions: Survey Results and Practice, Report by a working group established by the CGFS*. Basel: Bank for International Settlements. www.bis.org.

Crockett, Andrew. 1997. "Why Is Financial Stability a Goal of Public Policy?" In *Maintaining Financial Stability in a Global Economy, a Symposium*, edited by Jackson Hole. Wyoming: Federal Reserve Bank of Kansas City. www.kc.frb.org/publicat/econrev/pdf/4q97croc.pdf.

Demekas, D. G. 2015. *Designing Effective Macroprudential Stress Tests*. Washington, DC: IMF.

Dickey, D. A., and W. A. Fuller. 1979. "Distribution of the Estimators for Autoregressive Time Series with a Unit Root." *Journal of the American Statistical Association* 74: 427–31.

Easterly, W. 2002. *The Elusive Quest for Growth*. Cambridge, MA: MIT Press.

El Dahan, M., and A. Rasheed. 2023. *OPEC+ Announces Surprise Oil Output Cuts*, April. www.reuters.com/business/energy/sarabia-other-opec-producers-announce-voluntary-oil-output-cuts-2023-04–02/.

Elbadawi, I., and A. Gelb. 2010. "Oil, Economic Diversification and Development in the Arab World." ERF Policy Research Report No. 35, Cairo, Egypt.

Elbadawi, I., and S. Makdisi. 2011. "Democracy in the Arab World." In *Routledge Studies in Middle Eastern Politics*. London, UK.

Elbadawi, I., and R. Soto. 2012. "Resource Rents, Political institutions and Economic Growth." ERF Working Paper Series No. 678, Cairo, Egypt.

Ellestad, Myrvin H. 2003. *Stress Testing: Principles and Practice*, 10016. 5th ed. Oxford University Press Inc. (198 Madison Avenue, New York, New York). www.oup-usa.org.

Elliott, Graham, Thomas J. Rothenberg, and James H. Stock. 1996. "Efficient Tests for an Autoregressive Unit Root." *Econometrica* 64: 813–36.

Engle, Robert F., and C. W. J. Granger. 1987. "Co-integration and Error Correction: Representation, Estimation, and Testing." *Econometrica* 55: 251–76.

Evans, L., Arthur Grimes, Bryce Wilkinson, and David Teece. 1996. "Economic Reform in New Zealand 1984–95: The Pursuit of Efficiency." *Journal of Economic Literature* 34(4): 1856–902.

Feenstra, Robert C., Robert Inklaar, and Marcel P. Timmer. 2015. "The Next Generation of the Penn World Table." *American Economic Review* 105 (10): 3150–82. www.ggdc.net/pwt.

Frankel, Jeffrey. 2012. "The Natural Resource Curse: A Survey of Diagnoses and Some Prescriptions." HKS Faculty Research Working Paper Series (RWP12–014), Harvard Library. https://dash.harvard.edu/handle/1/8694932.

Friedman, Milton. 1957. "The Permanent Income Hypothesis." In *A Theory of the Consumption Function*, 20–37. Princeton: Princeton University Press.

Friedman, Milton. 1962. *Capitalism and Freedom*. 14th ed. Chicago and London: The University of Chicago Press.

Gillingham, Kenneth T., Arthur A. van Benthem, Stephanie Weber, Mohamed Al Saafi, and Xin He. 2023. "Has Consumer Acceptance of Electric Vehicles Been Increasing?

Evidence from Microdata on Every New Vehicle Sale in the United States." *AEA Papers and Proceedings* 113: 329–35.

Gonzalo, J. 1994. "Five Alternative Methods of Estimating Long-Run Equilibrium Relationships." *Journal of Econometrics* 60 (1–2): 203–33.

Gordon, J. 1999. "A peaceful, Silent, Deadly Remedy: the Ethics of Economic Sanctions." *Ethics and International Affairs* 13: 123–42. https:/doi.org/10.1111/j.1747-7093.1000.tb00330.x.

Hamilton, J. 1994. *Time Series Analysis*. Princeton, NJ: Princeton University Press.

Hayek, F. A. 1944. *The Road to Serfdom*. Chicago: University of Chicago Press.

Hayek, F. A. 2012. *Law, Legislation, and Liberty: A New Statement of the Liberal Principles of Justice and Political Economy*. London: Routledge.

Heitger, B. 2002. "Property Rights and Their Impact on the Wealth of Nations: Cross-Country Study." Keil Working Paper No. 1163.

Hsieh, Chang-Tai, and Peter J. Klenow. 2010. "Development Accounting." *American Economic Journal: Macroeconomics* 2 (1): 207–23.

IEA. 2023. *Net Zero Roadmap: A Global Pathway to Keep the 1.5 C Goal in Reach*. www.iea.org/reports/net-zero-roadmap-a-global-pathway-to-keep-the-15-0c-goal-in-reach.

Inklaar, Robert, Pieter Woltjer, and Daniel Gallardo Albarran. 2019. "The Composition of Capital and Cross-country Productivity Comparisons." *International Productivity Monitor* 36 (1): 34–52.

Isakin, M., and P. V. Ngo. 2020. "Variance Decomposition Analysis for Nonlinear Economic Models." *The Oxford Bulletin of Economics and Statistics* 82 (6): 1362–74.

Johansen, Søren. 1988. "Statistical Analysis of Cointegration Vectors." *Journal of Economics Dynamics and Control* 12: 231–54.

Johansen, Søren. 1991. "Estimation and Hypothesis Testing of Cointegration Vectors in Gaussian Vector Autoregressive Models." *Econometrica* 59: 1551–80.

Johansen, Søren. 1995. *Likelihood-based Inference in Cointegrated Vector Autoregressive Models*. Oxford: Oxford University Press.

Johansen, Søren, and Katarina Juselius. 1990. "Maximum Likelihood Estimation and Inferences on Cointegration – with applications to the demand for money." *Oxford Bulletin of Economics and Statistics* 52: 169–210.

Johnson, Richard A., and Dean W. Wichern. 1992. *Applied Multivariate Statistical Analysis*. 3rd ed. Upper Saddle River, NJ: Prentice-Hall, Inc.

Kanas, A., and P. Molyneux. 2018. "Macro Stress Testing the U.S. Banking System." *Journal of International Financial Markets, Institutions and Money* 54: 204–27 (ISSN 1042–4431). https://doi.org/10.1016/j.intfin.2017.12.006.

Knights, Michael. 2023. "Iraq Is Quietly Falling Apart." *Foreign Affairs*. https://www.foreignaffairs.com/iran/iraq-quietly-falling-apart.

Koop, G., M. H. Pesaran, and S. M. Potter. 1996. "Impulse Response Analysis in Nonlinear Multivariate Models." *Journal of Econometrics* 74: 119–47.

Koopmans, Tjalling C. 1965. "Chapter. 4: On the Concept of Optimal Economic Growth." In *Study Econometric Approach to Development Planning*, 225–87. Amsterdam: North-Holland Publishing Co.

Kormendi, R., and P. McGuire. 1985. "Macroeconomic Determinants of Growth: Cross-Section Evidence." *Journal of Monetary Economics* 16: 141–63.

Kwiatkowski, Denis, Peter C. B. Phillips, Peter Schmidt, and Yongcheol Shin. 1992. "Testing the Null Hypothesis of Stationary against the Alternative of a Unit Root." *Journal of Econometrics* 54: 159–78.

Laabas, B., and W. A. Razzak. 2011. "Economic Growth and The Quality of Human Capital." MPRA Paper No. 28727. https://mpra.ub.uni-muenchen.de/28727/.

Lott, B. 1956. "Executive Power in Venezuela." *American Political Science Review* 50 (2): 422–41. https://doi.org/10.2307/1951677. ISSN 0003-0554.

Lucas, Robert Jr. 1976. "Econometric Policy Evaluation: A Critique." In *The Phillips Curve and Labor Markets* (Rochester Conference Series on Public Policy), edited by K. Brunner and A. Meltzer, 19–46. Vol. 1. New York: American Elsevier.

MacKinnon, James G. 1996. "Numerical Distribution Functions for Unit Root and Cointegration Tests." *Journal of Applied Econometrics* 11: 601–18.

MacKinnon, James G., Alfred A. Haug, and Leo Michelis. 1999. "Numerical Distribution Functions of Likelihood Ratio Tests for Cointegration." *Journal of Applied Econometrics* 14: 563–77.

Maino, R., and K. I. Tintchev. 2012. *From Stress to Costress: Stress Testing Interconnected Banking System*. Washington, DC: IMF.

Mankiw, N. G., D. Romer, and D. N. Weil. 1992. "A Contribution to the Empirics of Economic Growth." *Quarterly Journal of Economics* 17 (2): 407–37.

Megson, T. H. G. 2019. *Structural and Stress Analysis*. 4th ed. Langford Lane, Kidlington, Oxford, UK: Elsevier, The Boulevard.

Miller, E. 2008. "An Assessment of CES and Cobb-Douglas Production Functions." *Congressional Budget Office*. https://www.cbo.gov/sites/default/files/cbofiles/ftpdocs/94xx/doc9497/2008-05.pdf.

Mokyr, J. 1990. *The Lever of Riches: Technological Creativity and Economic Progress*. New York: Oxford University Press.

Ng, Serena, and Pierre Perron. 2001. "Lag Length Selection and the Construction of Unit Root Tests with Good Size and Power." *Econometrica* 69: 1519–54.

Nickell, S. 2003. "Employment and Taxes." CESIFO Working Paper No. 1109, December. https://www.ifo.de/DocDL/cesifo1_wp1109.pdf.

North, Douglas, C., and Robert Paul Thomas. 1973. *The Rise of the Western World*. UK: Cambridge University Press.

O'Driscoll, G. Jr., and L. Hoskins. 2003. *Property Right: Key to Economic Development*. Washington, DC: Cato Institute.

OPEC Statement delivered at the UN Climate Change Conference. 2017. (by HE Mohammad Sanusi Barkindo, Secretary General, Bonn, Germany. www.opec.org/opec_web/en/press_room/4637.htm.

Orlov Dmitry, Zryumov Pavel, and Skrzypacz Andrzej. 2023. "The Design of Macroprudential Stress Tests." *The Review of Financial Studies*: 4460–501. https://doi.org/10.1093/rfs/hhad040.

Phillips, P. C. B. 2003. "Laws and Limits of Econometrics." *Economic Journal* 113 (486): C26–52.

Phillips, P. C. B., and M. Loretan. 1991. "Estimating Long-Run Equilibria." *Review of Economic Studies* 58 (3): 407–36.

Phillips, P. C. B., and S. Ouliaris. 1990. "Asymptotic Properties of Residual Based Tests for Cointegration." *Econometrica: Journal of the Econometric Society*: 165–93.

Phillips, P. C. B., and P. Perron. 1988. "Testing for a Unit Root in Time Series Regression." *Biometrika* 75: 335–46.

Pipes, R. 2000. *Private Property, Freedom and the Rule of Law*. Hoover Digest, Hoover Institution.

Prescott, E. C. 2004. "Why Do Americans Work So Much More Than Europeans?." *Federal Reserve Bank of Minneapolis Quarterly Review* 28 (1): 2–3.

Razzak, W. A. 2006. "Iraq: Private Ownership of Oil and the Quest for Democracy." MPRA, Paper 54, University Library of Munich, Germany.

Razzak, W. A. 2013. “Predicting Instability.” *Applied Economics, Taylor & Francis* 45 (23): 3305–15.

Razzak, W. A. 2022. *The Ownership of Oil, Democracy, and Iraq's Past, Present, and Future*. https://mpra.ub.uni-muenchen.de/111417/.

Razzak, W. A. 2023. *The Future of Economic Development in the Gulf Cooperation Council States – Evidence-Based Policy Analysis, Routledge Studies in the Modern World Economy*. London and New York: Taylor and Francis Group.

Rebonato, R. 2010. *Coherent Stress Testing: A Bayesian Approach to the Analysis of Financial Stress*. London, UK: Wiley.

Rosenberg, N., and L. E. Birdzell. 1986. *How the West Grew Rich: The Economic Transition of Industrial World*. New York: Basic Books.

Ross, M. L. 1999. “The Political Economy of the Resource Curse.” *World Politics* 51 (2): 297–322. https://doi.org/10.1017/S0043887100008200. S2CID 154826053.

Ross, M. L. 2001. “Does Oil Hinder Democracy?.” *World Politics* 53 (April): 325–61.

Rotunda, R. D. 2004. *Iraq, Oil and Democracy*. Washington, DC: Cato Institution.

Rudebusch, G. 1993. “The Uncertain Unit Root in Real GNP.” *American Economic Review* 83 (March): 264–72.

Sachs, Jeffrey, and Warner Andrew. 1995. “Natural Resource Abundance and Economic Growth.” NBER Working Paper 5398. https://doi.org/10.3386/w5398.

Said, Said E., and David A. Dickey. 1984. “Testing for Unit Roots in Autoregressive Moving Average Models of Unknown Order.” *Biometrika* 71: 599–607.

Saikkonen, Pentti. 1992. “Estimation and Testing of Cointegrated Systems by an Autoregressive Approximation.” *Econometric Theory* 8: 1–27.

Solow, R. and F. Y. Wan. 1976. “Extraction Costs in the Theory of Exhaustible Resources.” *The Bell Journal of Economics* 7 (2): 359–370.

Stiglitz, J. 1974. “Growth with Exhaustible Natural Resources: Efficient and Optimal Growth Paths.” *Review of Economic Studies*: 123–37.

Stock, J. H. 1991. “Confidence Intervals for the Largest Autoregressive Root in U.S. Macroeconomic Time Series.” *Journal of Monetary Economics* 28 (December): 435–59.

Stock, J. H., and Mark Watson. 1993. “A Simple Estimator of Cointegrating Vectors In Higher Order Integrated Systems.” *Econometrica* 61: 783–820.

UNFCCC, the Paris Agreement. 2015. “Conference Session COP21.” Paris Climate Change Conference – November 29, 2018.

Vahid, F., and R. Engle. 1993. “Common Trends and Common Cycles.” *Journal of Applied Econometrics* 8 (4): 341–60.

Vogelsang, Timothy J. 1993. *Unpublished Computer Program*.

Weber, Max. 1919. Politics as Vocation. Published as “Politik als Beruf,” Gesammelte Politische Schriften (Muenchen, 1921), pp. 396–450. Originally a speech at Munich University, 1918, published in 1919 by Duncker & Humblodt, Munich. From H.H. Gerth and C. Wright Mills (Translated and edited), From Max Weber: Essays in Sociology, pp. 77–128, New York: Oxford University Press, 1946.

White, Halbert. 1980. “A Heteroskedasticity-Consistent Covariance Matrix and a Direct Test for Heteroskedasticity.” *Econometrica* 48: 817–38.

Wolf, C. 2005. “Shareholders Don't Shoot Each Others.” https://www.rand.org/pubs/commentary/2005/11/shareholders-dont-shoot-each-other.html.

Index

Note: Page numbers in *italics* indicate figures, **bold** indicate tables in the text, and references following "n" refer notes.

For Product Safety Concerns and Information please contact our EU representative GPSR@taylorandfrancis.com Taylor & Francis Verlag GmbH, Kaufingerstraße 24, 80331 München, Germany